YALE BOOK OF AMERICAN VERSE

Published Under the Auspices

of the

Elizabethan Club

Yale University

Yale Book of American Verse

EDITED BY
THOMAS R. LOUNSBURY

New Haven: Yale University Press
London: Henry Frowde
Oxford University Press
MCMXII

Copyright, 1912
By Yale University Press

First printed September, 1912.   1250 copies

All rights reserved

COPYRIGHT NOTICE

All rights on poems in this work are reserved by the holders of the copyright. The publishers and others named in the subjoined list are the proprietors, either in their own right or as agents for the authors, of the books and poems of which the authorship and titles are given respectively, and of which the ownership is thus specifically noted and is hereby acknowledged.

Publishers of THE YALE BOOK OF AMERICAN VERSE.
1912.

MESSRS. D. APPLETON & Co., New York—W. C. Bryant: The Battle-Field, The Conqueror's Grave, The Crowded Street, The Death of the Flowers, A Forest Hymn, The Future Life, June, "Oh Mother of a Mighty Race," The Past, Planting of the Apple-Tree, The Snow-Shower, Song of Marion's Men, Thanatopsis, To a Waterfowl; Fitz-Greene Halleck: Alnwick Castle, Burns, Connecticut, Marco Bozzaris, On the Death of Joseph Rodman Drake, Red Jacket.

WILLIAM ALLEN BUTLER, JR.—William Allen Butler: The Incognita of Raphael, Nothing to Wear.

MRS. GEORGE WILLIAM CURTIS—George William Curtis: Egyptian Serenade, O Listen to the Sounding Sea, Spring Song.

MESSRS. DUFFIELD & COMPANY, New York—Edgar Allan Poe: Annabel Lee, The Bells, The Conqueror Worm, The Haunted Palace, The Raven, To Helen, To One in Paradise. (The Stedman-Woodberry text is herein used through the courtesy of Messrs. Duffield & Company, holders of the copyright.)

MESSRS. FUNK & WAGNALLS COMPANY, New York—John Williamson Palmer: The Fight at San Jacinto, Stonewall Jackson's Way.

MESSRS. HOUGHTON MIFFLIN COMPANY, Boston—Thomas Bailey Aldrich: Baby Bell, In an Atelier, Nocturne, On an Intaglio Head of Minerva, On Lynn Terrace, Palabras Cariñosas,

COPYRIGHT NOTICE

Song from the Persian; Phœbe Cary: Alas!, Nearer Home; Ralph Waldo Emerson: Browning, Brahma, Concord Hymn, Days, Fable, Heri, Cras, Hodie, The Humble Bee, Poet, The Problem, Rhodora, Sacrifice, Shakespeare, To Eva; William Lloyd Garrison: Freedom for the Mind; Richard Watson Gilder: Ah, Be Not False, The Heroic Age, Noël, Reform, The River Inn, Songs, A Woman's Thought; Francis Bret Harte: Chiquita, Dow's Flat, "Jim," Plain Language from Truthful James, The Society upon the Stanislaus, What the Engines Said; John Hay: Hymn of the Knights Templars, Jim Bludso, Mystery of Gilgal; Oliver Wendell Holmes: Ballad of the Oysterman, Chambered Nautilus, The Deacon's Masterpiece, The Dilemma, The Last Leaf, Lexington, The Music Grinders, My Aunt, On Lending a Punch-Bowl, The Parting Word, Philosopher to His Love, "Qui Vive," The Star and the Water-Lily, To the Portrait of a Lady, Under the Washington Elm, Cambridge, The Voice of the Loyal North, The Voiceless; Julia Ward Howe: Battle-Hymn of the Republic, Our Orders, The Summons; Lucy Larcom: Hannah Binding Shoes; Henry Wadsworth Longfellow: The Cumberland, The Day is Done, Endymion, Excelsior, Footsteps of Angels, Maidenhood, My Lost Youth, Nuremberg, The Psalm of Life, Resignation, Seaweed, Skeleton in Armor, Song of the Silent Land, The Village Blacksmith, Warden of the Cinque Ports; James Russell Lowell: Auf Wiedersehen, The Courtin', Credidimus Jovem Regnare, Ode Recited at the Harvard Commemoration, July 21, 1865, Palinode, The Petition, The Present Crisis, Song—"O Moonlight Deep and Tender," Telepathy, The Washers of the Shroud, What Mr. Robinson Thinks, Without and Within; William Vaughn Moody: Gloucester Moors, Ode in Time of Hesitation; Thomas William Parsons: Her Epitaph, Mary Booth, Obituary, On a Bust of Dante, Paradisi Gloria, Saint Peray; John Godfrey Saxe: Bereavement, Early Rising, Orpheus and Eurydice, Polyphemus and Ulysses;

COPYRIGHT NOTICE

Edward Rowland Sill: The Coup de Grace, The Fool's Prayer, The Lover's Song, Momentous Words, The Open Window, To a Maid Demure; Edmund Clarence Stedman: The Ballad of Lager Bier, Edged Tools, Hypatia, Kearny at Seven Pines, Pan in Wall Street, Provençal Lovers, Si Jeunesse Savait!, The Undiscovered Country, World Well Lost; William Wetmore Story: Black Eyes, Cleopatra, In the Rain, L'Abbate, Praxiteles and Phryne, Snowdrop; John Greenleaf Whittier: Barbara Frietchie, Barclay of Ury, Ichabod, Lines on the Death of S. O. Torrey, Maud Muller, My Playmate, The Old Burying-Ground, Proem to Poems of 1847, Dedication of "In War Time," Randolph of Roanoke, The Watchers, What the Birds Said.

MITCHELL KENNERLEY, New York—Walt Whitman: O Captain! My Captain!

MESSRS. J. B. LIPPINCOTT COMPANY—Thomas Buchanan Read: The Celestial Army, Sheridan's Ride, Some Things Love Me.

MESSRS. LOTHROP LEE & SHEPARD COMPANY, Boston—Marc Cook: Her Opinion of the Play.

MESSRS. CHARLES SCRIBNER'S SONS, New York—Henry Cuyler Bunner: Atlantic City, Candor, Chakey Einstein, The Chaperon, Da Capo, Feminine, Just a Love-Letter, She Was a Beauty, The Way to Arcady; Eugene Field: The Bibliomaniac's Prayer, Dear Old London, Dibden's Ghost, The Duel, Grandma's Prayer, In Amsterdam, The Little Peach, Lydia Dick, Preference Declared, The Tea-Gown; Sydney Lanier: Marshes of Glynn, Song of the Chattahoochee; Richard Henry Stoddard: The Flight of Youth, Without and Within, A Woman's Poem.

MESSRS. SMALL MAYNARD & COMPANY, INCORPORATED, Boston—Richard Hovey: At the End of the Day, Faith and Fate, Launa Dee, The Sea Gypsy, Unmanifest Destiny, Voices of Unseen Spirits, The Wander-Lovers.

MESSRS. THE JOHN C. WINSTON COMPANY, Philadelphia—Charles Fenno Hoffman: The Mint Julep, Monterey.

A WORD ABOUT ANTHOLOGIES

Aubrey de Vere tells us of three conversations he held the very same day on the very same subject with three different authors. Two of them were men of great poetic genius, the third was a man of distinct poetic talent. The topic of discussion in each case was the poetry of Burns. The difference of opinion expressed struck him as remarkable. The first with whom he talked was Tennyson. "Read the exquisite songs of Burns," exclaimed that poet, "in shape each of them has the perfection of the berry; in light the radiance of the dewdrop; you forget for its sake those stupid things, his serious pieces."

A little later in the day he met Wordsworth. Again the conversation fell on Burns. "Wordsworth," he writes, "praised him even more vehemently than Tennyson had done, as the great genius who had brought poetry back to nature. 'Of course,' he said in conclusion, 'I refer to his serious efforts, such as *The Cotter's Saturday Night;* those foolish little amatory songs of his one has to forget.'" On the evening of this same day he chanced to fall in with Henry Taylor. Him he told of the different views expressed by the two poets. The author of *Philip Van Artevelde* disposed of them both very summarily. "Burns' exquisite songs and Burns' serious efforts are to me alike tedious and disagreeable reading," was the comment he made.

The story is somewhat singular; but after all it is much more singular for the rapidity with which the expression of these varying views chanced to follow one another than for the views expressed. The disparagement of great poetic work by writers, themselves of great poetic power, and likewise the extraordinary praise lavished by them upon very ordinary verse, are both significant facts which can hardly fail to arrest at times the attention of the student of literature. The history of letters, in truth, abounds in singular judgments which men of genius have passed upon the productions of other men of genius. It is often hard to tell which is the more remarkable—the mean opinion which these entertain of what the rest of the world has approved, or the admiration they have or profess to have for what the rest of the world refuses to regard with favor.

Many will recall the lofty scorn which Matthew Arnold poured upon the men who for generations had admired and enjoyed Macaulay's *Lays of Ancient Rome*. He proclaimed that a man's power to detect the ring of false metal in these pieces was a good measure of his fitness to give an opinion about

A WORD ABOUT ANTHOLOGIES

poetical matters at all. The self-sufficiency of this utterance is as delicious as its positiveness. These Lays, it may be added, had been welcomed with such intense enthusiasm by Christopher North, the critical lawgiver of the generation of their appearance, that Macaulay felt himself constrained to make a personal acknowledgment of the cordiality of the greeting his work had met from the then all-powerful reviewer who had been one of his extreme political adversaries. But there is an even more amusing side to the affair. The self-satisfied criticism of Matthew Arnold could hardly have failed to bring to Trevelyan a half-malicious pleasure, when he revealed in his fascinating life of his uncle that it was the urgency of Arnold's own father that led Macaulay to complete and publish these Lays. They owed their conception to the theory of Niebuhr that the stories told in the first three or four books of Livy came from the lost ballads of the early Romans. This theory, Thomas Arnold adopted in his history as having been fully established. Macaulay also took the same view. Accordingly he amused himself, while in India, with the effort to restore some of these long-perished poems. Thomas Arnold died before the Lays were printed, but not before he had seen two of them in manuscript. These so impressed him that he wrote to Macaulay about them in terms of such eulogy that the latter was induced to go on with the completion and correction of them. In consequence the son was unconsciously exhibiting his own father as unfit to express any opinion about poetry at all.

The possession of creative power is indeed far from implying the possession of a corresponding degree of critical judgment. In literature all of us have our preferences and our aversions. Perhaps even more than their inferiors are men of genius susceptible to feelings of this nature and to the errors of judgment caused by them. The revelation of their likes and dislikes is in consequence apt to be more entertaining than edifying. At any rate, there is nothing surprising in itself that Tennyson and Wordsworth should each have cared in the poetry of Burns for what the other did not care at all. Each found in it that which appealed to him especially and also that which did not appeal to him in the slightest. It is but a single one of many proofs that the estimate taken by a man of genius of a particular work or writer is not necessarily of any more value than that taken by any other highly educated man, though it inevitably carries more weight with the general public. When, however, this estimate comes into direct conflict with the deliberate and settled opinion of the great body of cultivated readers, it is really of no value at all.

A WORD ABOUT ANTHOLOGIES

For the truth is that in the case of works of the imagination the settled judgment of the great body of cultivated men is infinitely superior to the judgment of any one man, however eminent. Very wisely that body will not in the long run, nor ordinarily even in the short run, accept the decision of any self-constituted censor which runs counter to its own conclusions. A genuinely great production will in the end find its own public which in time will become the public; and that public will not be deterred from admiring it by the most bitter attacks of the ablest writers in the most influential periodicals. In his estimate of works involving special knowledge, the individual wisely defers to the authority of experts. In works of the imagination, however, every man of culture is in varying degrees an expert himself. When dealing with productions of this class the right of private judgment overrides the authority of the highest court of criticism, reverses its decisions and frequently visits with contumely those who have pronounced its verdicts. For this view we have the authority of the acutest of observers and thinkers. Aristotle long ago pointed out that in the matter of music and poetry, the opinion of all men—of course he had in mind all those competent to be considered judges—was far more worthy of respect than the opinion of seemingly the greatest authority. "The people at large," said he, "however contemptible they may appear when taken individually, are not, when collectively considered, unworthy of sovereignty. They are the best judges of music and poetry. The general taste is not only better than that of the few, but even than that of any one man, howsoever discerning he may be."

It is not necessary to consider here the reasons which Aristotle adduced to establish the correctness of this view. It is enough for us to recognize the fact that the experience of men, rightly interpreted, bears witness to its truth. In each of the cases just mentioned the question has been settled accordingly. However wide differences of opinion may be as to the actual or comparative value of particular pieces, the verdict of the educated multitude has been given in approval of both the serious and the amatory poems of Burns. It has likewise been given in approval of the Roman lays of Macaulay. That individuals may plume themselves upon the peculiar exquisiteness of taste they exhibit in dissenting from the estimate taken by the public, does not affect the justice of that estimate any more than it does its permanence. It is full as often the fate of the too superior person, as it is that of the too inferior one, to show his lack of critical judgment by the judgment he shows.

Owing, however, to this wide diversity of taste, no

A WORD ABOUT ANTHOLOGIES

work of the nature of the present volume can ever be wholly satisfactory to any one save the compiler, if indeed it be so to him. As regards the rest of the world, he must content himself with at best a qualified approval even if he succeeds in avoiding general condemnation. An assumption that any collection made by a single person, no matter who he be, can possibly represent the final conclusions of the judgment of the collective body of cultivated men is as utterly unwarranted by experience as it is unsupported by reason. Yet it is an assumption which has more than once been made. Let us take, for example, the *Household Book of Poetry* brought out in 1857 by Charles Anderson Dana. This was an excellent compilation as well as the earliest with us of its special class. It was received with great favor and it deserved all the favor it received. Yet nothing more unwise or unwarranted could well have been written than the opening sentence of its preface. "The purpose of this book," said the editor, "is to comprise within the bounds of a single volume whatever is truly beautiful and admirable among the minor poems of the English language." No more suggestive comment need be given upon the claim then put forth than the remark contained in the advertisement prefixed to a subsequent edition. In that it was stated that some pieces originally included had been dropped and their places filled by others believed to possess greater merit.

A statement of the sort just made is based, in truth, not only upon the assumption that the editor's acquaintance with the poetical literature of our race is absolutely complete, but that his judgment of the comparative excellence of the pieces composing it is absolutely perfect. No one would be willing to concede the latter qualification and few the former. Every collection of poems must inevitably reflect to a great extent the limitation of the compiler's knowledge. Many pieces which he would have been glad to include, had he been aware of their existence, are likely to have escaped his observation. But were there no lack of knowledge, the choice he makes will be certain to reflect the nature of his literary sympathies, and even more the limitations of his literary taste; at all events its distinctive character. There are certain poems which it is always easy to select. Upon them the consent of the ages has already set the stamp of approval. Against this verdict of successive generations there may be protest upon the part of the individual; but from it there can be no valid appeal.

If, indeed, any one finds himself disliking something in which cultivated men of all periods have taken delight, it will be well for him to make a care-

A WORD ABOUT ANTHOLOGIES

ful examination of himself. The chances are that his own poor estimate of such work is due to a defect in himself and not in the poetry he undervalues. Few of us are sufficiently endowed with that broadmindedness of judgment and that catholicity of taste which enable its possessor to bring to poetry of essentially different kinds an equal capacity of appreciation. That may be a misfortune we cannot help; but we can free ourselves, at least, from the fancy of looking upon our own onesidedness and our inability to sympathize with the judgments of others whom we recognize to be our intellectual equals, as proof that we are in possession of a taste peculiarly refined.

For he indeed assumes a certain degree of risk who ventures to set up his own estimate of particular pieces in opposition to that which the large majority of cultivated men have apparently taken. Where something is plainly inferior or commonplace an editor may feel at liberty to exercise his own discretion as to its exclusion, no matter how popular it may be with thousands. But when it stands on the border line between the mediocre and the good, he ought, while preserving his independence, to have a certain hesitation in preferring his own taste to that of scores of educated men whom he recognizes to be as competent as he to sit in judgment. I have myself tried to conform to this dictum in the present

A WORD ABOUT ANTHOLOGIES

volume. There are certain cases in which I have inserted in it poems, not because of the estimate I personally entertain of their excellence, but because of the estimate entertained by others, whose critical opinion I respect. One or two specific instances will be given in the course of this essay in which I have submitted my own judgment to that of the large majority of critics, preferring to believe that my taste must be wrong, coming into conflict as it does with that of so many others. Furthermore, certain poems have been included here, commonplace enough so far as the words are concerned, but to which associations have come to attach themselves entirely independent of their literary quality. Popular interest or historic importance may be taken to indicate that there is warrant for their insertion. Every one would notice their absence; some would resent it. A notable instance of this is *Home, Sweet Home.*

Still, as regards poems which have received the approval of generations, there is generally little difficulty for the editor. But between the distinctly great pieces which all men competent to judge would accept without hesitation and the distinctly inferior pieces which these same persons would as summarily reject, there lies a vast body of verse. Here the world has not spoken authoritatively. Hence at this point comes in the play of individual choice. That

A WORD ABOUT ANTHOLOGIES

choice will be often widely different in the case of men apparently equal in knowledge and in critical judgment. One will rate a poem above the border line which separates excellence from mediocrity, the other will place it below. In each instance the influence of the personal equation becomes recognizable. To the one the poem may appeal because it calls up for him subtle trains of association, or because it revives for him certain feelings to which experiences of his own have made him keenly sensitive, or because it touches upon problems of life and conduct in which he is profoundly interested. To the other it conveys none of these things. Because it does not, he passes it by without interest and without regard.

It is further true that poetry which appeals to us at one period of life will sometimes not do so at another. The taste has changed; it is not necessary—it is certainly not discreet—to assume that it has improved. But far more influential than any other cause for difference of opinion are essential differences in men's natures which are sufficient to render the judgment partial. There exist among the most highly cultivated wide variations of taste—variations which extend to subject as well as treatment. A certain kind of verse is fairly sure to attract a certain class of minds—not necessarily to the exclusion of other kinds, but to a decided preference for it over them. One man is fond of meditative poetry; another of that which glitters with point and sparkle; another of that which deals in outbursts of intense feeling. It may be that this preference will exist with enjoyment and appreciation of a different kind of poetry, or indeed of all other kinds of poetry. It may be even that there will be an intellectual acknowledgment of the superiority of some other kind. Still the fact remains that this is the one kind which appeals to the man himself, the one kind that attracts and influences him.

Furthermore, there are certain moods of mind and states of experience in which a person is affected by the writings of one author and could not be influenced by those of another of equal or even greater powers. This is something entirely different from according to the author in question a supreme position, though it must be conceded that it has a tendency to elevate him to the highest. There is a very signal illustration of this fact in the account which John Stuart Mill gives in his autobiography of the crisis of mental depression through which he passed in his youth. In this he tried to find relief in poetry. To it he had previously paid little attention. He turned to Byron and found in him no help. That poet's state of mind was too like his own. Life was to him the vapid, uninteresting thing which it had become to the one who sought relief in his pages for his own dejection. It was in Wordsworth that he found relief—not in *The Excursion,* he tells us, from which he gained little or nothing, but from the miscellaneous poems which appeared in the edition of 1815. From the teachings of that poet he gradually emerged from the dejection which was threatening to become habitual. This instance is particularly worthy of notice because Mill was disposed to underrate Wordsworth. He did not place his work on a high level of achievement. Even in that writer's own age he thought there had been far greater poets. "I long continued to value Wordsworth," he wrote, "less according to his intrinsic merits than by the measure of what he had done for me. Compared with the greatest poets, he may be said to be the poet of unpoetical natures, possessed of quiet and contemplative tastes. But unpoetic natures are precisely those which require poetic cultivation. This cultivation Wordsworth is much more fitted to give than poets who are intrinsically far more poets than he."

The dissent which such a view of Wordsworth will awaken in that author's admirers renders distinct and marked the impossibility of bringing about harmony of view as to the comparative greatness of particular poets or as to the estimate which should be taken of the value of particular pieces. On such points the judgments of men of different natures can never be reconciled. If the fondness for any one sort of verse chances to be controlling, it is hard for its possessor to do justice to productions of a totally different character. The followers of poets of unlike types are fairly sure to be drawn up in different camps. They are not unfrequently found ranged in hostile ones. As a result the enthusiastic admirer of some particular author is seldom content with expressing what is for him a perfectly justifiable preference. He feels impelled to depreciate if not to deny totally the merits of some rival author with whom his own idol is constantly contrasted. He seems unaware that in thus giving vent to his hostility he is doing little more than betray his own limitations.

In this matter the difference in the point of view from which the works of different writers are looked at by different editors can be brought home to every one by comparing the poems taken from particular authors as found in this volume with those contained in the various anthologies which have been for some time before the public. It can be made still more emphatic by comparing these anthologies with one another. In all of them the influence of individual taste and preference makes itself distinctly felt. For obvious reasons the attention is here confined to the poetical collections brought out in this country. Of

A WORD ABOUT ANTHOLOGIES

these it is sufficient to say that during the last fifty or sixty years there have been published a full half-dozen which have aimed at completeness. As they set out to cover the whole field of English literature, much the largest proportion of what they contain has been taken from British authors. Still they have given full recognition to whatever has come from America which they have deemed worthy of inclusion.

The earliest of these works was Dana's *Household Book of Poetry* already mentioned. The second appeared in 1870. It was entitled *The Library of Poetry and Song*. To it was prefixed an introduction by William Cullen Bryant. Though not actually compiled by him, it passed under his supervision and revision. In so doing he added and excluded a good deal of matter; hence it came to go under his name. Then followed, in 1875, Emerson's collection entitled *Parnassus*, and the next year Whittier's *Songs of Three Centuries*. The fifth is the *Fireside Encyclopedia of Poetry*, which came out in 1878, edited by a Philadelphia publisher, Henry T. Coates. Finally appeared, in 1881, *Harper's Encyclopedia of British and American Poetry*, edited by Epes Sargent. To these six may fairly be added *The American Anthology* of Edmund Clarence Stedman which was published in 1900. This, indeed, differs from the others in character as well as in content. Like the earlier similar volume of Griswold, it was not designed as a collection of poems of undisputed worth, but as a general representation of the work of American authors who had written verse of various degrees of excellence.

Here, therefore, are seven volumes, six of which purport to contain nothing save what their compilers deemed to be of value in itself, as well as what would be generally conceded to be the best work of the best authors. Several of them were edited by men who had themselves attained the widest recognition as writers of verse. From these last one might naturally expect a fair degree of unanimity of opinion as to what pieces could be considered as most deserving of inclusion. As a matter of fact, nothing is more striking than the variations displayed in the selections made. The discrepancies of choice are so great as almost to deserve the epithet of startling, if indeed they may not be called amazing. And this difference of taste is not confined to the work of writers but little known. It is fully as remarkable in the case of American poets of the first rank, about the comparative value of whose production there might seem to have grown up an agreement of opinion which would make the task of selection comparatively easy.

Take for illustration the diversity of choice exhibited in the selections made from two or three of

A WORD ABOUT ANTHOLOGIES

the best known of these poets. Let us begin with Longfellow. He has been so much before the public and so popular that a general agreement would naturally be looked for as to those pieces of his which had received the approval of the whole circle of the most cultivated body of readers. Yet in his case a peculiarly wide discrepancy of choice has shown itself. Of the sixteen pieces of his which are found in this volume, one alone reaches the distinction of being contained in as many as four of the seven anthologies just mentioned. This is the *Psalm of Life*, or what the Heart of the Young Man said to the Psalmist. It is the most widely quoted of Longfellow's poems; to me it is one of the least worthy of quotation. It is largely a collection of observations which when they are not platitudinous, are not true. There is little use in telling us that the lives of great men remind us that we can make our own lives sublime. Most of us are perfectly well aware that the sublime lives of great men—and their lives have not unfrequently been petty—can not serve as examples to us, because we are not great men. Consequently we lack the ability to leave footprints on the sands of time, however much we may have the desire. Nor indeed does the particular method recommended strike one as practicable. The last place a rational man would choose for leaving a permanent footprint would be on the sandy beach bordering an ocean. The chance of its lasting long enough to be seen by any one sailing over life's solemn main would be too slight to make it worth while to take the trouble of implanting it. In truth this particular young man seems to have been very young. He is advised by his heart to be a hero not only in the battle but in the bivouac. If the psalmist had thought it worth while to reply, he would doubtless have informed the young man that the bivouac, in the modern sense of the word, affords little opportunity for one to show himself a hero, and that the best thing he could do there would be to act like one of the dumb driven cattle which his heart warns him not to imitate, and lie down and go peacefully to sleep. Yet with these views about the poem itself, I insert it in this collection in deference to a sentiment in which I do not share. On the other hand, were I asked to choose a piece which shows Longfellow at his best, it would be that which appeared originally as the proem to his collection entitled *The Waif*. This now usually receives, from its first line, the heading, *The Day is Done*. Yet out of these seven anthologies it is found only in that of Coates.

Let us consider now the selections from Bryant. In his case there is much more agreement among the compilers of these various anthologies than there is

A WORD ABOUT ANTHOLOGIES

in that of Longfellow. There are two of his poems which are contained in every one of them, and there are three or four others which have found a place in the majority. One of the two included by all is *The Waterfowl*. Apparently it is the correct thing to admire this particular piece. It is invariably or almost invariably printed in selections from Bryant's poetry. It is as regularly extolled as a singular proof of his genius. To me this most praised of his productions is the least worthy of those usually chosen as representative. It is merely a second-rate piece of work, whose inferiority forces itself upon the mind because it inevitably suggests a comparison it can not bear with the odes to the Skylark of Shelley, of Hogg and of Wordsworth. Yet it will be found here, not because of the opinion I entertain of its merit, but because its actual or assumed popularity with most educated men leads me to distrust my own judgment. On the other hand, the omission from these various anthologies of poems which fairly arrest attention strikes one as much more singular than some of the selections. Bryant and Stedman are the only editors who insert *The Snow-Shower*. The poet himself did not include in his own collection the poem of *June*, so warmly praised by Poe, nor *The Conqueror's Grave*, nor *The Future Life*. Of these three pieces which are peculiarly representative of

Bryant's finest work, the first two are found only in Stedman's and the last only in Sargent's collection.

The selections from Whittier exhibit even wider discrepancies of taste. In his *Songs of Three Centuries*, he included six of his own pieces. Literary history shows that poets themselves are frequently far from being the best judges of the comparative excellence of their own performances. The difference between the creative and the critical faculty often becomes at such times almost painfully marked. That, in my opinion, Whittier shared in this not uncommon defect may be inferred from the fact that not a single one of the six chosen by him can be found in the present volume. I have, however, the consolation of discovering that I am not alone in my blindness to their merits; that not a single one of them found its way into six of the anthologies which have been mentioned; and their verdict would have been unanimous had not one of the author's half-dozen somehow escaped into Coates's collection. On the other hand, four of those which are given in this work—*The Old Burying-Ground*, *Dedication* to the Sewalls of the volume entitled *In War Time*, *The Watchers*, and *Lines on the Death of O. S. Torrey*—have no place in a single one of the seven anthologies I have specified. Two other poems—*Randolph of Roanoke* and *What the Birds Said*—appear in but

A WORD ABOUT ANTHOLOGIES

a single one of these collections, in each case in a different one.

The comparison would be even more striking in the case of Oliver Wendell Holmes. There are over thirty of his pieces not found here which are included in some one of the seven volumes mentioned. Yet but a small proportion of the thirty appears in more than one of them. On the other hand, half a score of his poems which are here included cannot be found in a single one of these collections. But it is needless to go on giving illustrations of the wide divergencies of judgment and taste displayed in anthologies; for they could be multiplied almost endlessly. Facts of this nature prove conclusively to an editor that the selections he makes will never receive the full approval, not simply of all lovers of poetry, but of any individual among them. The impossibility of satisfying critics I take for granted, just as I would the impossibility of any one of them satisfying me, were he to undertake a similar task.

What, therefore, is incumbent to say here is to point out precisely what the aim is which has been kept in view in making this particular collection. It differs largely from most of the others which have been brought out. It puts forth no pretense of being representative or inclusive of American verse or verse-makers. Some names found in other anthologies do not appear here at all. Some again appear which are found in none of the others. This last was partly due to the fact that the plan of this work was to comprise kinds of verse which the plan of certain if not of all the others excluded. Had the whole field of English literature been open to draw from, it would have been easy from the abundance of material to restrict the selection to what might be distinctly called poetry pure and simple. Confined as this volume is to the comparatively scanty body of American verse, liberty of choice of this nature did not exist. Such a limitation was practically impossible. Yet had there been for it a demand, it would not have seemed to me desirable. Every kind of verse worth reading at all has a right to be represented; all that can fairly be demanded is that the poem chosen should be good in its kind, though the kind itself may be distinctly inferior. Accordingly specimens of all sorts of poetry can be found in the present volume—the serious, the light, the contemplative, the pathetic, the humorous and the satiric. Not even has the travesty been excluded; and there are a goodly number of specimens of that sort of verse which in our tongue lacks a recognized name and appears under the foreign title of *vers de société*. Perhaps, indeed, disproportionate space has been given to the representatives of these minor classes. Yet this is a fault,

A WORD ABOUT ANTHOLOGIES

if it be a fault, which the general reader will be disposed to pardon, however much the severe student of poetry may disapprove.

As the authors from whom selections were made were required to follow one another in chronological order, there was no choice save to begin with specimens of religious poetry; for only in that is found the very little of our early verse that can be deemed worthy of citation at all. Few will be disposed to deny that Joel Barlow's version of the one hundred and thirty-seventh psalm is worth more, poetically considered, than the whole of his laborious epic, to say nothing of his other pieces. Curiously enough, not even his name, as well as that of one or two others represented in this volume, appears in Stedman's supposedly all-embracing anthology. The fact that Barlow's version of this psalm is rarely found in modern hymnals, is another justification for its inclusion in this work. Still, in the case of religious poetry, it must be confessed, the choice is so hard as to be almost perilous. "A good hymn," said Tennyson, "is the most difficult thing in the world to write. For a good hymn you have to be commonplace and poetical. The moment you cease to be commonplace and put in an expression at all out of the common, it ceases to be a hymn." But if difficulties of this sort beset the writer, full as perplexing ones beset the editor. Most hymns that have any enduring popularity are almost invariably set to particular tunes. The permanent addition of music to the words blunts in time the critical sense. The two are at last so blended in the minds of those by whom they are heard frequently that it becomes practically impossible to dissociate them and judge the value of each independently. Hence the compiler is always in danger of choosing pieces not so much on account of the poetic merit they possess as of the music to which they are set; for he cannot tell where the influence of the one begins and that of the other ends. It may therefore be that he who comes to the consideration of some of these pieces without any associations save those purely literary may find them unworthy of being included.

Of the earlier writers represented in this collection, the two who seem to have given most promise of future performance were cut off prematurely. These were Joseph Rodman Drake and Edward Coate Pinkney. Both suffered long from disease, both lived only about a quarter of a century. For most of us the memory of Drake has been better preserved by the lines Halleck wrote on his death than by anything he himself produced. Of the two, indeed, Pinkney's was the more poetic nature. There is something peculiarly pathetic in the following passage from one of his poems, revealing as it does the sickness of heart that comes from failing hope and the depression of spirit which the shadow of death had already begun to cast upon his life:

> A sense it was, that I could see
>   The angel leave my side—
> That thenceforth my prosperity
>   Must be a falling tide;
> A strange and ominous belief
> That in spring-time the yellow leaf
>   Had fallen on my hours;
> And that all hope must be most vain,
> Of finding on my path again,
>   Its former, vanished flowers.

Pinkney is best known by his piece entitled, *A Health;* and it would be difficult to find anywhere in English literature a more exquisite tribute paid to womanhood. It is unquestionably the most perfect of his productions; but there is excellence enough in his other work to make keenly felt the loss which American literature suffered from his prolonged illness and the consequent despondency which hung over much of his life and ceased only with his untimely death.

    No small number of authors will be found represented in this collection by a single piece only. There is nothing peculiar in itself in the fact. Writers of established reputation in English literature there are who continue to flourish—if that verb can be properly used in such cases—almost entirely on the strength of one, two or three short poems. They may have produced a large body of other verse and usually have done so. This may have had too in its own day great vogue; but it is now unfamiliar to all save literary scholars or rather literary antiquaries. Take as an illustration the case of Edmund Waller. He was so much a favorite writer of the seventeenth century that by large numbers he was regarded as the greatest poet of his time. His first collected volume of verse belongs to 1645, the year which witnessed a similar venture on the part of Milton. The immediate fortunes of the two works were, however, distinctly different. Three editions of Waller's volume appeared the first year of its publication. Before his death in 1687 four others had followed, to say nothing of his many productions published separately. Yet so far now as he retains acceptance with the mass of educated men, his repute rests upon two or three short pieces, in very deed mainly upon one.

Nevertheless, it is a good deal of an achievement to have produced even a single piece of poetry which the men of aftertimes will continue to cherish as part of the intellectual riches of the race. The fact is that in the same way as many persons are capable of writing but one good work of fiction, so many persons are capable of writing but one really excellent poem. Their other productions may possess merit of a sort; only one stands out so conspicuously among its fellows that the world recognizes its superiority the moment it chances to be brought to its attention. This truth is illustrated frequently in this volume. The *Florence Vane* of Philip Pendleton Cooke; the *Two Villages* of Rose Terry Cooke; the *After the Ball* of Nora Perry; the *Ships at Sea* of Robert Barry Coffin, and several others which could be mentioned, are so much better than anything besides, which each of these authors has written, that it perhaps tends to render the critic unjust to whatever else they have accomplished. Still to be judged by his best performance always tends to add more to the credit of the writer than if the attention were distracted from it to other pieces, which even if good in themselves are distinctly inferior to the one selected as representative.

It has been part of my plan to give those pieces dealing with the feelings and fortunes of the combatants during the long and desperate struggle that went on between North and South, the poetical merits of which might seem to justify their insertion. A large body of verse came then into being and even afterward. Much of it naturally owed the favorable reception it met to the fact that it appealed to the excited passions of the moment. Its literary quality came little into consideration. Still there are poems occasioned by the Civil War which are worthy of a place in any American anthology. Of the lyrics then produced two stand out as of exceptional excellence. One is *My Maryland*, the impassioned appeal of James Ryder Randall, then resident in Louisiana, to his native state to join the South in its resistance to Northern aggression. The other is Julia Ward Howe's *Battle-Hymn of the Republic*, in which the fiery anti-slavery zeal of a minority, soon to become a majority, found its most adequate expression. Yet in spite not only of the fervor but of the exquisite literary finish of the latter poem, it seems to me decidedly inferior as a martial lyric to the stirring strains of the former.

Here again some pieces have been included, not so much on the score of their literary excellence as for the reason that they came to be endeared to those participating in the conflict in consequence of serving as a solace to their feelings or an inspiration to their acts. Verses which operate upon the hearts of multitudes and express their emotions deserve recognition in any anthology even if their literary merit is so far from being of the highest type that it is not in fact very high. This itself is a sufficient reason

A WORD ABOUT ANTHOLOGIES

for including Palmer's *Stonewall Jackson's Way,* and above all *Dixie,* which in its literary form, as contrasted with its popular one, was singularly enough the production of a man of Massachusetts birth who never saw the South until after he had reached his majority.

It is a peculiarity of many of these Civil War poems that their content would frequently fail to reveal the section of country from which they came. This indeed might naturally be expected to happen when the combatants on each side had not the slightest doubt in their minds that in taking the course they did, they were doing their best to carry out the purposes of the Lord. In consequence there is often nothing in the words themselves to reveal the place of their origin. Such, for instance, is the case with Cutler's *Volunteer* and *The Thousand and Thirty-Seven* of Halpine. Even the dedication of Whittier's volume entitled *In War Time,* dealing as it does with the widespread sorrow reaching then every home from the lakes to the gulf, might as easily have been written by a Southern fire-eater as by a Northern abolitionist. In truth Ethel Lynn Beers's *All Quiet Along the Potomac* has been claimed by, or at least has been attributed to, several persons, among them one who was a Mississippian and another a Georgian. Furthermore, to this day it has not been definitely

A WORD ABOUT ANTHOLOGIES

settled from which quarter came the popular poem sometimes entitled *Civil War* and sometimes *The Fancy Shot*. It appeared originally in the London periodical, *Once a Week*, for October 5, 1861. There the title given was *Civile Bellum*, and the poem itself was signed "From the Once United States." In this collection I have followed hesitatingly the authorities which attribute its composition to Charles Dawson Shanley.

Among the poems begotten of this prolonged conflict, which are to be found in this volume, is one which I have included with hesitation because I am ignorant whether its author, whoever he or she was, is living or dead. I have never met it in any collection, and it was under somewhat peculiar circumstances that I came across it myself. On the march to Gettysburg the army had gone one night into camp, when I picked up a torn piece of newspaper which was fluttering about. As anything to be read of any sort was then far from abundant, I looked it over. From the character of the contents of what little had been preserved, it was manifestly an antislavery sheet, though there was nothing left to tell which one it was of the several then published. What arrested my attention, however, were certain verses headed, if I remember aright, *Home Wounded*. At all events, the production was manifestly suggested

A WORD ABOUT ANTHOLOGIES

by Gerald Massey's poem with that title. But though it reminded one of it, beyond the idea underlying its conception it was indebted to it for only two or three words and phrases.

No name of writer appeared on this torn fragment as I found it; in fact, no space was left for one. Even the last word of the poem had disappeared, though it was easily supplied by the sense and ryme. It could have been written by either man or woman, though in my ignorance about its authorship I should attribute it to a woman. It was further characteristic of the similar way in which the intense feeling which prevailed on both sides then manifested itself, that, though the verses appeared in an anti-slavery journal, they could as well have been written in the South as in the North, were it not for a single line in the last stanza. I was so struck at the time by the poem that I cut it out of the torn piece of paper containing it. Naturally this soon disappeared. The words, however, remained in my mind. I have reproduced them from memory, and though after the lapse of so many years I can not be sure that what is printed here is an absolutely exact transcript of the lines as I found them, I am confident that it is not much out of the way.

Still while there are many creditable pieces of poetry that owe their existence to the passions aroused by the Civil War, there are comparatively few that by the most liberal charity attain sufficient distinction to deserve reception in the most hospitable of anthologies. Unfortunately for literature, the expression of feeling is rarely on a level with its intensity. This accounts largely for the inferiority of national hymns. As a general rule these are not of a high order from the point of view of literature; in no case that I am acquainted with are they of the highest. The patriotism of men has to supply an inspiration which the words themselves lack. As such poems almost invariably owe their origin to the excitement and emotion attending some passing moment or movement there is little chance of their ever being produced to order; for though the order for the poetry may be pecuniarily high, the result is little likely to be of a high order of poetry.

The best of our own national hymns—in fact, the only one worth mentioning for its verse—is *The Star-Spangled Banner*. This need not fear comparison on its literary merits with other productions of this class; but it is hopelessly handicapped by being set to a tune, in part of which no respect is paid to the capabilities of the ordinary human voice. This is all the more to be regretted, because it has led to the frequent employment by us of the distinctively English national air as if it were our own. There is nothing more impudent in the history of plagiarism than our appropriation of *God Save the King* and dubbing it *America*. Such appropriations have not been uncommon with individuals; but it is apparently the first time that the act has been perpetrated by a people. It was bad enough to steal the tune; but to marry it to the feeble words which were set to it was adding insult to injury. The English poem is far from being literature of a high type. No one is likely to maintain that

> Confound their politics,
> Frustrate their knavish tricks,

is great poetry. But it means something. It has vigor. It is written by a man for men, and it conveys the feelings of men. But such sentimental twaddle as

> I love thy rocks and rills,
> Thy woods and templed hills,

such apostrophes to one's country as "sweet land of liberty," is a sort of stuff which might appeal to the feelings of a body of gushing schoolgirls, but is hopelessly out of place in the expression of fervent patriotic sentiment. The wretchedness of taste displayed by the average man is forced painfully upon

A WORD ABOUT ANTHOLOGIES

the attention as a consequence of the wide acceptance which these vapid verses have attained.

No limitations beyond the consent of owners of copyright were placed upon the choice of poems to be included in this volume save that their authors must have added to their other distinctions the all-essential one of being dead. The persistence of certain persons in living has in consequence prevented me from inserting here a number of poems which I should have been particularly glad to include. Furthermore, a few pieces which I was anxious to insert have been reluctantly left out because of the inability to ascertain who the authors of them were, and in consequence whether they were alive or dead or whether they were English or American. Still, after what I have said in the earlier part of this introductory essay, no one will expect me to assume that even with the allowances that ought to be made, the selections here given will recommend themselves to the approval of all. Especially will the failure to meet the views and tastes of many show itself in the case of the more recent writers. The work of compilation would in truth have been much easier, and its outcome, so far as it went, would have been likely to prove more satisfactory, had the collection been limited to the productions of such authors as had died by the beginning of the present century. The

A WORD ABOUT ANTHOLOGIES

work of our closest contemporaries is usually hardest to estimate impartially. Time has not brought sufficient familiarity of acquaintance to test, nor sufficient cumulativeness of judgment to decide upon the permanent value of what has been written. One must therefore follow one's own individual preferences. I have indeed striven desperately to find certain poems admirable which others, whose judgment I respect, much admire. In a few cases, as has been remarked already, I have sufficiently overcome the scruples of my literary conscience as to insert them; but in general the work represents my own taste or, if critics so prefer to consider it, my want of taste.

For in this volume no small number of authors of more or less note in American literature are not represented at all. These, in the opinion of some, if not of many, ought to have been included. Again, authors who have been included will be found represented by poems, which some, and perhaps many, will deem no better than others omitted, if indeed as good. It is not because the work of certain well-known names is in itself poor that they are not found here. On the contrary, it is often very good—some of it indeed so good that an editor feels at times a doubt as to his having done wisely in letting it go unrepresented. Yet, though it may be good in general, no one production seems to stand out with so manifest superiority as to justify its insertion into an anthology. They are all excellent in their way. But each and every one of them lacks distinctiveness, not to speak of distinction, whether that distinctiveness be of pure poetry or merely that of wit or humorous observation, or quaint conceit. Still, no sensible man will venture to set up his own judgment as an infallible standard. All he can hope or reasonably expect is that the reader who regrets not to find here poems which, in his opinion, ought not to have been excluded, will take no serious exception to the large majority of those which have been included.

It remains to say one word about the methods adopted in the preparation of this volume. An effort has been made to follow, as far as practicable, the latest text which passed under the author's own supervision. This task has been rendered in most instances comparatively easy by the opportunity afforded of consulting the extraordinary and invaluable collection of the various editions of American authors which has been presented to the Yale University library by the munificence of Owen Franklin Aldis of the Class of 1874. As a result verbal alterations have been made at times from what is perhaps to many the familiar reading. These collectively are,

A WORD ABOUT ANTHOLOGIES

however, neither numerous nor important. Furthermore, thanks are due in particular to the several American publishers who have granted permission to make selections from works of which they own the copyright. Without their consent the publication of this work would have been impossible.

T. R. L.

August 1, 1912.

TABLE OF CONTENTS

ALDRICH, THOMAS BAILEY
    Baby Bell 427
    In an Atelier 433
    Nocturne 440
    On an Intaglio Head of Minerva 438
    On Lynn Terrace 436
    Palabras Cariñosas 432
    Song from the Persian 431

ALLEN, ELIZABETH ANN (CHASE) (AKERS)
    Last 397
    Left Behind 398
    Rock Me to Sleep 395

ANONYMOUS
    Home Wounded 468

BARLOW, JOEL
    Babylonian Captivity, The. Psalm CXXXVII 3

BROWN, PHEBE (HINSDALE)
    Private Devotion 6

BRYANT, WILLIAM CULLEN
    Battle-Field, The 53
    Conqueror's Grave, The 60
    Crowded Street, The 56
    Death of the Flowers, The 46
    Forest Hymn, A 40
    Future Life, The 55
    June 44
    "Oh Mother of a Mighty Race" 58
    Past, The 48
    Planting of the Apple-Tree, The 63
    Snow-Shower, The 66

TABLE OF CONTENTS

    Song of Marion's Men 51
    Thanatopsis 36
    To a Waterfowl 39

BUNNER, HENRY CUYLER
    Atlantic City 525
    Candor 517
    Chakey Einstein 520
    Chaperon, The 519
    Da Capo 529
    Feminine 516
    Just a Love-Letter 531
    She Was a Beauty 516
    Way to Arcady, The 512
    Wed 518

BUTLER, WILLIAM ALLEN
    Incognita of Raphael, The 346
    Nothing to Wear 348

CARY, PHŒBE
    Alas! 345
    Nearer Home 344

COFFIN, ROBERT BARRY
    Ships at Sea 379

COOK, MARC
    Her Opinion of the Play 510

COOKE, PHILIP PENDLETON
    Florence Vane 251

COOKE, ROSE (TERRY)
    Two Villages, The 385

CURTIS, GEORGE WILLIAM
    Egyptian Serenade 343
    O Listen to the Sounding Sea 342
    Spring Song 342

TABLE OF CONTENTS

Cutler, Elbridge Jefferson
    Volunteer, The 394

Doane, George Washington
    Evening 72

Drake, Joseph Rodman
    American Flag, The 69

Dwight, Timothy
    Love to the Church 1

Emerson, Ralph Waldo
    Borrowing 86
    Brahma 87
    Concord Hymn 85
    Days 84
    Fable 83
    Heri, Cras, Hodie 86
    Humble-Bee, The 80
    Poet 85
    Problem, The 77
    Rhodora, The 79
    Sacrifice 86
    Shakespeare 86
    To Eva 84

Field, Eugene
    Bibliomaniac's Prayer, The 498
    Dear Old London 494
    Dibdin's Ghost 499
    Duel, The 508
    Grandma's Prayer 507
    In Amsterdam 496
    Little Peach, The 503
    Lydia Dick 504
    Preference Declared, The 507
    Tea-Gown, The 502

TABLE OF CONTENTS

GARRISON, WILLIAM LLOYD
    Freedom for the Mind 88

GILDER, RICHARD WATSON
    Ah, Be Not False 492
    Heroic Age, The 493
    Noël 491
    Reform 490
    River Inn, The 489
    Songs 492
    Woman's Thought, A 488

HALLECK, FITZ-GREENE
    Alnwick Castle 14
    Burns 18
    Connecticut 30
    Marco Bozzaris 10
    On the Death of Joseph Rodman Drake 25
    Red Jacket 26

HALPINE, CHARLES GRAHAM
    Thousand and Thirty-Seven, The 389

HARTE, FRANCIS BRET
    Chiquita 462
    Dow's Flat 456
    "Jim" 460
    Plain Language from Truthful James 454
    Society upon the Stanislaus, The 452
    What the Engines Said 465

HASTINGS, THOMAS
    In Sorrow 8
    Latter Day, The 7

HAY, JOHN
    Hymn of the Knights Templars 447
    Jim Bludso 443
    Mystery of Gilgal, The 445

TABLE OF CONTENTS

HOFFMAN, CHARLES FENNO
    Mint Julep, The 93
    Monterey 92

HOLMES, OLIVER WENDELL
    Ballad of the Oysterman, The 216
    Chambered Nautilus, The 226
    Deacon's Masterpiece, The 218
    Dilemma, The 195
    Last Leaf, The 193
    Lexington 203
    Music-Grinders, The 200
    My Aunt 197
    On Lending a Punch-Bowl 206
    Parting Word, The 210
    Philosopher to His Love, The 215
    "Qui Vive" 223
    Star and the Water-Lily, The 213
    To the Portrait of "A Lady" 199
    Under the Washington Elm, Cambridge 225
    Voice of the Loyal North, A 228
    Voiceless, The 224

HOVEY, RICHARD
    At the End of Day 539
    Faith and Fate 546
    Launa Dee 541
    Sea Gypsy, The 540
    Unmanifest Destiny 543
    Voices of Unseen Spirits 545
    Wander-Lovers, The 536

HOWE, JULIA WARD
    Battle-Hymn of the Republic 317
    Our Orders 318
    Summons, The 319

TABLE OF CONTENTS

HOWELLS, ELIZABETH (LLOYD)
    Milton's Prayer of Patience 232

INGALLS, JOHN JAMES
    Opportunity 426

KEY, FRANCIS SCOTT
    Star-Spangled Banner, The 4

LANIER, SIDNEY
    Marshes of Glynn, The 482
    Song of the Chattahoochee 480

LARCOM, LUCY
    Hannah Binding Shoes 377

LONGFELLOW, HENRY WADSWORTH
    Arsenal at Springfield, The 113
    Cumberland, The 131
    Day is Done, The 119
    Endymion 108
    Excelsior 111
    Footsteps of Angels 96
    Maidenhood 109
    My Lost Youth 127
    Nuremberg 115
    Psalm of Life, The 95
    Resignation 123
    Seaweed 121
    Skeleton in Armor, The 99
    Song of the Silent Land 98
    Village Blacksmith, The 106
    Warden of the Cinque Ports, The 125

LOWELL, JAMES RUSSELL
    Auf Wiedersehen 302
    Courtin', The 270
    Credidimus Jovem Regnare 307

TABLE OF CONTENTS

 Ode Recited at the Harvard Commemoration, July 21,
  1865 286
 Palinode 303
 Petition, The 306
 Present Crisis, The 275
 Song—"O Moonlight Deep and Tender"............. 274
 Telepathy 306
 Washers of the Shroud, The 282
 What Mr. Robinson Thinks 268
 Without and Within 304

LYTLE, WILLIAM HAINES
 Antony and Cleopatra 381

MCMASTER, GUY HUMPHREYS
 Carmen Bellicosum 387

MESSINGER, ROBERT HINCKLEY
 Winter Wish, A 234

MOODY, WILLIAM VAUGHN
 Gloucester Moors 556
 Ode in Time of Hesitation, An 547

O'HARA, THEODORE
 Bivouac of the Dead, The 332

PALMER, JOHN WILLIAMSON
 Fight at the San Jacinto, The 361
 Stonewall Jackson's Way 364

PALMER, RAY
 Faith 168

PARSONS, THOMAS WILLIAM
 Her Epitaph 326
 Mary Booth 325
 Obituary 327
 On a Bust of Dante 323

TABLE OF CONTENTS

    Paradisi Gloria 328
    Saint Peray 329

PERRY, NORA
    After the Ball 477

PIKE, ALBERT
    Dixie 230

PINKNEY, EDWARD COATE
    Health, A 74
    Parting, A 76
    Serenade, A 73
    Song—"We Break the Glass" 73
    Widow's Song, The 76

PRATT, GEORGE
    Pen of Steel, A 401

POE, EDGAR ALLAN
    Annabel Lee 186
    Bells, The 182
    Conqueror Worm, The 180
    Haunted Palace, The 178
    Raven, The 170
    To Helen 192
    To One in Paradise 177
    Ulalume 188

RANDALL, JAMES RYDER
    My Maryland 449

READ, THOMAS BUCHANAN
    Celestial Army, The 337
    Sheridan's Ride 339
    Some Things Love Me 336

SARGENT, EPES
    Life on the Ocean Wave, A 239

TABLE OF CONTENTS

Saxe, John Godfrey
    Bereavement 250
    Early Rising 240
    Orpheus and Eurydice 245
    Polyphemus and Ulysses 242

Shanly, Charles Dawson
    Fancy Shot, The 237

Sill, Edward Rowland
    Coup de Grace, The 476
    Fool's Prayer, The 470
    Lover's Song, The 475
    Momentous Words 474
    Open Window, The 471
    To a Maid Demure 473

Stedman, Edmund Clarence
    Ballad of Lager Bier, The 406
    Edged Tools 413
    Hypatia 422
    Kearny at Seven Pines 420
    Pan in Wall Street 403
    Provençal Lovers 418
    Si Jeunesse Savait! 417
    Undiscovered Country, The 415
    World Well Lost, The 416

Stoddard, Richard Henry
    Flight of Youth, The 366
    Without and Within 367
    Woman's Poem, A 372

Story, William Wetmore
    Black Eyes 264
    Cleopatra 253
    In the Rain 266
    L'Abbate 260

TABLE OF CONTENTS

    Praxiteles and Phryne 258
    Snowdrop 267

TAPPAN, WILLIAM BINGHAM
    Hour of Peaceful Rest, The 35

TIMROD, HENRY
    Charleston 391
    Ode 393

WAKEFIELD, NANCY AMELIA WOODBURY (PRIEST)
    Over the River 441

WHITMAN, WALT
    O Captain! My Captain! 321

WHITTIER, JOHN GREENLEAF
    Barbara Frietchie 163
    Barclay of Ury 139
    Dedication of "In War Time" 159
    Ichabod 146
    Lines on the Death of S. O. Torrey 144
    Maud Muller 148
    My Playmate 153
    Old Burying-Ground, The 155
    Proem to Poems of 1847.......................... 133
    Randolph of Roanoke 134
    Watchers, The 160
    What the Birds Said 166

WILLARD, EMMA (HART)
    Rocked in the Cradle of the Deep 9

WILLIS, NATHANIEL PARKER
    Love in a Cottage 90
    Unseen Spirits 89

YALE BOOK OF AMERICAN VERSE

TIMOTHY DWIGHT 1752–1817

Love to the Church

I love thy kingdom, Lord,
   The house of thine abode,
The church our blest Redeemer saved
   With his own precious blood.

I love thy church, O God!
   Her walls before thee stand,
Dear as the apple of thine eye,
   And graven on thy hand.

If e'er to bless thy sons
   My voice or hands deny,
These hands let useful skill forsake,
   This voice in silence die.

For her my tears shall fall,
   For her my prayers ascend;
To her my cares and toils be given
   Till toils and cares shall end.

Beyond my highest joy
   I prize her heavenly ways,
Her sweet communion, solemn vows,
   Her hymns of love and praise.

Jesus, thou friend divine,
   Our Saviour and our King,
Thy hand from every snare and foe
   Shall great deliverance bring.

TIMOTHY DWIGHT 1752–1817

Sure as thy truth shall last,
  To Zion shall be given
The brightest glories earth can yield,
  And brighter bliss of heaven.

JOEL BARLOW 1755–1812

Psalm CXXXVII

The Babylonian Captivity

Along the banks where Babel's current flows
   Our captive bands in deep despondence stray'd,
While Zion's fall in sad remembrance rose,
   Her friends, her children mingled with the dead.

The tuneless harp, that once with joy we strung,
   When praise employ'd and mirth inspir'd the lay,
In mournful silence on the willows hung;
   And growing grief prolong'd the tedious day.

The barbarous tyrants, to increase the woe,
   With taunting smiles a song of Zion claim;
Bid sacred praise in strains melodious flow,
   While they blaspheme the great Jehovah's name.

But how, in heathen chains and lands unknown,
   Shall Israel's sons a song of Zion raise?
O hapless Salem, God's terrestrial throne,
   Thou land of glory, sacred mount of praise.

If e'er my memory lose thy lovely name,
   If my cold heart neglect my kindred race,
Let dire destruction seize this guilty frame;
   My hand shall perish and my voice shall cease.

Yet shall the Lord, who hears when Zion calls,
   O'ertake her foes with terror and dismay,
His arm avenge her desolated walls,
   And raise her children to eternal day.

FRANCIS SCOTT KEY 1779–1843

The Star-Spangled Banner

O say, can you see, by the dawn's early light,
What so proudly we hailed at the twilight's last gleaming?
Whose broad stripes and bright stars through the perilous fight,
O'er the ramparts we watched were so gallantly streaming;
And the rocket's red glare, the bombs bursting in air,
Gave proof through the night that our flag was still there;
O say, does that star-spangled banner yet wave
O'er the land of the free, and the home of the brave?

On the shore dimly seen through the mists of the deep,
Where the foe's haughty host in dread silence reposes,
What is that which the breeze, o'er the towering steep,
As it fitfully blows, now conceals, now discloses?
Now it catches the gleam of the morning's first beam,
In full glory reflected now shines on the stream;
'Tis the star-spangled banner; O long may it wave
O'er the land of the free, and the home of the brave!

And where is that band who so vauntingly swore
That the havoc of war and the battle's confusion
A home and a country should leave us no more?
Their blood has washed out their foul footsteps' pollution.

FRANCIS SCOTT KEY 1779–1843

No refuge could save the hireling and slave,
From the terror of flight and the gloom of the grave;
And the star-spangled banner in triumph doth wave
O'er the land of the free, and the home of the brave!

O! thus be it ever, when freemen shall stand
Between their loved homes and the war's desolation!
Blest with victory and peace, may the heav'n-rescued land,
Praise the power that hath made and preserved us a nation.
Then conquer we must, for our cause it is just.
And this be our motto—"In God is our trust;"
And the star-spangled banner in triumph shall wave
O'er the land of the free, and the home of the brave.

PHEBE (HINSDALE) BROWN 1783–1861

Private Devotion

I love to steal awhile away
    From every cumbering care,
And spend the hours of setting day
    In humble, grateful prayer.

I love, in solitude, to shed
    The penitential tear;
And all His promises to plead,
    When none but God can hear.

I love to think on mercies past,
    And future good implore;
And all my cares and sorrows cast
    On Him whom I adore.

I love, by faith, to take a view
    Of brighter scenes in heaven;
The prospect doth my strength renew,
    While here by tempests driven.

Thus, when life's toilsome day is o'er,
    May its departing ray
Be calm as this impressive hour,
    And lead to endless day.

THOMAS HASTINGS 1784–1872

The Latter Day

Hail to the brightness of Zion's glad morning;
    Joy to the lands that in darkness have lain;
Hushed be the accents of sorrow and mourning;
    Zion in triumph begins her mild reign!

Hail to the brightness of Zion's glad morning,
    Long by the prophets of Israel foretold;
Hail to the millions from bondage returning;
    Gentiles and Jews the blest vision behold!

Lo, in the desert rich flowers are springing;
    Streams ever copious are gliding along;
Loud from the mountain-tops echoes are ringing;
    Wastes rise in verdure, and mingle in song.

See, from all lands, from the isles of the ocean,
    Praise to Jehovah ascending on high;
Fallen are the engines of war and commotion;
    Shouts of salvation are rending the sky!

THOMAS HASTINGS 1784–1872

In Sorrow

Gently, Lord, oh, gently lead us,
   Pilgrims in this vale of tears,
Through the trials yet decreed us,
   Till our last great change appears.
When temptation's darts assail us,
   When in devious paths we stray,
Let thy goodness never fail us,
   Lead us in thy perfect way.

In the hour of pain and anguish,
   In the hour when death draws near,
Suffer not our hearts to languish,
   Suffer not our souls to fear;
And, when mortal life is ended,
   Bid us in thine arms to rest,
Till, by angel bands attended,
   We awake among the blest.

EMMA (HART) WILLARD 1787–1870

Rocked in the Cradle of the Deep

Rocked in the cradle of the deep
I lay me down in peace to sleep;
Secure I rest upon the wave,
For Thou, O Lord! hast power to save.
I know Thou wilt not slight my call,
For Thou dost mark the sparrow's fall;
And calm and peaceful shall I sleep,
Rocked in the cradle of the deep.

When in the dead of night I lie
And gaze upon the trackless sky,
The star-bespangled heavenly scroll,
The boundless waters as they roll,—
I feel Thy wondrous power to save
From perils of the stormy wave:
Rocked in the cradle of the deep,
I calmly rest and soundly sleep.

And such the trust that still were mine,
Though stormy winds swept o'er the brine,
Or though the tempest's fiery breath
Roused me from sleep to wreck and death.
In ocean cave, still safe with Thee
The germ of immortality!
And calm and peaceful shall I sleep,
Rocked in the cradle of the deep.

FITZ-GREENE HALLECK 1790–1867

Marco Bozzaris

At midnight, in his guarded tent,
   The Turk was dreaming of the hour
When Greece, her knee in suppliance bent,
   Should tremble at his power;
In dreams, through camp and court, he bore
The trophies of a conqueror;
   In dreams his song of triumph heard;
Then wore his monarch's signet-ring:
Then pressed that monarch's throne—a king;
As wild his thoughts, and gay of wing,
   As Eden's garden bird.

At midnight, in the forest shades,
   Bozzaris ranged his Suliote band,
True as the steel of their tried blades,
   Heroes in heart and hand.
There had the Persian's thousands stood,
There had the glad earth drunk their blood—
   On old Platæa's day;
And now there breathed that haunted air
The sons of sires who conquered there,
With arm to strike, and soul to dare,
   As quick, as far as they.

An hour passed on—the Turk awoke:
   That bright dream was his last;
He woke—to hear his sentries shriek,
   "To arms! they come! the Greek! the Greek!"

FITZ-GREENE HALLECK 1790–1867

He woke—to die midst flame, and smoke,
And shout, and groan, and sabre-stroke,
  And death-shots falling thick and fast
As lightnings from the mountain-cloud;
And heard, with voice as trumpet loud,
  Bozzaris cheer his band:
"Strike—till the last armed foe expires;
Strike—for your altars and your fires;
Strike—for the green graves of your sires;
  God—and your native land!"

They fought—like brave men, long and well;
  They piled that ground with Moslem slain,
They conquered—but Bozzaris fell,
  Bleeding at every vein.
His few surviving comrades saw
His smile when rang their proud hurrah,
  And the red field was won;
Then saw in death his eyelids close
Calmly, as to a night's repose,
  Like flowers at set of sun.

Come to the bridal-chamber, Death!
  Come to the mother's, when she feels,
For the first time, her first-born's breath;
  Come when the blessèd seals
That close the pestilence are broke,
And crowded cities wail its stroke;
Come in consumption's ghastly form,
The earthquake shock, the ocean storm;

FITZ-GREENE HALLECK 1790–1867

Come when the heart beats high and warm,
   With banquet-song, and dance and wine;
And thou art terrible—the tear,
The groan, the knell, the pall, the bier;
And all we know, or dream, or fear
   Of agony, are thine.

But to the hero, when his sword
   Has won the battle for the free,
Thy voice sounds like a prophet's word;
And in its hollow tones are heard
   The thanks of millions yet to be.
Come, when his task of fame is wrought—
Come, with her laurel-leaf, blood-bought—
   Come in her crowning hour—and then
Thy sunken eye's unearthly light
To him is welcome as the sight
   Of sky and stars to prisoned men:
Thy grasp is welcome as the hand
Of brother in a foreign land;
Thy summons welcome as the cry
That told the Indian isles were nigh
   To the world-seeking Genoese,
When the land wind, from woods of palm,
And orange groves, and fields of balm,
   Blew o'er the Haytian seas.

Bozzaris! with the storied brave
   Greece nurtured in her glory's time,
Rest thee—there is no prouder grave,
   Even in her own proud clime.

FITZ-GREENE HALLECK 1790–1867

She wore no funeral weeds for thee,
   Nor bade the dark hearse wave its plume,
Like torn branch from death's leafless tree,
In sorrow's pomp and pageantry,
   The heartless luxury of the tomb:
But she remembers thee as one
Long loved, and for a season gone.
For thee her poet's lyre is wreathed,
Her marble wrought, her music breathed;
For thee she rings the birthday bells;
Of thee her babes' first lisping tells;
For thine her evening prayer is said
At palace couch and cottage bed;
Her soldier, closing with the foe,
Gives for thy sake a deadlier blow;
His plighted maiden, when she fears
For him, the joy of her young years,
Thinks of thy fate, and checks her tears:
   And she, the mother of thy boys,
Though in her eye and faded cheek
Is read the grief she will not speak,
   The memory of her buried joys,
And even she who gave thee birth,
Will, by her pilgrim-circled hearth,
   Talk of thy doom without a sigh:
For thou art Freedom's now, and Fame's;
One of the few, the immortal names,
   That were not born to die.

FITZ-GREENE HALLECK 1790–1867

Alnwick Castle

Home of the Percys' high-born race,
   Home of their beautiful and brave,
Alike their birth and burial place,
   Their cradle and their grave!
Still sternly o'er the castle gate
Their house's Lion stands in state,
   As in his proud departed hours;
And warriors frown in stone on high,
And feudal banners "flout the sky"
   Above his princely towers.

A gentle hill its side inclines,
   Lovely in England's fadeless green,
To meet the quiet stream which winds
   Through this romantic scene
As silently and sweetly still,
As when, at evening, on that hill,
   While summer's wind blew soft and low,
Seated by gallant Hotspur's side,
His Katherine was a happy bride,
   A thousand years ago.

Gaze on the Abbey's ruined pile:
   Does not the succoring ivy, keeping
Her watch around it, seem to smile,
   As o'er a loved one sleeping?
One solitary turret gray
   Still tells, in melancholy glory,

FITZ-GREENE HALLECK 1790–1867

The legend of the Cheviot day,
   The Percys' proudest border story.
That day its roof was triumph's arch;
   Then rang, from isle to pictured dome,
The light step of the soldier's march,
   The music of the trump and drum;
And babe, and sire, the old, the young,
And the monk's hymn, and minstrel's song,
And woman's pure kiss, sweet and long,
   Welcomed her warrior home.

Wild roses by the Abbey towers
   Are gay in their young bud and bloom:
They were born of a race of funeral flowers
That garlanded, in long-gone hours,
   A templar's knightly tomb.
He died, the sword in his mailed hand,
On the holiest spot of the Blessed land,
   Where the Cross was damped with his dying breath,
When blood ran free as festal wine,
And the sainted air of Palestine
   Was thick with the darts of death.

Wise with the lore of centuries,
What tales, if there be "tongues in trees,"
   Those giant oaks could tell,
Of beings born and buried here;
Tales of the peasant and the peer,
Tales of the bridal and the bier,
   The welcome and farewell,

Since on their boughs the startled bird
First, in her twilight slumbers, heard
   The Norman's curfew-bell!

I wandered through the lofty halls
   Trod by the Percys of old fame,
And traced upon the chapel walls
   Each high heroic name,
From him who once his standard set
Where now, o'er mosque and minaret,
   Glitter the Sultan's crescent moons;
To him who, when a younger son,
Fought for King George at Lexington,
   A major of dragoons.

That last half stanza—it has dashed
   From my warm lips the sparkling cup;
The light that o'er my eyebeam flashed,
   The power that bore my spirit up
Above this bank-note world—is gone;
And Alnwick's but a market town,
And this, alas! its market day,
And beasts and borderers throng the way;
Oxen and bleating lambs in lots,
Northumbrian boors and plaided Scots,
   Men in the coal and cattle line;
From Teviot's bard and hero land,
From royal Berwick's beach of sand,
From Wooller, Morpeth, Hexham, and
   Newcastle-upon-Tyne.

FITZ-GREENE HALLECK 1790–1867

These are not the romantic times
So beautiful in Spenser's rhymes,
   So dazzling to the dreaming boy:
Ours are the days of fact, not fable,
Of knights, but not of the round table,
   Of Bailie Jarvie, not Rob Roy:
'T is what "our President" Monroe
   Has called "the era of good feeling":
The Highlander, the bitterest foe
To modern laws, has felt their blow,
Consented to be taxed, and vote,
And put on pantaloons and coat,
   And leave off cattle-stealing:
Lord Stafford mines for coal and salt,
The Duke of Norfolk deals in malt,
   The Douglas in red herrings;
And noble name and cultured land,
Palace, and park, and vassal band,
Are powerless to the notes of hand
   Of Rothschild or the Barings.

The age of bargaining, said Burke,
Has come: to-day the turbaned Turk
(Sleep, Richard of the lion heart!
Sleep on, nor from your cerements start),
   Is England's friend and fast ally;
The Moslem tramples on the Greek,
   And on the Cross and altar-stone,
   And Christendom looks tamely on,

And hears the Christian maiden shriek,
   And sees the Christian father die;
And not a sabre-blow is given
For Greece and fame, for faith and heaven,
   By Europe's craven chivalry.

You'll ask if yet the Percy lives
   In the armed pomp of feudal state?
The present representatives
   Of Hotspur and his "gentle Kate,"
Are some half-dozen serving-men
In the drab coat of William Penn;
   A chambermaid, whose lip and eye,
And cheek, and brown hair, bright and curling,
   Spoke nature's aristocracy;
And one, half groom, half seneschal,
Who bowed me through court, bower, and hall,
From donjon-keep to turret wall,
   For ten-and-sixpence sterling.

Burns

To a Rose, brought from near Alloway Kirk, in Ayrshire, in the Autumn of 1822

Wild rose of Alloway! my thanks;
   Thou 'mindst me of that autumn noon
When first we met upon "the banks
   And braes o' bonny Doon."

Like thine, beneath the thorn-tree's bough,
  My sunny hour was glad and brief,
We've crossed the winter sea, and thou
  Art withered—flower and leaf.

And will not thy death-doom be mine—
  The doom of all things wrought of clay—
And withered my life's leaf like thine,
  Wild rose of Alloway?

Not so his memory,—for whose sake
  My bosom bore thee far and long,
His—who a humbler flower could make
  Immortal as his song.

The memory of Burns—a name
  That calls, when brimmed her festal cup,
A nation's glory and her shame,
  In silent sadness up.

A nation's glory—be the rest
  Forgot—she's canonized his mind;
And it is joy to speak the best
  We may of human kind.

I've stood beside the cottage-bed
  Where the Bard-peasant first drew breath;
A straw-thatched roof above his head,
  A straw-wrought couch beneath.

FITZ-GREENE HALLECK 1790–1867

And I have stood beside the pile,
   His monument—that tells to Heaven
The homage of earth's proudest isle
   To that Bard-peasant given!

Bid thy thoughts hover o'er that spot,
   Boy-Minstrel, in thy dreaming hour;
And know, however low his lot,
   A Poet's pride and power:

The pride that lifted Burns from earth,
   The power that gave a child of song
Ascendency o'er rank and birth,
   The rich, the brave, the strong;

And if despondency weigh down
   Thy spirit's fluttering pinions then,
Despair—thy name is written on
   The roll of common men.

There have been loftier themes than his,
   And longer scrolls, and louder lyres,
And lays lit up with Poesy's
   Purer and holier fires:

Yet read the names that know not death;
   Few nobler ones than Burns are there;
And few have won a greener wreath
   Than that which binds his hair.

FITZ-GREENE HALLECK 1790–1867

His is that language of the heart,
   In which the answering heart would speak,
Thought, word, that bids the warm tear start,
   Or the smile light the cheek;

And his that music, to whose tone
   The common pulse of man keeps time,
In cot or castle's mirth or moan,
   In cold or sunny clime.

And who hath heard his song, nor knelt
   Before its spell with willing knee,
And listened, and believed, and felt
   The Poet's mastery

O'er the mind's sea, in calm and storm,
   O'er the heart's sunshine and its showers,
O'er Passion's moments bright and warm,
   O'er Reason's dark, cold hours;

On fields where brave men "die or do,"
   In halls where rings the banquet's mirth,
Where mourners weep, where lovers woo,
   From throne to cottage-hearth?

What sweet tears dim the eye unshed,
   What wild vows falter on the tongue,
When "Scots wha hae wi' Wallace bled,"
   Or "Auld Lang Syne" is sung!

FITZ-GREENE HALLECK 1790–1867

Pure hopes, that lift the soul above,
   Come with his Cotter's hymn of praise,
And dreams of youth, and truth, and love,
   With "Logan's" banks and braes.

And when he breathes his master-lay
   Of Alloway's witch-haunted wall,
All passions in our frames of clay
   Come thronging at his call.

Imagination's world of air,
   And our own world, its gloom and glee,
Wit, pathos, poetry, are there,
   And death's sublimity.

And Burns—though brief the race he ran,
   Though rough and dark the path he trod,
Lived—died—in form and soul a Man,
   The image of his God.

Through care and pain, and want, and woe,
   With wounds that only death could heal,
Tortures—the poor alone can know,
   The proud alone can feel;

He kept his honesty and truth,
   His independent tongue and pen,
And moved, in manhood as in youth,
   Pride of his fellow-men.

FITZ-GREENE HALLECK 1790–1867

Strong sense, deep feeling, passions strong,
   A hate of tyrant and of knave,
A love of right, a scorn of wrong,
   Of coward and of slave;

A kind, true heart, a spirit high,
   That could not fear and would not bow,
Were written in his manly eye
   And on his manly brow.

Praise to the bard! his words are driven,
   Like flower-seeds by the far winds sown,
Where'er, beneath the sky of heaven,
   The birds of fame have flown.

Praise to the man! a nation stood
   Beside his coffin with wet eyes,
Her brave, her beautiful, her good,
   As when a loved one dies.

And still, as on his funeral day,
   Men stand his cold earth-couch around,
With the mute homage that we pay
   To consecrated ground.

And consecrated ground it is,
   The last, the hallowed home of one
Who lives upon all memories,
   Though with the buried gone.

Such graves as his are pilgrim shrines,
   Shrines to no code or creed confined—
The Delphian vales, the Palestines,
   The Meccas of the mind.

Sages, with wisdom's garland wreathed,
   Crowned kings, and mitred priests of power,
And warriors with their bright swords sheathed,
   The mightiest of the hour;

And lowlier names, whose humble home
   Is lit by Fortune's dimmer star,
Are there—o'er wave and mountain come,
   From countries near and far;

Pilgrims whose wandering feet have pressed
   The Switzer's snow, the Arab's sand,
Or trod the piled leaves of the West,
   My own green forest-land.

All ask the cottage of his birth,
   Gaze on the scenes he loved and sung,
And gather feelings not of earth
   His fields and streams among.

They linger by the Doon's low trees,
   And pastoral Nith, and wooded Ayr,
And round thy sepulchres, Dumfries!
   The poet's tomb is there.

But what to them the sculptor's art,
   His funeral columns, wreaths and urns?
Wear they not graven on the heart
   The name of Robert Burns?

On the Death of Joseph Rodman Drake

Green be the turf above thee,
   Friend of my better days!
None knew thee but to love thee,
   Nor named thee but to praise.

Tears fell, when thou wert dying,
   From eyes unused to weep,
And long where thou art lying,
   Will tears the cold turf steep.

When hearts, whose truth was proven,
   Like thine, are laid in earth,
There should a wreath be woven
   To tell the world their worth;

And I, who woke each morrow
   To clasp thy hand in mine,
Who shared thy joy and sorrow,
   Whose weal and woe were thine:

It should be mine to braid it
  Around thy faded brow,
But I 've in vain essayed it,
  And feel I can not now.

While memory bids me weep thee,
  Nor thoughts nor words are free,
The grief is fixed too deeply
  That mourns a man like thee.

Red Jacket

Cooper, whose name is with his country's woven,
  First in her files, her Pioneer of mind—
A wanderer now in other climes, has proven
  His love for the young land he left behind;

And throned her in the senate-hall of nations,
  Robed like the deluge rainbow, heaven-wrought;
Magnificent as his own mind's creations,
  And beautiful as its green world of thought:

And faithful to the Act of Congress, quoted
  As law authority, it passed *nem. con.;*
He writes that we are, as ourselves have voted,
  The most enlightened people ever known.

FITZ-GREENE HALLECK 1790–1867

That all our week is happy as a Sunday
   In Paris, full of song, and dance, and laugh;
And that, from Orleans to the Bay of Fundy,
   There's not a bailiff or an epitaph;

And furthermore—in fifty years, or sooner,
   We shall export our poetry and wine;
And our brave fleet, eight frigates and a schooner,
   Will sweep the seas from Zembla to the Line.

If he were with me, King of Tuscarora!
   Gazing, as I, upon thy portrait now,
In all its medalled, fringed, and beaded glory,
   Its eye's dark beauty, and its thoughtful brow—

Its brow, half martial and half diplomatic,
   Its eye, upsoaring like an eagle's wings,
Well might he boast that we, the Democratic,
   Outrival Europe, even in our Kings!

For thou wast monarch born. Tradition's pages
   Tell not the planting of thy parent tree,
But that the forest tribes have bent for ages
   To thee, and to thy sires, the subject knee.

Thy name is princely—if no poet's magic
   Could make Red Jacket grace an English rhyme,
Though some one with a genius for the tragic
   Hath introduced it in a pantomine,

Yet it is music in the language spoken
  Of thine own land, and on her herald-roll;
As bravely fought for, and as proud a token
  As Cœur de Lion's of a warrior's soul.

Thy garb—though Austria's bosom-star would frighten
  That medal pale, as diamonds the dark mine,
And George the Fourth wore, at his court at Brighton,
  A more becoming evening dress than thine;

Yet 't is a brave one, scorning wind and weather,
  And fitted for thy couch, on field and flood,
As Rob Roy's tartan for the Highland heather,
  Or forest green for England's Robin Hood.

Is strength a monarch's merit, like a whaler's?
  Thou art as tall, as sinewy, and as strong
As earth's first kings—the Argo's gallant sailors,
  Heroes in history and gods in song.

Is beauty?—Thine has with thy youth departed;
  But the love-legends of thy manhood's years,
And she who perished, young and broken-hearted,
  Are—but I rhyme for smiles and not for tears.

Is eloquence?—Her spell is thine that reaches
  The heart, and makes the wisest head its sport;
And there's one rare, strange virtue in thy speeches,
  The secret of their mastery—they are short.

FITZ-GREENE HALLECK 1790–1867

The monarch mind, the mystery of commanding,
   The birth-hour gift, the art Napoleon,
Of winning, fettering, moulding, wielding, banding
   The hearts of millions till they move as one:

Thou hast it. At thy bidding men have crowded
   The road to death as to a festival;
And minstrels, at their sepulchres, have shrouded
   With banner-folds of glory the dark pall.

Who will believe? Not I—for in deceiving
   Lies the dear charm of life's delightful dream;
I cannot spare the luxury of believing
   That all things beautiful are what they seem;

Who will believe that, with a smile whose blessing
   Would, like the Patriarch's, soothe a dying hour,
With voice as low, as gentle, and caressing,
   As e'er won maiden's lip in moonlit bower;

With look like patient Job's eschewing evil;
   With motions graceful as a bird's in air;
Thou art, in sober truth, the veriest devil
   That e'er clinched fingers in a captive's hair!

That in thy breast there springs a poison fountain
   Deadlier than that where bathes the Upas-tree;
And in thy wrath, a nursing cat-o'-mountain
   Is calm as her babe's sleep compared with thee!

And underneath that face, like summer ocean's,
   Its lip as moveless, and its cheek as clear,
Slumbers a whirlwind of the heart's emotions,
   Love, hatred, pride, hope, sorrow—all save fear.

Love—for thy land, as if she were thy daughter,
   Her pipe in peace, her tomahawk in wars;
Hatred—of missionaries and cold water;
   Pride—in thy rifle trophies and thy scars;

Hope—that thy wrongs may be, by the Great Spirit,
   Remembered and revenged when thou art gone;
Sorrow—that none are left thee to inherit
   Thy name, thy fame, thy passions, and thy throne!

Connecticut

—Still her gray rocks tower above the sea
   That crouches at their feet, a conquered wave;
'T is a rough land of earth, and stone, and tree,
   Where breathes no castled lord or cabined slave;
Where thoughts, and tongues, and hands are bold and free,
   And friends will find a welcome, foes a grave;
And where none kneel, save when to Heaven they pray,
Nor even then, unless in their own way.

FITZ-GREENE HALLECK 1790–1867

Theirs is a pure republic, wild, yet strong,
   A "fierce democracie," where all are true
To what themselves have voted—right or wrong—
   And to their laws, denominated blue;
(If red, they might to Draco's code belong);
   A vestal state, which power could not subdue,
Nor promise win—like her own eagle's nest,
Sacred—the San Marino of the West.

A justice of the peace, for the time being,
   They bow to, but may turn him out next year:
They reverence their priest, but disagreeing
   In price or creed, dismiss him without fear;
They have a natural talent for foreseeing
   And knowing all things; and should Park appear
From his long tour in Africa, to show
The Niger's source, they 'd meet him with—"we know!"

They love their land, because it is their own,
   And scorn to give aught other reason why;
Would shake hands with a king upon his throne,
   And think it kindness to his majesty;
A stubborn race, fearing and flattering none.
   Such are they nurtured, such they live and die:
All—but a few apostates, who are meddling
With merchandise, pounds, shillings, pence and peddling;

Or wandering through the southern countries teaching
   The A B C from Webster's spelling-book;
Gallant and godly, making love and preaching,
   And gaining, by what they call "hook and crook,"

And what the moralists call over-reaching,
   A decent living. The Virginians look
Upon them with as favorable eyes
As Gabriel on the devil in Paradise.

But these are but their outcasts. View them near
   At home, where all their worth and pride is placed;
And there their hospitable fires burn clear,
   And there the lowliest farmhouse hearth is graced
With manly hearts, in piety sincere,
   Faithful in love, in honor stern and chaste,
In friendship warm and true, in danger brave,
Beloved in life, and sainted in the grave.

And minds have there been nurtured, whose control
   Is felt even in the nation's destiny;
Men who swayed senates with a statesman's soul,
   And looked on armies with a leader's eye;
Names that adorn and dignify the scroll,
   Whose leaves contain their country's history,
And tales of love and war—listen to one
Of the Green-Mountaineer—the Stark of Bennington.

When on that field his band the Hessians fought,
   Briefly he spoke before the fight began:
"Soldiers! Those German gentlemen are bought
   For four pounds eight and sevenpence per man,
By England's king; a bargain, as is thought.
   Are we worth more? Let's prove it now we can;
For we must beat them, boys, ere set of sun,
Or Mary Stark's a widow." It was done.

. . . . .

FITZ-GREENE HALLECK 1790–1867

Hers are not Tempe's nor Arcadia's spring,
   Nor the long summer of Cathayan vales,
The vines, the flowers, the air, the skies, that fling
   Such wild enchantment o'er Boccaccio's tales
Of Florence and the Arno; yet the wing
   Of life's best angel, Health, is on her gales
Through sun and snow; and, in the autumn time
Earth has no purer and no lovelier clime.

Her clear, warm heaven at noon,—the mist that shrouds
   Her twilight hills—her cool and starry eves,
The glorious splendor of her sunset clouds,
   The rainbow beauty of her forest leaves,
Come o'er the eye, in solitude and crowds,
   Where'er his web of song her poet weaves;
And his mind's brightest vision but displays
The autumn scenery of his boyhood's days.

And when you dream of woman, and her love;
   Her truth, her tenderness, her gentle power;
The maiden, listening in the moonlight grove,
   The mother, smiling in her infant's bower;
Forms, features, worshipped while we breathe or move,
   Be by some spirit of your dreaming hour
Borne, like Loretto's chapel, through the air
To the green land I sing, then wake, you'll find them
   there.

JOHN HOWARD PAYNE 1791-1852

Home, Sweet Home

From the Opera of "Clari, the Maid of Milan"

Mid pleasures and palaces though we may roam,
Be it ever so humble there's no place like home!
A charm from the sky seems to hallow us there,
Which, seek through the world, is ne'er met with elsewhere.
    Home! home! sweet, sweet home!
    There's no place like home!

An exile from home, splendor dazzles in vain:
O, give me my lowly thatched cottage again!
The birds singing gayly that came at my call;—
Give me them,—and the peace of mind dearer than all!
    Home! home! sweet, sweet home!
    There's no place like home!

How sweet 't is to sit 'neath a fond father's smile,
And the cares of a mother to soothe and beguile!
Let others delight mid new pleasures to roam,
But give me, oh, give me, the pleasures of home!
    Home! home! sweet, sweet home!
    There's no place like home!

To thee I'll return, overburdened with care;
The heart's dearest solace will smile on me there;
No more from that cottage again will I roam;
Be it ever so humble, there's no place like home.
    Home! home! sweet, sweet home!
    There's no place like home!

WILLIAM BINGHAM TAPPAN 1794–1849

The Hour of Peaceful Rest

There is an hour of peaceful rest
  To mourning wanderers given;
There is a joy for souls distrest,
A balm for every wounded breast,
  'T is found alone in heaven.

There is a soft, a downy bed,
  Far from these shades of even—
A couch for weary mortals spread,
Where they may rest the aching head,
  And find repose, in heaven.

There is a home for weary souls
  By sin and sorrow driven;
When tossed on life's tempestuous shoals,
Where storms arise, and ocean rolls,
  And all is drear but heaven.

There faith lifts up her cheerful eye,
  To brighter prospects given;
And views the tempest passing by,
The evening shadows quickly fly,
  And all serene in heaven.

There fragrant flowers immortal bloom,
  And joys supreme are given;
There rays divine disperse the gloom:
Beyond the confines of the tomb
  Appears the dawn of heaven.

WILLIAM CULLEN BRYANT 1794-1878

Thanatopsis

To him who in the love of Nature holds
Communion with her visible forms, she speaks
A various language; for his gayer hours
She has a voice of gladness, and a smile
And eloquence of beauty, and she glides
Into his darker musings, with a mild
And healing sympathy, that steals away
Their sharpness, ere he is aware. When thoughts
Of the last bitter hour come like a blight
Over thy spirit, and sad images
Of the stern agony, and shroud, and pall,
And breathless darkness, and the narrow house,
Make thee to shudder, and grow sick at heart;—
Go forth under the open sky, and list
To Nature's teachings, while from all around—
Earth and her waters, and the depths of air—
Comes a still voice—Yet a few days, and thee
The all-beholding sun shall see no more
In all his course; nor yet in the cold ground,
Where thy pale form was laid, with many tears,
Nor in the embrace of ocean, shall exist
Thy image. Earth, that nourished thee, shall claim
Thy growth, to be resolved to earth again,
And, lost each human trace, surrendering up
Thine individual being, shalt thou go
To mix forever with the elements;
To be a brother to the insensible rock,

WILLIAM CULLEN BRYANT 1794–1878

And to the sluggish clod, which the rude swain
Turns with his share, and treads upon. The oak
Shall send his roots abroad, and pierce thy mould.
   Yet not to thine eternal resting-place
Shalt thou retire alone, nor couldst thou wish
Couch more magnificent. Thou shalt lie down
With patriarchs of the infant world,—with kings,
The powerful of the earth,—the wise, the good,
Fair forms, and hoary seers of ages past,
All in one mighty sepulchre. The hills
Rock-ribbed and ancient as the sun; the vales
Stretching in pensive quietness between;
The venerable woods—rivers that move
In majesty, and the complaining brooks
That make the meadows green; and, poured round all,
Old Ocean's gray and melancholy waste,—
Are but the solemn decorations all
Of the great tomb of man! The golden sun,
The planets, all the infinite host of heaven,
Are shining on the sad abodes of death,
Through the still lapse of ages. All that tread
The globe are but a handful to the tribes
That slumber in its bosom.—Take the wings
Of morning, pierce the Barcan wilderness,
Or lose thyself in the continuous woods
Where rolls the Oregon, and hears no sound,
Save his own dashings,—yet the dead are there:
And millions in those solitudes, since first
The flight of years began, have laid them down

In their last sleep—the dead reign there alone.
So shalt thou rest; and what if thou withdraw
In silence from the living, and no friend
Take note of thy departure? All that breathe
Will share thy destiny. The gay will laugh
When thou art gone, the solemn brood of care
Plod on, and each one as before will chase
His favorite phantom; yet all these shall leave
Their mirth and their employments, and shall come
And make their bed with thee. As the long train
Of ages glide away, the sons of men,
The youth in life's green spring, and he who goes
In the full strength of years, matron and maid,
The speechless babe, and the gray-headed man—
Shall one by one be gathered to thy side
By those, who in their turn shall follow them.

   So live, that when thy summons comes to join
The innumerable caravan which moves
To that mysterious realm, where each shall take
His chamber in the silent halls of death,
Thou go not, like the quarry-slave at night,
Scourged to his dungeon, but, sustained and soothed
By an unfaltering trust, approach thy grave
Like one who wraps the drapery of his couch
About him, and lies down to pleasant dreams.

WILLIAM CULLEN BRYANT 1794–1878

To a Waterfowl

Whither, midst falling dew,
While glow the heavens with the last steps of day,
Far, through their rosy depths, dost thou pursue
    Thy solitary way?

Vainly the fowler's eye
Might mark thy distant flight to do thee wrong,
As, darkly seen against the crimson sky,
    Thy figure floats along.

Seek'st thou the plashy brink
Of weedy lake, or marge of river wide,
Or where the rocking billows rise and sink
    On the chafed ocean-side?

There is a Power whose care
Teaches thy way along that pathless coast—
The desert and illimitable air—
    Lone wandering, but not lost.

All day thy wings have fanned,
At that far height, the cold, thin atmosphere,
Yet stoop not, weary, to the welcome land,
    Though the dark night is near.

And soon that toil shall end;
Soon shalt thou find a summer home, and rest,
And scream among thy fellows; reeds shall bend,
    Soon, o'er thy sheltered nest.

Thou 'rt gone, the abyss of heaven
Hath swallowed up thy form; yet, on my heart
Deeply hath sunk the lesson thou hast given,
    And shall not soon depart.

    He who, from zone to zone,
Guides through the boundless sky thy certain flight,
In the long way that I must tread alone,
    Will lead my steps aright.

A Forest Hymn

    The groves were God's first temples. Ere man learned
To hew the shaft, and lay the architrave,
And spread the roof above them—ere he framed
The lofty vault, to gather and roll back
The sound of anthems; in the darkling wood,
Amidst the cool and silence, he knelt down,
And offered to the Mightiest solemn thanks
And supplication. For his simple heart
Might not resist the sacred influences
Which, from the stilly twilight of the place,
And from the gray old trunks that high in heaven
Mingled their mossy boughs, and from the sound
Of the invisible breath that swayed at once
All their green tops, stole over him, and bowed
His spirit with the thought of boundless power
And inaccessible majesty. Ah, why

WILLIAM CULLEN BRYANT 1794–1878

Should we, in the world's riper years, neglect
God's ancient sanctuaries, and adore
Only among the crowd, and under roofs
That our frail hands have raised? Let me, at least,
Here, in the shadow of this aged wood,
Offer one hymn—thrice happy if it find
Acceptance in His ear.

           Father, thy hand
Hath reared these venerable columns, thou
Didst weave this verdant roof. Thou didst look down
Upon the naked earth, and, forthwith, rose
All these fair ranks of trees. They, in thy sun,
Budded, and shook their green leaves in thy breeze,
And shot towards heaven. The century-living crow,
Whose birth was in their tops, grew old and died
Among their branches, till, at last, they stood,
As now they stand, massy, and tall, and dark,
Fit shrine for humble worshipper to hold
Communion with his Maker. These dim vaults,
These winding aisles, of human pomp or pride
Report not. No fantastic carvings show
The boast of our vain race to change the form
Of thy fair works. But thou art here—thou fill'st
The solitude. Thou art in the soft winds
That run along the summit of these trees
In music; thou art in the cooler breath
That from the inmost darkness of the place
Comes, scarcely felt; the barky trunks, the ground,
The fresh moist ground, are all instinct with thee.

WILLIAM CULLEN BRYANT 1794–1878

Here is continual worship;—Nature, here,
In the tranquillity that thou dost love,
Enjoys thy presence. Noiselessly, around,
From perch to perch, the solitary bird
Passes; and yon clear spring, that, midst its herbs,
Wells softly forth and wandering steeps the roots
Of half the mighty forest, tells no tale
Of all the good it does. Thou hast not left
Thyself without a witness, in these shades,
Of thy perfections. Grandeur, strength, and grace,
Are here to speak of thee. This mighty oak,—
By whose immovable stem I stand and seem
Almost annihilated—not a prince,
In all that proud old world beyond the deep,
E'er wore his crown as loftily as he
Wears the green coronal of leaves with which
Thy hand has graced him. Nestled at his root
Is beauty, such as blooms not in the glare
Of the broad sun. That delicate forest flower,
With scented breath and look so like a smile,
Seems, as it issues from the shapeless mould,
An emanation of the indwelling Life,
A visible token of the upholding Love,
That are the soul of this great universe.

   My heart is awed within me when I think
Of the great miracle that still goes on,
In silence, round me—the perpetual work
Of thy creation, finished, yet renewed
Forever. Written on thy works I read

WILLIAM CULLEN BRYANT 1794–1878

The lesson of thy own eternity.
Lo! all grow old and die—but see again,
How on the faltering footsteps of decay
Youth presses,—ever-gay and beautiful youth
In all its beautiful forms. These lofty trees
Wave not less proudly that their ancestors
Moulder beneath them. O, there is not lost
One of earth's charms: upon her bosom yet,
After the flight of untold centuries,
The freshness of her far beginning lies
And yet shall lie. Life mocks the idle hate
Of his arch-enemy Death—yea, seats himself
Upon the tyrant's throne—the sepulchre,
And of the triumphs of his ghastly foe
Makes his own nourishment. For he came forth
From thine own bosom, and shall have no end.

There have been holy men who hid themselves
Deep in the woody wilderness, and gave
Their lives to thought and prayer, till they outlived
The generation born with them, nor seemed
Less aged than the hoary trees and rocks
Around them;—and there have been holy men
Who deemed it were not well to pass life thus.
But let me often to these solitudes
Retire, and in thy presence reassure
My feeble virtue. Here its enemies,
The passions, at thy plainer footsteps shrink
And tremble and are still. O God! when thou
Dost scare the world with tempests, set on fire

The heavens with falling thunderbolts, or fill,
With all the waters of the firmament,
The swift dark whirlwind that uproots the woods
And drowns the villages; when, at thy call,
Uprises the great deep and throws himself
Upon the continent, and overwhelms
Its cities—who forgets not, at the sight
Of these tremendous tokens of thy power,
His pride, and lays his strifes and follies by?
O, from these sterner aspects of thy face
Spare me and mine, nor let us need the wrath
Of the mad, unchainèd elements to teach
Who rules them. Be it ours to meditate,
In these calm shades, thy milder majesty,
And to the beautiful order of thy works
Learn to conform the order of our lives.

June

I gazed upon the glorious sky
    And the green mountains round,
And thought that when I came to lie
    At rest within the ground,
'T were pleasant, that in flowery June,
When brooks send up a cheerful tune,
    And groves a joyous sound,
The sexton's hand, my grave to make,
The rich, green mountain-turf should break.

WILLIAM CULLEN BRYANT 1794–1878

A cell within the frozen mould,
   A coffin borne through sleet,
And icy clods above it rolled,
   While fierce the tempests beat—
Away!—I will not think of these—
Blue be the sky and soft the breeze,
   Earth green beneath the feet,
And be the damp mould gently pressed
Into my narrow place of rest.

There through the long, long summer hours
   The golden light should lie,
And thick young herbs and groups of flowers
   Stand in their beauty by.
The oriole should build and tell
His love-tale close beside my cell;
   The idle butterfly
Should rest him there, and there be heard
The housewife bee and humming-bird.

And what if cheerful shouts at noon
   Come, from the village sent,
Or song of maids, beneath the moon
   With fairy laughter blent?
And what if, in the evening light,
Betrothèd lovers walk in sight
   Of my low monument?
I would the lovely scene around
Might know no sadder sight nor sound.

I know that I no more should see
    The season's glorious show,
Nor would its brightness shine for me,
    Nor its wild music flow;
But if, around my place of sleep,
The friends I love should come to weep,
    They might not haste to go.
Soft airs, and song, and light, and bloom
Should keep them lingering by my tomb.

These to their softened hearts should bear
    The thought of what has been,
And speak of one who cannot share
    The gladness of the scene;
Whose part, in all the pomp that fills
The circuit of the summer hills,
    Is that his grave is green;
And deeply would their hearts rejoice
To hear again his living voice.

The Death of the Flowers

The melancholy days have come, the saddest of the year,
Of wailing winds, and naked woods, and meadows brown and sere;
Heaped in the hollows of the grove, the autumn leaves lie dead;
They rustle to the eddying gust, and to the rabbit's tread;

WILLIAM CULLEN BRYANT 1794–1878

The robin and the wren are flown, and from the shrubs the jay,
And from the wood-top calls the crow through all the gloomy day.

Where are the flowers, the fair young flowers, that lately sprang and stood
In brighter light and softer airs, a beauteous sisterhood?
Alas! they all are in their graves, the gentle race of flowers
Are lying in their lowly beds with the fair and good of ours.
The rain is falling where they lie, but the cold November rain
Calls not from out the gloomy earth the lovely ones again.

The wind-flower and the violet, they perished long ago,
And the brier-rose and the orchis died amid the summer glow;
But on the hill the goldenrod, and the aster in the wood,
And the yellow sunflower by the brook in autumn beauty stood,
Till fell the frost from the clear cold heaven, as falls the plague on men,
And the brightness of their smile was gone, from upland, glade, and glen.

And now, when comes the calm mild day, as still such days will come,
To call the squirrel and the bee from out their winter home;

When the sound of dropping nuts is heard, though all the trees are still,
And twinkle in the smoky light the waters of the rill,
The south wind searches for the flowers whose fragrance late he bore,
And sighs to find them in the wood and by the stream no more.

And then I think of one who in her youthful beauty died,
The fair meek blossom that grew up and faded by my side.
In the cold moist earth we laid her, when the forests cast the leaf,
And we wept that one so lovely should have a life so brief:
Yet not unmeet it was that one, like that young friend of ours,
So gentle and so beautiful, should perish with the flowers.

The Past

    Thou unrelenting Past!
Strong are the barriers round thy dark domain,
    And fetters, sure and fast,
Hold all that enter thy unbreathing reign.

    Far in thy realm withdrawn
Old empires sit in sullenness and gloom,
    And glorious ages gone
Lie deep within the shadow of thy womb.

WILLIAM CULLEN BRYANT 1794–1878

  Childhood, with all its mirth,
Youth, Manhood, Age that draws us to the ground,
  And last, Man's Life on earth,
Glide to thy dim dominions, and are bound.

  Thou hast my better years;
Thou hast my earlier friends, the good, the kind,
  Yielded to thee with tears—
The venerable form, the exalted mind.

  My spirit yearns to bring
The lost ones back—yearns with desire intense,
  And struggles hard to wring
Thy bolts apart, and pluck thy captives thence.

  In vain; thy gates deny
All passage save to those who hence depart;
  Nor to the streaming eye
Thou giv'st them back—nor to the broken heart.

  In thy abysses hide
Beauty and excellence unknown; to thee
  Earth's wonder and her pride
Are gathered, as the waters to the sea;

  Labors of good to man,
Unpublished charity, unbroken faith,
  Love, that midst grief began,
And grew with years, and faltered not in death.

WILLIAM CULLEN BRYANT 1794–1878

    Full many a mighty name
Lurks in thy depths, unuttered, unrevered;
    With thee are silent fame,
Forgotten arts, and wisdom disappeared.

    Thine for a space are they—
Yet shalt thou yield thy treasures up at last:
    Thy gates shall yet give way,
Thy bolts shall fall, inexorable Past!

    All that of good and fair
Has gone into thy womb from earliest time,
    Shall then come forth to wear
The glory and the beauty of its prime.

    They have not perished—no!
Kind words, remembered voices once so sweet,
    Smiles, radiant long ago,
And features, the great soul's apparent seat.

    All shall come back; each tie
Of pure affection shall be knit again;
    Alone shall Evil die,
And Sorrow dwell a prisoner in thy reign.

    And then shall I behold
Him, by whose kind paternal side I sprung,
    And her, who, still and cold,
Fills the next grave—the beautiful and young.

WILLIAM CULLEN BRYANT 1794–1878

Song of Marion's Men

Our band is few but true and tried,
    Our leader frank and bold;
The British soldier trembles
    When Marion's name is told.
Our fortress is the good greenwood,
    Our tent the cypress-tree;
We know the forest round us,
    As seamen know the sea.
We know its walls of thorny vines,
    Its glades of reedy grass,
Its safe and silent islands
    Within the dark morass.

Woe to the English soldiery
    That little dread us near!
On them shall light at midnight
    A strange and sudden fear:
When, waking to their tents on fire,
    They grasp their arms in vain,
And they who stand to face us
    Are beat to earth again;
And they who fly in terror deem
    A mighty host behind,
And hear the tramp of thousands
    Upon the hollow wind.

Then sweet the hour that brings release
   From danger and from toil;
We talk the battle over,
   And share the battle's spoil.
The woodland rings with laugh and shout,
   As if a hunt were up,
And woodland flowers are gathered
   To crown the soldier's cup.
With merry songs we mock the wind
   That in the pine-top grieves,
And slumber long and sweetly
   On beds of oaken leaves.

Well knows the fair and friendly moon
   The band that Marion leads—
The glitter of their rifles,
   The scampering of their steeds.
'T is life to guide the fiery barb
   Across the moonlit plain;
'T is life to feel the night-wind
   That lifts his tossing mane.
A moment in the British camp—
   A moment—and away
Back to the pathless forest,
   Before the peep of day.

Grave men there are by broad Santee,
   Grave men with hoary hairs;
Their hearts are all with Marion,
   For Marion are their prayers.

And lovely ladies greet our band
   With kindliest welcoming,
With smiles like those of summer,
   And tears like those of spring.
For them we wear these trusty arms,
   And lay them down no more
Till we have driven the Briton,
   Forever, from our shore.

The Battle-Field

Once this soft turf, this rivulet's sands,
   Were trampled by a hurrying crowd,
And fiery hearts and armèd hands
   Encountered in the battle-cloud.

Ah! never shall the land forget
   How gushed the life-blood of her brave—
Gushed, warm with hope and courage yet,
   Upon the soil they fought to save.

Now all is calm, and fresh, and still;
   Alone the chirp of flitting bird,
And talk of children on the hill,
   And bell of wandering kine, are heard.

No solemn host goes trailing by
   The black-mouthed gun and staggering wain;
Men start not at the battle-cry,—
   O, be it never heard again!

WILLIAM CULLEN BRYANT 1794–1878

Soon rested those who fought; but thou
   Who minglest in the harder strife
For truths which men receive not now,
   Thy warfare only ends with life.

A friendless warfare! lingering long
   Through weary day and weary year;
A wild and many-weaponed throng
   Hang on thy front, and flank, and rear.

Yet nerve thy spirit to the proof,
   And blench not at thy chosen lot,
The timid good may stand aloof,
   The sage may frown—yet faint thou not.

Nor heed the shaft too surely cast,
   The foul and hissing bolt of scorn;
For with thy side shall dwell, at last,
   The victory of endurance born.

Truth, crushed to earth, shall rise again;
   The eternal years of God are hers;
But Error, wounded, writhes in pain,
   And dies among his worshippers.

Yea, though thou lie upon the dust,
   When they who helped thee flee in fear,
Die full of hope and manly trust,
   Like those who fell in battle here.

WILLIAM CULLEN BRYANT 1794–1878

    Another hand thy sword shall wield,
        Another hand the standard wave,
    Till from the trumpet's mouth is pealed
        The blast of triumph o'er thy grave.

The Future Life

How shall I know thee in the sphere which keeps
    The disembodied spirits of the dead,
When all of thee that time could wither sleeps
    And perishes among the dust we tread?

For I shall feel the sting of ceaseless pain
    If there I meet thy gentle presence not;
Nor hear the voice I love, nor read again
    In thy serenest eyes the tender thought.

Will not thy own meek heart demand me there?
    That heart whose fondest throbs to me were given—
My name on earth was ever in thy prayer,
    And wilt thou never utter it in heaven?

In meadows fanned by heaven's life-breathing wind,
    In the resplendence of that glorious sphere,
And larger movements of the unfettered mind,
    Wilt thou forget the love that joined us here?

The love that lived through all the stormy past,
    And meekly with my harsher nature bore,
And deeper grew, and tenderer to the last,
    Shall it expire with life, and be no more?

A happier lot than mine, and larger light,
   Await thee there, for thou hast bowed thy will
In cheerful homage to the rule of right,
   And lovest all, and renderest good for ill.

For me, the sordid cares in which I dwell
   Shrink and consume my heart as heat the scroll;
And wrath has left its scar—that fire of hell
   Has left its frightful scar upon my soul.

Yet, though thou wear'st the glory of the sky,
   Wilt thou not keep the same belovèd name,
The same fair thoughtful brow, and gentle eye,
   Lovelier in heaven's sweet climate, yet the same?

Shalt thou not teach me, in that calmer home,
   The wisdom that I learned so ill in this—
The wisdom which is love—till I become
   Thy fit companion in that land of bliss?

The Crowded Street

Let me move slowly through the street,
   Filled with an ever-shifting train,
Amid the sound of steps that beat
   The murmuring walks like autumn rain.

How fast the flitting figures come!
   The mild, the fierce, the stony face;
Some bright with thoughtless smiles, and some
   Where secret tears have left their trace.

WILLIAM CULLEN BRYANT 1794–1878

They pass—to toil, to strife, to rest;
   To halls in which the feast is spread;
To chambers where the funeral guest
   In silence sits beside the dead.

And some to happy homes repair,
   Where children, pressing cheek to cheek,
With mute caresses shall declare
   The tenderness they cannot speak.

And some, who walk in calmness here,
   Shall shudder as they reach the door
Where one who made their dwelling dear,
   Its flower, its light, is seen no more.

Youth, with pale cheek and slender frame,
   And dreams of greatness in thine eye!
Go'st thou to build an early name,
   Or early in the task to die?

Keen son of trade, with eager brow!
   Who is now fluttering in thy snare?
Thy golden fortunes, tower they now,
   Or melt the glittering spires in air?

Who of this crowd to-night shall tread
   The dance till daylight gleam again?
Who sorrow o'er the untimely dead?
   Who writhe in throes of mortal pain?

Some, famine-struck, shall think how long
   The cold dark hours, how slow the light;
And some, who flaunt amid the throng,
   Shall hide in dens of shame to-night.

Each, where his tasks or pleasures call,
   They pass, and heed each other not.
There is who heeds, who holds them all,
   In His large love and boundless thought.

These struggling tides of life that seem
   In wayward, aimless course to tend,
Are eddies of the mighty stream
   That rolls to its appointed end.

"Oh Mother of a Mighty Race"

Oh mother of a mighty race,
Yet lovely in thy youthful grace!
The elder dames, thy haughty peers,
Admire and hate thy blooming years.
     With words of shame
And taunts of scorn they join thy name.

For on thy cheeks the glow is spread
That tints thy morning hills with red;
Thy step—the wild deer's rustling feet
Within thy woods are not more fleet;
     Thy hopeful eye
Is bright as thine own sunny sky.

WILLIAM CULLEN BRYANT 1794–1878

Ay, let them rail—those haughty ones,
While safe thou dwellest with thy sons.
They do not know how loved thou art,
How many a fond and fearless heart
      Would rise to throw
Its life between thee and the foe.

They know not, in their hate and pride,
What virtues with thy children bide;
How true, how good, thy graceful maids
Make bright, like flowers, the valley-shades;
      What generous men
Spring, like thine oaks, by hill and glen.

What cordial welcomes greet the guest
By thy lone rivers of the West;
How faith is kept, and truth revered,
And man is loved, and God is feared,
      In woodland homes,
And where the ocean-border foams.

There's freedom at thy gates and rest
For Earth's down-trodden and opprest,
A shelter for the hunted head,
For the starved laborer toil and bread.
      Power, at thy bounds,
Stops and calls back his baffled hounds.

Oh, fair young mother! on thy brow
Shall sit a nobler grace than now.
Deep in the brightness of the skies

The thronging years in glory rise,
      And, as they fleet,
Drop strength and riches at thy feet.

Thine eye, with every coming hour,
Shall brighten, and thy form shall tower;
And when thy sisters, elder born,
Would brand thy name with words of scorn,
      Before thine eye,
Upon their lips the taunt shall die.

The Conqueror's Grave

Within this lowly grave a Conqueror lies,
   And yet the monument proclaims it not,
   Nor round the sleeper's name hath chisel wrought
The emblems of a fame that never dies,—
Ivy and amaranth, in a graceful sheaf,
Twined with the laurel's fair, imperial leaf.
     A simple name alone,
     To the great world unknown,
Is graven here, and wild-flowers, rising round,
Meek meadow-sweet and violets of the ground,
   Lean lovingly against the humble stone.

Here, in the quiet earth, they laid apart
   No man of iron mould and bloody hands,
   Who sought to wreak upon the cowering lands
The passions that consumed his restless heart;

WILLIAM CULLEN BRYANT 1794–1878

But one of tender spirit and delicate frame,
    Gentlest, in mien and mind,
    Of gentle womankind,
Timidly shrinking from the breath of blame:
One in whose eyes the smile of kindness made
    Its haunt, like flowers by sunny brooks in May,
Yet, at the thought of others' pain, a shade
    Of sweeter sadness chased the smile away.

Nor deem that when the hand that moulders here
Was raised in menace, realms were chilled with fear,
    And armies mustered at the sign, as when
Clouds rise on clouds before the rainy East—
    Gray captains leading bands of veteran men
And fiery youths to be the vulture's feast.
Not thus were waged the mighty wars that gave
The victory to her who fills this grave;
    Alone her task was wrought,
    Alone the battle fought;
Through that long strife her constant hope was staid
On God alone, nor looked for other aid.

She met the hosts of Sorrow with a look
    That altered not beneath the frown they wore,
And soon the lowering brood were tamed, and took,
    Meekly, her gentle rule, and frowned no more.
Her soft hand put aside the assaults of wrath,
    And calmly broke in twain
    The fiery shafts of pain,

And rent the nets of passion from her path.
   By that victorious hand despair was slain.
With love she vanquished hate and overcame
Evil with good, in her Great Master's name.

Her glory is not of this shadowy state,
   Glory that with the fleeting season dies;
But when she entered at the sapphire gate
   What joy was radiant in celestial eyes!
How heaven's bright depths with sounding welcomes
       rung,
And flowers of heaven by shining hands were flung!
     And He who, long before,
      Pain, scorn, and sorrow bore,
The Mighty Sufferer, with aspect sweet,
Smiled on the timid stranger from his seat;
He who returning, glorious, from the grave,
Dragged Death, disarmed, in chains, a crouching slave.

See, as I linger here, the sun grows low;
   Cool airs are murmuring that the night is near.
O gentle sleeper, from thy grave I go
   Consoled though sad, in hope and yet in fear.
     Brief is the time, I know,
      The warfare scarce begun;
Yet all may win the triumphs thou hast won.
Still flows the fount whose waters strengthened thee,
   The victors' names are yet too few to fill
Heaven's mighty roll; the glorious armory,
   That ministered to thee, is open still.

WILLIAM CULLEN BRYANT 1794–1878

The Planting of the Apple-Tree

   Come, let us plant the apple-tree.
Cleave the tough greensward with the spade;
Wide let its hollow bed be made;
There gently lay the roots, and there
Sift the dark mould with kindly care,
   And press it o'er them tenderly,
As, round the sleeping infant's feet,
We softly fold the cradle sheet;
   So plant we the apple-tree.

   What plant we in this apple-tree?
Buds, which the breath of summer days
Shall lengthen into leafy sprays;
Boughs where the thrush, with crimson breast,
Shall haunt and sing and hide her nest;
   We plant, upon the sunny lea,
A shadow for the noontide hour,
A shelter from the summer shower,
   When we plant the apple-tree.

   What plant we in this apple-tree?
Sweets for a hundred flowery springs
To load the May-wind's restless wings,
When, from the orchard row, he pours
Its fragrance through our open doors;
   A world of blossoms for the bee,
Flowers for the sick girl's silent room,
For the glad infant sprigs of bloom,
   We plant with the apple-tree.

WILLIAM CULLEN BRYANT 1794-1878

What plant we in this apple-tree!
Fruits that shall swell in sunny June,
And redden in the August noon,
And drop, when gentle airs come by,
That fan the blue September sky,
   While children come, with cries of glee,
And seek them where the fragrant grass
Betrays their bed to those who pass,
   At the foot of the apple-tree.

And when, above this apple-tree,
The winter stars are quivering bright,
And winds go howling through the night,
Girls, whose young eyes o'erflow with mirth,
Shall peel its fruit by cottage-hearth,
   And guests in prouder homes shall see,
Heaped with the grape of Cintra's vine
And golden orange of the line,
   The fruit of the apple-tree.

The fruitage of this apple-tree
Winds and our flag of stripe and star
Shall bear to coasts that lie afar,
Where men shall wonder at the view,
And ask in what fair groves they grew;
   And sojourners beyond the sea
Shall think of childhood's careless day
And long, long hours of summer play,
   In the shade of the apple-tree.

WILLIAM CULLEN BRYANT 1794–1878

    Each year shall give this apple-tree
A broader flush of roseate bloom,
A deeper maze of verdurous gloom,
And loosen, when the frost-clouds lower,
The crisp brown leaves in thicker shower;
    The years shall come and pass, but we
Shall hear no longer, where we lie,
The summer's songs, the autumn's sigh,
    In the boughs of the apple-tree.

    And time shall waste this apple-tree.
Oh, when its aged branches throw
Thin shadows on the ground below,
Shall fraud and force and iron will
Oppress the weak and helpless still?
    What shall the tasks of mercy be,
Amid the toils, the strifes, the tears
Of those who live when length of years
    Is wasting this little apple-tree?

    "Who planted this old apple-tree?"
The children of that distant day
Thus to some aged man shall say;
And, gazing on its mossy stem,
The gray-haired man shall answer them:
    "A poet of the land was he,
Born in the rude but good old times;
'T is said he made some quaint old rhymes
    On planting the apple-tree."

WILLIAM CULLEN BRYANT 1794–1878

The Snow-Shower

Stand here by my side and turn, I pray,
    On the lake below thy gentle eyes;
The clouds hang over it, heavy and gray,
    And dark and silent the water lies;
And out of that frozen mist the snow
In wavering flakes begins to flow;
              Flake after flake
They sink in the dark and silent lake.

See how in a living swarm they come
    From the chambers beyond that misty veil;
Some hover awhile in air, and some
    Rush prone from the sky like summer hail.
All, dropping swiftly or settling slow,
Meet and are still in the depths below;
              Flake after flake
Dissolved in the dark and silent lake.

Here delicate snow-stars, out of the cloud,
    Come floating downward in airy play,
Like spangles dropped from the glistening crowd
    That whiten by night the milky-way;
There broader and burlier masses fall;
The sullen water buries them all—
              Flake after flake
All drowned in the dark and silent lake.

WILLIAM CULLEN BRYANT 1794–1878

And some, as on tender wings they glide
   From their chilly birth-cloud, dim and gray,
Are joined in their fall, and, side by side,
   Come clinging along their unsteady way;
As friend with friend, or husband with wife,
Makes hand in hand the passage of life;
             Each mated flake
Soon sinks in the dark and silent lake.

Lo! while we are gazing, in swifter haste
   Stream down the snows, till the air is white,
As, myriads by myriads madly chased,
   They fling themselves from their shadowy height.
The fair, frail creatures of middle sky,
What speed they make, with their grave so nigh;
             Flake after flake,
To lie in the dark and silent lake!

I see in thy gentle eyes a tear;
   They turn to me in sorrowful thought;
Thou thinkest of friends, the good and dear,
   Who were for a time and now are not;
Like these fair children of cloud and frost,
That glisten a moment and then are lost,
             Flake after flake—
All lost in the dark and silent lake.

Yet look again, for the clouds divide;
  A gleam of blue on the water lies;
And far away, on the mountain-side,
  A sunbeam falls from the opening skies.
But the hurrying host that flew between
The cloud and the water, no more is seen;
              Flake after flake,
At rest in the dark and silent lake.

JOSEPH RODMAN DRAKE 1795–1820

The American Flag

When Freedom from her mountain height
   Unfurled her standard to the air,
She tore the azure robe of night,
   And set the stars of glory there.
She mingled with its gorgeous dyes
The milky baldric of the skies,
And striped its pure celestial white
With streakings of the morning light;
Then from his mansion in the sun
She called her eagle bearer down,
And gave into his mighty hand
The symbol of her chosen land.

Majestic monarch of the cloud,
   Who rear'st aloft thy regal form,
To hear the tempest trumpings loud
And see the lightning lances driven,
   When strive the warriors of the storm,
And rolls the thunder-drum of heaven,
Child of the sun! to thee 't is given
   To guard the banner of the free,
To hover in the sulphur smoke,
To ward away the battle stroke,
And bid its blendings shine afar,
Like rainbows on the cloud of war,
   The harbingers of victory!

JOSEPH RODMAN DRAKE 1795–1820

Flag of the brave! thy folds shall fly,
The sign of hope and triumph high,
When speaks the signal trumpet tone,
And the long line comes gleaming on.
Ere yet the life-blood, warm and wet,
Has dimmed the glistening bayonet,
Each soldier eye shall brightly turn
To where thy sky-born glories burn,
And, as his springing steps advance,
Catch war and vengeance from the glance.
And when the cannon-mouthings loud
Heave in wild wreaths the battle shroud,
And gory sabres rise and fall
Like shoots of flame on midnight's pall;
   Then shall thy meteor glances glow,
And cowering foes shall shrink beneath
   Each gallant arm that strikes below
That lovely messenger of death.

Flag of the seas! on ocean wave
Thy stars shall glitter o'er the brave;
When death, careering on the gale,
Sweeps darkly round the bellied sail,
And frighted waves rush wildly back
Before the broadside's reeling rack,
Each dying wanderer of the sea
Shall look at once to heaven and thee,
And smile to see thy splendors fly
In triumph o'er his closing eye.

JOSEPH RODMAN DRAKE 1795–1820

Flag of the free heart's hope and home!
    By angel hands to valor given;
Thy stars have lit the welkin dome,
    And all thy hues were born in heaven.
Forever float that standard sheet!
    Where breathes the foe but falls before us,
With Freedom's soil beneath our feet,
    And Freedom's banner streaming o'er us?

GEORGE WASHINGTON DOANE 1799–1859

Evening

Psalm CXLI. 2

Softly now the light of day
Fades upon my sight away;
Free from care, from labor free,
Lord, I would commune with Thee:

Thou, whose all-pervading eye
Naught escapes, without, within,
Pardon each infirmity,
Open fault, and secret sin.

Soon, for me, the light of day
Shall for ever pass away;
Then, from sin and sorrow free,
Take me, Lord, to dwell with Thee:

Thou, who, sinless, yet hast known
All of man's infirmity;
Then, from Thine eternal throne,
Jesus, look with pitying eye.

EDWARD COATE PINKNEY 1802–1828

Song

We break the glass, whose sacred wine
   To some beloved health we drain,
Lest future pledges, less divine,
   Should e'er the hallowed toy profane;
And thus I broke a heart, that poured
   Its tide of feelings out for thee,
In draughts, by after-times deplored,
   Yet dear to memory.

But still the old, empassioned ways
   And habits of my mind remain,
And still unhappy light displays
   Thine image chambered in my brain,
And still it looks as when the hours
   Went by like flights of singing birds,
Or that soft chain of spoken flowers,
   And airy gems, thy words.

A Serenade

Look out upon the stars, my love,
   And shame them with thine eyes,
On which, than on the lights above,
   There hang more destinies.
Night's beauty is the harmony
   Of blending shades and light;
Then, Lady, up,—look out, and be
   A sister to the night!—

Sleep not!—thine image wakes for aye,
    Within my watching breast:
Sleep not!—from her soft sleep should fly,
    Who robs all hearts of rest.
Nay, Lady, from thy slumbers break,
    And make this darkness gay,
With looks, whose brightness well might make
    Of darker nights a day.

A Health

I fill this cup to one made up of loveliness alone,
A woman, of her gentle sex the seeming paragon;
To whom the better elements and kindly stars have given
A form so fair, that, like the air, 't is less of earth than
    heaven.

Her every tone is music's own, like those of morning
    birds,
And something more than melody dwells ever in her
    words;
The coinage of her heart are they, and from her lips each
    flows
As one may see the burthened bee forth issue from the
    rose.

EDWARD COATE PINKNEY 1802–1828

Affections are as thoughts to her, the measures of her hours;
Her feelings have the fragrancy, the freshness, of young flowers;
And lovely passions, changing oft, so fill her, she appears
The image of themselves by turns,—the idol of past years!

Of her bright face one glance will trace a picture on the brain,
And of her voice in echoing hearts a sound must long remain;
But memory such as mine of her so very much endears,
When death is nigh my latest sigh will not be life's but hers.

I filled this cup to one made up of loveliness alone,
A woman, of her gentle sex the seeming paragon—
Her health! and would on earth there stood some more of such a frame,
That life might be all poetry, and weariness a name.

EDWARD COATE PINKNEY 1802–1828

The Widow's Song

I burn no incense, hang no wreath,
    On this, thine early tomb:
Such cannot cheer the place of death,
    But only mock its gloom.
Here odorous smoke and breathing flower
    No grateful influence shed;
They lose their perfume and their power,
    When offered to the dead.

And if, as is the Afghaun's creed,
    The spirit may return,
A disembodied sense to feed,
    On fragrance, near its urn—
It is enough, that she, whom thou
    Did'st love in living years,
Sits desolate beside it now,
    And falls these heavy tears.

A Parting

Alas! our pleasant moments fly
    On rapid wings away,
While those recorded with a sigh,
    Mock us by long delay.

Time—envious time—loves not to be
    In company with mirth,
But makes malignant pause to see
    The work of pain on earth.

RALPH WALDO EMERSON 1803–1882

The Problem

I like a church; I like a cowl;
I love a prophet of the soul;
And on my heart monastic aisles
Fall like sweet strains, or pensive smiles;
Yet not for all his faith can see
Would I that cowlèd churchman be.
Why should the vest on him allure,
Which I could not on me endure?

Not from a vain or shallow thought
His awful Jove young Phidias brought;
Never from lips of cunning fell
The thrilling Delphic oracle:
Out from the heart of nature rolled
The burdens of the Bible old;
The litanies of nations came,
Like the volcano's tongue of flame,
Up from the burning core below,—
The canticles of love and woe;
The hand that rounded Peter's dome,
And groined the aisles of Christian Rome,
Wrought in a sad sincerity;
Himself from God he could not free;
He builded better than he knew;—
The conscious stone to beauty grew.

RALPH WALDO EMERSON 1803–1882

Know'st thou what wove yon woodbird's nest
Of leaves, and feathers from her breast?
Or how the fish outbuilt her shell,
Painting with morn each annual cell?
Or how the sacred pine tree adds
To her old leaves new myriads?
Such and so grew these holy piles,
Whilst love and terror laid the tiles.
Earth proudly wears the Parthenon,
As the best gem upon her zone;
And Morning opes with haste her lids,
To gaze upon the Pyramids;
O'er England's abbeys bends the sky,
As on its friends, with kindred eye;
For, out of Thought's interior sphere,
These wonders rose to upper air;
And Nature gladly gave them place,
Adopted them into her race,
And granted them an equal date
With Andes and with Ararat.

These temples grew as grows the grass;
Art might obey, but not surpass.
The passive Master lent his hand
To the vast soul that o'er him planned;
And the same power that reared the shrine,
Bestrode the tribes that knelt within.
Ever the fiery Pentecost
Girds with one flame the countless host,

RALPH WALDO EMERSON 1803–1882

Trances the heart through chanting choirs,
And through the priest the mind inspires.

The word unto the prophet spoken
Was writ on tables yet unbroken;
The word by seers or sibyls told,
In groves of oak, or fanes of gold,
Still floats upon the morning wind,
Still whispers to the willing mind.
One accent of the Holy Ghost
The heedless world hath never lost.
I know what say the fathers wise,—
The Book itself before me lies,—
Old *Chrysostom,* best Augustine,
And he who blent both in his line,
The younger *Golden Lips* or mines,
Taylor, the Shakespeare of divines.
His words are music in my ear,
I see his cowlèd portrait dear;
And yet, for all his faith could see,
I would not this good bishop be.

The Rhodora

On Being Asked Whence Is the Flower

In May, when sea-winds pierced our solitudes,
I found the fresh Rhodora in the woods,
Spreading its leafless blooms in a damp nook,
To please the desert and the sluggish brook.

The purple petals, fallen in the pool,
Made the black water with their beauty gay;
Here might the red-bird come his plumes to cool,
And court the flower that cheapens his array.
Rhodora! if the sages ask thee why
This charm is wasted on the earth and sky,
Tell them, dear, that if eyes were made for seeing,
Then Beauty is its own excuse for being:
Why thou wert there, O rival of the rose!
I never thought to ask, I never knew:
But, in my simple ignorance, suppose
The self-same Power that brought me there brought you.

The Humble-Bee

Burly, dozing humble-bee,
Where thou art is clime for me.
Let them sail for Porto Rique,
Far-off heats through seas to seek;
I will follow thee alone,
Thou animated torrid-zone!
Zigzag steerer, desert cheerer,
Let me chase thy waving lines;
Keep me nearer, me thy hearer,
Singing over shrubs and vines.

Insect lover of the sun,
Joy of thy dominion!
Sailor of the atmosphere;
Swimmer through the waves of air;

RALPH WALDO EMERSON 1803–1882

Voyager of light and noon;
Epicurean of June;
Wait, I prithee, till I come
Within earshot of thy hum,—
All without is martyrdom.

When the south wind, in May days,
With a net of shining haze
Silvers the horizon wall,
And, with softness touching all,
Tints the human countenance
With a color of romance,
And, infusing subtle heats,
Turns the sod to violets,
Thou, in sunny solitudes,
Rover of the underwoods,
The green silence dost displace
With thy mellow, breezy bass.

Hot midsummer's petted crone,
Sweet to me thy drowsy tone
Tells of countless sunny hours,
Long days, and solid banks of flowers;
Of gulfs of sweetness without bound
In Indian wildernesses found;
Of Syrian peace, immortal leisure,
Firmest cheer, and bird-like pleasure.

RALPH WALDO EMERSON 1803–1882

Aught unsavory or unclean
Hath my insect never seen;
But violets and bilberry bells,
Maple-sap, and daffodels,
Grass with green flag half-mast high,
Succory to match the sky,
Columbine with horn of honey,
Scented fern, and agrimony,
Clover, catchfly, adder's-tongue
And brier-roses, dwelt among;
All beside was unknown waste,
All was picture as he passed.

Wiser far than human seer,
Yellow-breeched philosopher!
Seeing only what is fair,
Sipping only what is sweet,
Thou dost mock at fate and care,
Leave the chaff, and take the wheat.
When the fierce northwestern blast
Cools sea and land so far and fast,
Thou already slumberest deep;
Woe and want thou canst outsleep;
Want and woe, which torture us,
Thy sleep makes ridiculous.

RALPH WALDO EMERSON 1803-1882

Fable

The mountain and the squirrel
Had a quarrel;
And the former called the latter "Little Prig."
Bun replied,
"You are doubtless very big;
But all sorts of things and weather
Must be taken in together,
To make up a year
And a sphere.
And I think it no disgrace
To occupy my place.
If I'm not as large as you,
You are not so small as I,
And not half so spry.
I'll not deny you make
A very pretty squirrel track;
Talents differ; all is well and wisely put;
If I cannot carry forests on my back,
Neither can you crack a nut."

RALPH WALDO EMERSON 1803–1882

To Eva

O fair and stately maid, whose eyes
Were kindled in the upper skies
   At the same torch that lighted mine;
For so I must interpret still
Thy sweet dominion o'er my will,
   A sympathy divine.

Ah! let me blameless gaze upon
Features that seem at heart my own;
   Nor fear those watchful sentinels,
Who charm the more their glance forbids,
Chaste-glowing, underneath their lids,
   With fire that draws while it repels.

Days

Daughters of Time, the hypocritic Days,
Muffled and dumb like barefoot dervishes,
And marching single in an endless file,
Bring diadems and fagots in their hands.
To each they offer gifts after his will,
Bread, kingdoms, stars, and sky that holds them all.
I, in my pleachèd garden, watched the pomp,
Forgot my morning wishes, hastily
Took a few herbs and apples, and the Day
Turned and departed silent. I, too late,
Under her solemn fillet saw the scorn.

RALPH WALDO EMERSON 1803–1882

Concord Hymn

Sung at the Completion of the Battle Monument, April 19, 1836

By the rude bridge that arched the flood,
   Their flag to April's breeze unfurled,
Here once the embattled farmers stood,
   And fired the shot heard round the world.

The foe long since in silence slept;
   Alike the conqueror silent sleeps;
And Time the ruined bridge has swept
   Down the dark stream which seaward creeps.

On this green bank, by this soft stream,
   We set to-day a votive stone;
That memory may their deed redeem,
   When, like our sires, our sons are gone.

Spirit, that made those heroes dare
   To die, and leave their children free,
Bid Time and Nature gently spare
   The shaft we raise to them and thee.

Poet

To clothe the fiery thought
In simple words succeeds,
For still the craft of genius is
To mask a king in weeds.

RALPH WALDO EMERSON 1803–1882

Borrowing

From the French

Some of the hurts you have cured,
And the sharpest you still have survived,
But what torments of grief you endured
From evils which never arrived!

Heri, Cras, Hodie

Shines the last age, the next with hope is seen,
To-day slinks poorly off unmarked between:
Future or Past no rich secret folds,
O friendless Present! than thy bosom holds.

Sacrifice

Though love repine, and reason chafe,
There came a voice without reply,—
" 'T is man's perdition to be safe,
When for the truth he ought to die."

Shakespeare

I see all human wits
Are measured but a few;
Unmeasured still my Shakespeare sits,
Lone as the blessed Jew.

RALPH WALDO EMERSON   1803–1882

Brahma

If the red slayer think he slays,
   Or if the slain think he is slain,
They know not well the subtle ways
   I keep, and pass, and turn again.

Far or forgot to me is near;
   Shadow and sunlight are the same;
The vanished gods to me appear;
   And one to me are shame and fame.

They reckon ill who leave me out;
   When me they fly, I am the wings;
I am the doubter and the doubt,
   And I the hymn the Brahmin sings.

The strong gods pine for my abode,
   And pine in vain the sacred Seven;
But thou, meek lover of the good!
   Find me, and turn thy back on heaven.

WILLIAM LLOYD GARRISON 1805–1879

Freedom for the Mind

High walls and huge the body may confine,
And iron grates obstruct the prisoner's gaze,
And massive bolts may baffle his design,
And vigilant keepers watch his devious ways:
Yet scorns the immortal mind this base control!
No chains can bind it, and no cell enclose:
Swifter than light, it flies from pole to pole,
And, in a flash, from earth to heaven it goes!
It leaps from mount to mount—from vale to vale
It wanders, plucking honeyed fruits and flowers;
It visits home, to hear the fireside tale,
Or in sweet converse pass the joyous hours.
'T is up before the sun, roaming afar,
And, in its watches, wearies every star!

NATHANIEL PARKER WILLIS 1806–1867

Unseen Spirits

The shadows lay along Broadway,
   'T was near the twilight-tide—
And slowly there a lady fair
   Was walking in her pride.
Alone walked she; but, viewlessly,
   Walked spirits at her side.

Peace charmed the street beneath her feet,
   And Honor charmed the air;
And all astir looked kind on her,
   And called her good as fair—
For all God ever gave to her
   She kept with chary care.

She kept with care her beauties rare
   From lovers warm and true—
For her heart was cold to all but gold,
   And the rich came not to woo—
But honored well are charms to sell
   If priests the selling do.

Now walking there was one more fair—
   A slight girl, lily-pale;
And she had unseen company
   To make the spirit quail—
'Twixt Want and Scorn she walked forlorn,
   And nothing could avail.

No mercy now can clear her brow
    For this world's peace to pray;
For, as love's wild prayer dissolved in air,
    Her woman's heart gave way!—
But the sin forgiven by Christ in heaven
    By man is cursed alway!

Love in a Cottage

They may talk of love in a cottage,
    And bowers of trellised vine—
Of nature bewitchingly simple,
    And milkmaids half divine;
They may talk of the pleasure of sleeping
    In the shade of a spreading tree,
And a walk in the fields at morning,
    By the side of a footstep free!

But give me a sly flirtation
    By the light of a chandelier—
With music to play in the pauses,
    And nobody very near;
Or a seat on a silken sofa,
    With a glass of pure old wine,
And mamma too blind to discover
    The small white hand in mine.

NATHANIEL PARKER WILLIS 1806–1867

Your love in a cottage is hungry,
   Your vine is a nest for flies—
Your milkmaid shocks the Graces,
   And simplicity talks of pies!
You lie down to your shady slumber
   And wake with a bug in your ear,
And your damsel that walks in the morning
   Is shod like a mountaineer.

True love is at home on a carpet,
   And mightily likes his ease—
And true love has an eye for a dinner,
   And starves beneath shady trees.
His wing is the fan of a lady,
   His foot's an invisible thing,
And his arrow is tipp'd with a jewel
   And shot from a silver string.

CHARLES FENNO HOFFMAN 1806–1884

Monterey

We were not many—we who stood
   Before the iron sleet that day—
Yet many a gallant spirit would
Give half his years if he then could
   Have been with us at Monterey.

Now here, now there, the shot, it hailed
   In deadly drifts of fiery spray,
Yet not a single soldier quailed
When wounded comrades round them wailed
   Their dying shout at Monterey.

And on—still on our column kept
   Through walls of flame its withering way;
Where fell the dead, the living stept,
Still charging on the guns which swept
   The slippery streets of Monterey.

The foe himself recoiled aghast,
   When, striking where he strongest lay,
We swooped his flanking batteries past,
And braving full their murderous blast,
   Stormed home the towers of Monterey.

Our banners on those turrets wave,
   And there our evening bugles play;
Where orange boughs above their grave
Keep green the memory of the brave
   Who fought and fell at Monterey.

CHARLES FENNO HOFFMAN 1806–1884

We are not many,—we who pressed
   Beside the brave who fell that day;
But who of us has not confessed
He'd rather share their warrior rest
   Than not have been at Monterey?

The Mint Julep

'T is said that the gods, on Olympus of old
   (And who the bright legend profanes with a doubt),
One night, mid their revels, by Bacchus were told
   That his last butt of nectar had somehow run out!

But determined to send round the goblet once more,
   They sued to their fairer immortals for aid
In composing a draught, which, till drinking were o'er,
   Should cast every wine ever drank in the shade.

Grave Ceres herself blithely yielded her corn,
   And the spirit that lives in each amber-hued grain,
And which first had its birth from the dew of the morn,
   Was taught to steal out in bright dewdrops again,

Pomona, whose choicest of fruits on the board
   Were scatter'd profusely in every one's reach,
When call'd on a tribute to cull from the hoard,
   Express'd the mild juice of the delicate peach.

CHARLES FENNO HOFFMAN 1806–1884

The liquids were mingled while Venus look'd on
   With glances so fraught with sweet magical power,
That the honey of Hybla, e'en when they were gone,
   Has never been miss'd in the draught from that hour.

Flora then, from her bosom of fragrancy, shook,
   And with roseate fingers press'd down in the bowl,
All dripping and fresh as it came from the brook,
   The herb whose aroma should flavor the whole.

The draught was delicious, and loud the acclaim,
   Though something seemed wanting for all to bewail;
But Juleps the drink of immortals became,
   When Jove himself added a handful of hail.

HENRY WADSWORTH LONGFELLOW 1807–1882

A Psalm of Life

What the Heart of the Young Man Said to the Psalmist

Tell me not, in mournful numbers,
    Life is but an empty dream!—
For the soul is dead that slumbers,
    And things are not what they seem.

Life is real! Life is earnest!
    And the grave is not its goal;
Dust thou art, to dust returnest,
    Was not spoken of the soul.

Not enjoyment, and not sorrow,
    Is our destined end or way;
But to act, that each to-morrow
    Find us farther than to-day.

Art is long, and Time is fleeting,
    And our hearts, though stout and brave,
Still, like muffled drums, are beating
    Funeral marches to the grave.

In the world's broad field of battle,
    In the bivouac of Life,
Be not like dumb, driven cattle!
    Be a hero in the strife!

Trust no Future, howe'er pleasant!
    Let the dead Past bury its dead!
Act,—act in the living Present!
    Heart within, and God o'erhead!

HENRY WADSWORTH LONGFELLOW 1807–1882

Lives of great men all remind us
   We can make our lives sublime,
And, departing, leave behind us
   Footprints on the sands of time;

Footprints, that perhaps another,
   Sailing o'er life's solemn main,
A forlorn and shipwrecked brother,
   Seeing, shall take heart again.

Let us, then, be up and doing,
   With a heart for any fate;
Still achieving, still pursuing,
   Learn to labor and to wait.

Footsteps of Angels

When the hours of Day are numbered,
   And the voices of the Night
Wake the better soul, that slumbered,
   To a holy, calm delight;

Ere the evening lamps are lighted,
   And, like phantoms grim and tall,
Shadows from the fitful firelight
   Dance upon the parlor wall;

HENRY WADSWORTH LONGFELLOW 1807–1882

Then the forms of the departed
   Enter at the open door;
The beloved, the true-hearted,
   Come to visit me once more;

He, the young and strong, who cherished
   Noble longings for the strife,
By the roadside fell and perished,
   Weary with the march of life!

They, the holy ones and weakly,
   Who the cross of suffering bore,
Folded their pale hands so meekly,
   Spake with us on earth no more!

And with them the Being Beauteous,
   Who unto my youth was given,
More than all things else to love me,
   And is now a saint in heaven.

With a slow and noiseless footstep
   Comes that messenger divine,
Takes the vacant chair beside me,
   Lays her gentle hand in mine.

And she sits and gazes at me
   With those deep and tender eyes,
Like the stars, so still and saint-like,
   Looking downward from the skies.

Uttered not, yet comprehended,
   Is the spirit's voiceless prayer,
Soft rebukes, in blessings ended,
   Breathing from her lips of air.

Oh, though oft depressed and lonely,
   All my fears are laid aside,
If I but remember only
   Such as these have lived and died!

Song of the Silent Land
(Lied: Ins Stille Land)

BY JOHANN GAUDENZ VON SALIS-SEEWIS

Into the Silent Land!
Ah! who shall lead us thither?
Clouds in the evening sky more darkly gather,
And shattered wrecks lie thicker on the strand.
Who leads us with a gentle hand
Thither, oh, thither,
Into the Silent Land?

Into the Silent Land!
To you, ye boundless regions
Of all perfection! Tender morning-visions
Of beauteous souls! The Future's pledge and band!
Who in Life's battle firm doth stand,
Shall bear Hope's tender blossoms
Into the Silent Land!

HENRY WADSWORTH LONGFELLOW 1807–1882

O Land! O Land!
For all the broken-hearted
The mildest herald by our fate allotted,
Beckons, and with inverted torch doth stand
To lead us with a gentle hand
To the land of the great Departed,
Into the Silent Land!

The Skeleton in Armor

"Speak! speak! thou fearful guest!
Who, with thy hollow breast
Still in rude armor drest,
   Comest to daunt me!
Wrapt not in Eastern balms,
But with thy fleshless palms
Stretched, as if asking alms,
   Why dost thou haunt me?"

Then, from those cavernous eyes
Pale flashes seemed to rise,
As when the Northern skies
   Gleam in December;
And, like the water's flow
Under December's snow,
Came a dull voice of woe
   From the heart's chamber.

HENRY WADSWORTH LONGFELLOW 1807–1882

"I was a Viking old!
My deeds, though manifold,
No Skald in song has told,
   No Saga taught thee!
Take heed, that in thy verse
Thou dost the tale rehearse,
Else dread a dead man's curse;
   For this I sought thee.

"Far in the Northern Land,
By the wild Baltic's strand,
I, with my childish hand,
   Tamed the gerfalcon;
And, with my skates fast-bound,
Skimmed the half-frozen Sound,
That the poor whimpering hound
   Trembled to walk on.

"Oft to his frozen lair
Tracked I the grisly bear,
While from my path the hare
   Fled like a shadow;
Oft through the forest dark
Followed the were-wolf's bark,
Until the soaring lark
   Sang from the meadow.

HENRY WADSWORTH LONGFELLOW 1807–1882

"But when I older grew,
Joining a corsair's crew,
O'er the dark sea I flew
  With the marauders.
Wild was the life we led;
Many the souls that sped,
Many the hearts that bled,
  By our stern orders.

"Many a wassail-bout
Wore the long Winter out;
Often our midnight shout
  Set the cocks crowing,
As we the Berserk's tale
Measured in cups of ale,
Draining the oaken pail,
  Filled to o'erflowing.

"Once as I told in glee
Tales of the stormy sea,
Soft eyes did gaze on me,
  Burning yet tender;
And as the white stars shine
On the dark Norway pine,
On that dark heart of mine
  Fell their soft splendor.

HENRY WADSWORTH LONGFELLOW 1807–1882

"I wooed the blue-eyed maid,
Yielding, yet half afraid,
And in the forest's shade
  Our vows were plighted.
Under its loosened vest
Fluttered her little breast,
Like birds within their nest
  By the hawk frighted.

"Bright in her father's hall
Shields gleamed upon the wall,
Loud sang the minstrels all,
  Chanting his glory;
When of old Hildebrand
I asked his daughter's hand,
Mute did the minstrels stand
  To hear my story.

"While the brown ale he quaffed,
Loud then the champion laughed,
And as the wind-gusts waft
  The sea-foam brightly,
So the loud laugh of scorn,
Out of those lips unshorn,
From the deep drinking-horn
  Blew the foam lightly.

HENRY WADSWORTH LONGFELLOW 1807–1882

"She was a Prince's child,
I but a Viking wild,
And though she blushed and smiled,
   I was discarded!
Should not the dove so white
Follow the sea-mew's flight,
Why did they leave that night
   Her nest unguarded?

"Scarce had I put to sea,
Bearing the maid with me,
Fairest of all was she
   Among the Norsemen!
When on the white sea-strand,
Waving his armèd hand,
Saw we old Hildebrand,
   With twenty horsemen.

"Then launched they to the blast,
Bent like a reed each mast,
Yet we were gaining fast,
   When the wind failed us;
And with a sudden flaw
Came round the gusty Skaw,
So that our foe we saw
   Laugh as he hailed us.

"And as to catch the gale
Round veered the flapping sail,
'Death!' was the helmsman's hail,
    'Death without quarter!'
Mid-ships with iron keel
Struck we her ribs of steel;
Down her black hulk did reel
    Through the black water!

"As with his wings aslant,
Sails the fierce cormorant,
Seeking some rocky haunt,
    With his prey laden,
So toward the open main,
Beating to sea again,
Through the wild hurricane,
    Bore I the maiden.

"Three weeks we westward bore,
And when the storm was o'er,
Cloud-like we saw the shore
    Stretching to leeward;
There for my lady's bower
Built I the lofty tower,
Which, to this very hour,
    Stands looking seaward.

HENRY WADSWORTH LONGFELLOW 1807–1882

"There lived we many years;
Time dried the maiden's tears;
She had forgot her fears,
   She was a mother;
Death closed her mild blue eyes,
Under that tower she lies;
Ne'er shall the sun arise
   On such another!

"Still grew my bosom then,
Still as a stagnant fen!
Hateful to me were men,
   The sunlight hateful!
In the vast forest here,
Clad in my warlike gear,
Fell I upon my spear,
   Oh, death was grateful!

"Thus, seamed with many scars,
Bursting these prison bars,
Up to its native stars
   My soul ascended!
There from the flowing bowl
Deep drinks the warrior's soul,
Skoal! to the Northland! *skoal!*"
   Thus the tale ended.

HENRY WADSWORTH LONGFELLOW 1807–1882

The Village Blacksmith

Under a spreading chestnut tree
   The village smithy stands;
The smith, a mighty man is he,
   With large and sinewy hands;
And the muscles of his brawny arms
   Are strong as iron bands.

His hair is crisp, and black, and long,
   His face is like the tan;
His brow is wet with honest sweat,
   He earns whate'er he can,
And looks the whole world in the face,
   For he owes not any man.

Week in, week out, from morn till night,
   You can hear his bellows blow;
You can hear him swing his heavy sledge
   With measured beat and slow,
Like a sexton ringing the village bell,
   When the evening sun is low.

And children coming home from school
   Look in at the open door;
They love to see the flaming forge,
   And hear the bellows roar,
And watch the burning sparks that fly
   Like chaff from a threshing-floor.

HENRY WADSWORTH LONGFELLOW 1807–1882

He goes on Sunday to the church,
   And sits among his boys;
He hears the parson pray and preach,
   He hears his daughter's voice,
Singing in the village choir,
   And it makes his heart rejoice.

It sounds to him like her mother's voice,
   Singing in Paradise!
He needs must think of her once more,
   How in the grave she lies;
And with his hard, rough hand he wipes
   A tear out of his eyes.

Toiling,—rejoicing,—sorrowing,
   Onward through life he goes;
Each morning sees some task begin,
   Each evening sees it close;
Something attempted, something done,
   Has earned a night's repose.

Thanks, thanks to thee, my worthy friend,
   For the lesson thou hast taught!
Thus at the flaming forge of life
   Our fortunes must be wrought;
Thus on its sounding anvil shaped
   Each burning deed and thought!

HENRY WADSWORTH LONGFELLOW 1807–1882

Endymion

The rising moon has hid the stars;
Her level rays, like golden bars,
    Lie on the landscape green,
    With shadows brown between.

And silver white the river gleams,
As if Diana, in her dreams,
    Had dropt her silver bow
    Upon the meadows low.

On such a tranquil night as this,
She woke Endymion with a kiss,
    When, sleeping in the grove,
    He dreamed not of her love.

Like Dian's kiss, unasked, unsought,
Love gives itself, but is not bought;
    Nor voice, nor sound betrays
    Its deep, impassioned gaze.

It comes,—the beautiful, the free,
The crown of all humanity,—
    In silence and alone
    To seek the elected one.

It lifts the boughs, whose shadows deep
Are Life's oblivion, the soul's sleep,
    And kisses the closed eyes
    Of him who slumbering lies.

HENRY WADSWORTH LONGFELLOW 1807–1882

O weary hearts! O slumbering eyes!
O drooping souls, whose destinies
    Are fraught with fear and pain,
    Ye shall be loved again!

No one is so accursed by fate,
No one so utterly desolate,
    But some heart, though unknown,
    Responds unto his own.

Responds,—as if with unseen wings,
An angel touched its quivering strings;
    And whispers, in its song,
    "Where hast thou stayed so long?"

Maidenhood

Maiden! with the meek, brown eyes,
In whose orbs a shadow lies
Like the dusk in evening skies!

Thou whose locks outshine the sun,
Golden tresses, wreathed in one,
As the braided streamlets run!

Standing, with reluctant feet,
Where the brook and river meet,
Womanhood and childhood fleet!

HENRY WADSWORTH LONGFELLOW 1807–1882

Gazing, with a timid glance,
On the brooklet's swift advance,
On the river's broad expanse!

Deep and still, that gliding stream
Beautiful to thee must seem,
As the river of a dream.

Then why pause with indecision,
When bright angels in thy vision
Beckon thee to fields Elysian?

Seest thou shadows sailing by,
As the dove, with startled eye
Sees the falcon's shadow fly?

Hearest thou voices on the shore,
That our ears perceive no more,
Deafened by the cataract's roar?

Oh, thou child of many prayers!
Life hath quicksands, Life hath snares!
Care and age come unawares!

Like the swell of some sweet tune
Morning rises into noon,
May glides onward into June.

Childhood is the bough, where slumbered
Birds and blossoms many numbered;—
Age, that bough with snows encumbered.

HENRY WADSWORTH LONGFELLOW 1807–1882

Gather, then, each flower that grows,
When the young heart overflows,
To embalm that tent of snows.

Bear a lily in thy hand;
Gates of brass cannot withstand
One touch of that magic wand.

Bear through sorrow, wrong, and ruth
In thy heart the dew of youth,
On thy lips the smile of truth.

O, that dew, like balm, shall steal
Into wounds, that cannot heal
Even as sleep our eyes doth seal;

And that smile, like sunshine, dart
Into many a sunless heart,
For a smile of God thou art.

Excelsior

The shades of night were falling fast,
As through an Alpine village passed
A youth, who bore, 'mid snow and ice,
A banner with the strange device,
    Excelsior!

HENRY WADSWORTH LONGFELLOW 1807–1882

His brow was sad; his eye beneath,
Flashed like a falchion from its sheath,
And like a silver clarion rung
The accents of that unknown tongue,
      Excelsior!

In happy homes he saw the light
Of household fires gleam warm and bright;
Above, the spectral glaciers shone,
And from his lips escaped a groan,
      Excelsior!

"Try not the Pass!" the old man said;
"Dark lowers the tempest overhead,
The roaring torrent is deep and wide!"
And loud that clarion voice replied,
      Excelsior!

"Oh, stay," the maiden said, "and rest
Thy weary head upon this breast!"
A tear stood in his bright blue eye,
But still he answered, with a sigh,
      Excelsior!

"Beware the pine-tree's withered branch!
Beware the awful avalanche!"
This was the peasant's last Good-night,
A voice replied, far up the height,
      Excelsior!

HENRY WADSWORTH LONGFELLOW 1807–1882

At break of day, as heavenward
The pious monks of Saint Bernard
Uttered the oft-repeated prayer,
A voice cried through the startled air,
    Excelsior!

A traveller, by the faithful hound,
Half-buried in the snow was found,
Still grasping in his hand of ice
That banner with the strange device,
    Excelsior!

There, in the twilight cold and gray,
Lifeless, but beautiful, he lay,
And from the sky, serene and far,
A voice fell, like a falling star,
    Excelsior!

The Arsenal at Springfield

This is the Arsenal. From floor to ceiling,
  Like a huge organ, rise the burnished arms;
But from their silent pipes no anthem pealing
  Startles the villages with strange alarms.

Ah! what a sound will rise, how wild and dreary,
  When the death-angel touches those swift keys!
What loud lament and dismal Miserere
  Will mingle with their awful symphonies!

HENRY WADSWORTH LONGFELLOW 1807–1882

I hear even now the infinite fierce chorus,
   The cries of agony, the endless groan,
Which, through the ages that have gone before us,
   In long reverberations reach our own.

On helm and harness rings the Saxon hammer,
   Through Cimbric forest roars the Norseman's song,
And loud, amid the universal clamor,
   O'er distant deserts sounds the Tartar gong.

I hear the Florentine, who from his palace
   Wheels out his battle-bell with dreadful din,
And Aztec priests upon their teocallis
   Beat the wild war-drums made of serpent's skin;

The tumult of each sacked and burning village;
   The shouts that every prayer for mercy drowns;
The soldiers' revels in the midst of pillage;
   The wail of famine in beleaguered towns;

The bursting shell, the gateway wrenched asunder,
   The rattling musketry, the clashing blade;
And ever and anon, in tones of thunder
   The diapason of the cannonade.

Is it, O man, with such discordant noises,
   With such accursed instruments as these,
Thou drownest Nature's sweet and kindly voices,
   And jarrest the celestial harmonies?

Were half the power, that fills the world with terror,
  Were half the wealth bestowed on camps and courts,
Given to redeem the human mind from error,
  There were no need of arsenals or forts:

The warrior's name would be a name abhorrèd!
  And every nation, that should lift again
Its hand against a brother, on its forehead
  Would wear forevermore the curse of Cain!

Down the dark future, through long generations,
  The echoing sounds grow fainter and then cease;
And like a bell, with solemn, sweet vibrations,
  I hear once more the voice of Christ say, "Peace!"

Peace! and no longer from its brazen portals
  The blast of War's great organ shakes the skies!
But beautiful as songs of the immortals,
  The holy melodies of love arise.

Nuremberg

In the valley of the Pegnitz, where across broad meadow-lands
Rise the blue Franconian mountains, Nuremberg, the ancient, stands.

Quaint old town of toil and traffic, quaint old town of art and song,
Memories haunt thy pointed gables, like the rooks that round them throng:

Memories of the Middle Ages, when the emperors, rough and bold,
Had their dwelling in thy castle, time-defying, centuries old;

And thy brave and thrifty burghers boasted, in their uncouth rhyme,
That their great imperial city stretched its hand through every clime.

In the court-yard of the castle, bound with many an iron band,
Stands the mighty linden planted by Queen Cunigunde's hand;

On the square the oriel window, where in old heroic days
Sat the poet Melchior singing Kaiser Maximilian's praise.

Everywhere I see around me rise the wondrous world of Art:
Fountains wrought with richest sculpture standing in the common mart;

And above cathedral doorways saints and bishops carved in stone,
By a former age commissioned as apostles to our own.

In the church of sainted Sebald sleeps enshrined his holy dust,
And in bronze the Twelve Apostles guard from age to age their trust;

HENRY WADSWORTH LONGFELLOW 1807–1882

In the church of sainted Lawrence stands a pix of sculpture rare,
Like the foamy sheaf of fountains, rising through the painted air.

Here, when Art was still religion, with a simple, reverent heart,
Lived and labored Albrecht Dürer, the Evangelist of Art;

Hence in silence and in sorrow, toiling still with busy hand,
Like an emigrant he wandered, seeking for the Better Land.

Emigravit is the inscription on the tombstone where he lies;
Dead he is not, but departed,—for the artist never dies.

Fairer seems the ancient city, and the sunshine seems more fair,
That he once has trod its pavement, that he once has breathed its air!

Through these streets so broad and stately, these obscure and dismal lanes,
Walked of yore the Mastersingers, chanting rude poetic strains.

From remote and sunless suburbs came they to the friendly guild,
Building nests in Fame's great temple, as in spouts the swallows build.

As the weaver plied the shuttle, wove he too the mystic rhyme,
And the smith his iron measures hammered to the anvil's chime;

Thanking God, whose boundless wisdom makes the flowers of poesy bloom
In the forge's dust and cinders, in the tissues of the loom.

Here Hans Sachs, the cobbler-poet, laureate of the gentle craft,
Wisest of the Twelve Wise Masters, in huge folios sang and laughed.

But his house is now an ale-house, with a nicely sanded floor,
And a garland in the window, and his face above the door;

Painted by some humble artist, as in Adam Puschman's song,
As the old man gray and dove-like, with his great beard white and long.

And at night the swart mechanic comes to drown his cark and care,
Quaffing ale from pewter tankards, in the master's antique chair.

Vanished is the ancient splendor, and before my dreamy eye
Wave these mingled shapes and figures, like a faded tapestry.

HENRY WADSWORTH LONGFELLOW 1807–1882

Not thy Councils, not thy Kaisers, win for thee the
    world's regard;
But thy painter, Albrecht Dürer, and Hans Sachs, thy
    cobbler bard.

Thus, O Nuremberg, a wanderer from a region far away,
As he paced thy streets and court-yards, sang in thought
    his careless lay:

Gathering from the pavement's crevice, as a floweret of
    the soil,
The nobility of labor,—the long pedigree of toil.

The Day is Done

    The day is done, and the darkness
        Falls from the wings of Night,
    As a feather is wafted downward
        From an eagle in his flight.

    I see the lights of the village
        Gleam through the rain and the mist,
    And a feeling of sadness comes o'er me
        That my soul cannot resist:

    A feeling of sadness and longing,
        That is not akin to pain,
    And resembles sorrow only
        As the mist resembles the rain.

HENRY WADSWORTH LONGFELLOW 1807–1882

Come, read to me some poem,
 Some simple and heartfelt lay,
That shall soothe this restless feeling,
 And banish the thoughts of day.

Not from the grand old masters,
 Not from the bards sublime,
Whose distant footsteps echo
 Through the corridors of Time.

For, like strains of martial music,
 Their mighty thoughts suggest
Life's endless toil and endeavor;
 And to-night I long for rest.

Read from some humbler poet,
 Whose songs gushed from his heart,
As showers from the clouds of summer,
 Or tears from the eyelids start;

Who, through long days of labor,
 And nights devoid of ease,
Still heard in his soul the music
 Of wonderful melodies.

Such songs have power to quiet
 The restless pulse of care,
And come like the benediction
 That follows after prayer.

Then read from the treasured volume
    The poem of thy choice,
And lend to the rhyme of the poet
    The beauty of thy voice.

And the night shall be filled with music,
    And the cares, that infest the day,
Shall fold their tents, like the Arabs,
    And as silently steal away.

Seaweed

When descends on the Atlantic
    The gigantic
Storm-wind of the equinox,
Landward in his wrath he scourges
    The toiling surges,
Laden with seaweed from the rocks:

From Bermuda's reefs; from edges
    Of sunken ledges,
In some far-off, bright Azore;
From Bahama, and the dashing,
    Silver-flashing
Surges of San Salvador;

From the tumbling surf, that buries
    The Orkneyan skerries,
Answering the hoarse Hebrides;

And from wrecks of ships, and drifting
    Spars, uplifting
On the desolate, rainy seas;—

Ever drifting, drifting, drifting
    On the shifting
Currents of the restless main;
Till in sheltered coves, and reaches
    Of sandy beaches,
All have found repose again.

So when storms of wild emotion
    Strike the ocean
Of the poet's soul, erelong
From each cave and rocky fastness,
    In its vastness,
Floats some fragment of a song:

From the far-off isles enchanted,
    Heaven has planted
With the golden fruit of Truth;
From the flashing surf, whose vision
    Gleams Elysian
In the tropic clime of Youth;

From the strong Will, and the Endeavor
    That forever
Wrestle with the tides of Fate;
From the wreck of Hopes far-scattered,
    Tempest-shattered,
Floating waste and desolate;—

HENRY WADSWORTH LONGFELLOW 1807–1882

    Ever drifting, drifting, drifting
        On the shifting
    Currents of the restless heart;
    Till at length in books recorded,
        They, like hoarded
    Household words, no more depart.

Resignation

There is no flock, however watched and tended,
    But one dead lamb is there!
There is no fireside, howsoe'er defended,
    But has one vacant chair!

The air is full of farewells to the dying,
    And mournings for the dead;
The heart of Rachel, for her children crying,
    Will not be comforted!

Let us be patient! These severe afflictions
    Not from the ground arise,
But oftentimes celestial benedictions
    Assume this dark disguise.

We see but dimly through the mists and vapors;
    Amid these earthly damps
What seem to us but sad, funereal tapers
    May be heaven's distant lamps.

HENRY WADSWORTH LONGFELLOW 1807–1882

There is no Death! What seems so is transition;
    This life of mortal breath
Is but a suburb of the life elysian,
    Whose portal we call Death.

She is not dead,—the child of our affection,—
    But gone unto that school
Where she no longer needs our poor protection,
    And Christ himself doth rule.

In that great cloister's stillness and seclusion,
    By guardian angels led,
Safe from temptation, safe from sin's pollution,
    She lives, whom we call dead.

Day after day we think what she is doing
    In those bright realms of air;
Year after year, her tender steps pursuing,
    Behold her grown more fair.

Thus do we walk with her, and keep unbroken
    The bond which nature gives,
Thinking that our remembrance, though unspoken,
    May reach her where she lives.

Not as a child shall we again behold her;
    For when with raptures wild
In our embraces we again enfold her,
    She will not be a child;

HENRY WADSWORTH LONGFELLOW 1807–1882

But a fair maiden, in her Father's mansion,
   Clothed with celestial grace;
And beautiful with all the soul's expansion
   Shall we behold her face.

And though at times impetuous with emotion
   And anguish long suppressed,
The swelling heart heaves moaning like the ocean,
   That cannot be at rest,—

We will be patient, and assuage the feeling
   We may not wholly stay;
By silence sanctifying, not concealing,
   The grief that must have way.

The Warden of the Cinque Ports

A mist was driving down the British Channel,
   The day was just begun,
And through the window-panes, on floor and panel,
   Streamed the red autumn sun.

It glanced on flowing flag and rippling pennon,
   And the white sails of ships;
And, from the frowning rampart, the black cannon
   Hailed it with feverish lips.

HENRY WADSWORTH LONGFELLOW 1807–1882

Sandwich and Romney, Hastings, Hithe, and Dover,
    Were all alert that day,
To see the French war-steamers speeding over,
    When the fog cleared away.

Sullen and silent, and like couchant lions,
    Their cannon, through the night,
Holding their breath, had watched, in grim defiance,
    The sea-coast opposite.

And now they roared at drum-beat from their stations,
    On every citadel;
Each answering each, with morning salutations,
    That all was well.

And down the coast, all taking up the burden,
    Replied the distant forts,
As if to summon from his sleep the Warden
    And Lord of the Cinque Ports.

Him shall no sunshine from the fields of azure,
    No drum-beat from the wall,
No morning gun from the black fort's embrasure,
    Awaken with its call!

No more, surveying with an eye impartial
    The long line of the coast,
Shall the gaunt figure of the old Field Marshal
    Be seen upon his post!

For in the night, unseen, a single warrior,
    In sombre harness mailed,
Dreaded of man, and surnamed the Destroyer,
    The rampart wall had scaled.

He passed into the chamber of the sleeper,
    The dark and silent room,
And as he entered, darker grew, and deeper,
    The silence and the gloom.

He did not pause to parley or dissemble,
    But smote the Warden hoar;
Ah! what a blow! that made all England tremble
    And groan from shore to shore.

Meanwhile, without, the surly cannon waited,
    The sun rose bright o'erhead;
Nothing in Nature's aspect intimated
    That a great man was dead.

My Lost Youth

Often I think of the beautiful town
   That is seated by the sea;
Often in thought go up and down
The pleasant streets of that dear old town,
   And my youth comes back to me.
     And a verse of a Lapland song
     Is haunting my memory still:
    "A boy's will is the wind's will,
And the thoughts of youth are long, long thoughts."

HENRY WADSWORTH LONGFELLOW 1807–1882

I can see the shadowy lines of its trees,
   And catch, in sudden gleams,
The sheen of the far-surrounding seas,
And islands that were the Hesperides
   Of all my boyish dreams.
      And the burden of that old song,
        It murmurs and whispers still:
      "A boy's will is the wind's will,
And the thoughts of youth are long, long thoughts."

I remember the black wharves and the slips,
   And the sea-tides tossing free;
And Spanish sailors with bearded lips,
And the beauty and mystery of the ships,
   And the magic of the sea.
      And the voice of that wayward song
        Is singing and saying still:
      "A boy's will is the wind's will,
And the thoughts of youth are long, long thoughts."

I remember the bulwarks by the shore,
   And the fort upon the hill;
The sunrise gun, with its hollow roar,
The drum-beat repeated o'er and o'er,
   And the bugle wild and shrill.
      And the music of that old song
        Throbs in my memory still:
      "A boy's will is the wind's will,
And the thoughts of youth are long, long thoughts."

HENRY WADSWORTH LONGFELLOW 1807–1882

I remember the sea-fight far away,
  How it thundered o'er the tide!
And the dead captains, as they lay
In their graves, o'erlooking the tranquil bay,
    Where they in battle died.
    And the sound of that mournful song
    Goes through me with a thrill:
    "A boy's will is the wind's will,
And the thoughts of youth are long, long thoughts."

I can see the breezy dome of groves,
  The shadows of Deering's Woods;
And the friendships old and the early loves
Come back with a Sabbath sound, as of doves
    In quiet neighborhoods.
    And the verse of that sweet old song,
    It flutters and murmurs still:
    "A boy's will is the wind's will,
And the thoughts of youth are long, long thoughts."

I remember the gleams and glooms that dart
  Across the school-boy's brain;
The song and the silence in the heart,
That in part are prophecies, and in part
    Are longings wild and vain.
    And the voice of that fitful song
    Sings on, and is never still:
    "A boy's will is the wind's will,
And the thoughts of youth are long, long thoughts."

HENRY WADSWORTH LONGFELLOW 1807-1882

There are things of which I may not speak;
   There are dreams that cannot die;
There are thoughts that make the strong heart weak,
And bring a pallor into the cheek,
   And a mist before the eye.
      And the words of that fatal song
      Come over me like a chill:
      "A boy's will is the wind's will,
And the thoughts of youth are long, long thoughts."

Strange to me now are the forms I meet
   When I visit the dear old town;
But the native air is pure and sweet,
And the trees that o'ershadow each well-known street,
   As they balance up and down,
      Are singing the beautiful song,
      Are sighing and whispering still:
      "A boy's will is the wind's will,
And the thoughts of youth are long, long thoughts."

And Deering's Woods are fresh and fair,
   And with joy that is almost pain
My heart goes back to wander there,
And among the dreams of the days that were,
   I find my lost youth again.
      And the strange and beautiful song,
      The groves are repeating it still:
      "A boy's will is the wind's will,
And the thoughts of youth are long, long thoughts."

HENRY WADSWORTH LONGFELLOW 1807–1882

The Cumberland

At anchor in Hampton Roads we lay,
  On board of the Cumberland, sloop-of-war;
And at times from the fortress across the bay
    The alarum of drums swept past,
      Or a bugle blast
  From the camp on the shore.

Then far away to the south uprose
  A little feather of snow-white smoke,
And we knew that the iron ship of our foes
    Was steadily steering its course
      To try the force
  Of our ribs of oak.

Down upon us heavily runs,
  Silent and sullen, the floating fort;
Then comes a puff of smoke from her guns,
    And leaps the terrible death,
      With fiery breath,
  From each open port.

We are not idle, but send her straight
  Defiance back in a full broadside!
As hail rebounds from a roof of slate,
    Rebounds our heavier hail
      From each iron scale
  Of the monster's hide.

HENRY WADSWORTH LONGFELLOW 1807–1882

"Strike your flag!" the rebel cries,
   In his arrogant old plantation strain.
"Never!" our gallant Morris replies;
     "It is better to sink than to yield!"
     And the whole air pealed
   With the cheers of our men.

Then, like a kraken huge and black,
   She crushed our ribs in her iron grasp!
Down went the Cumberland all a wrack,
     With a sudden shudder of death,
     And the cannon's breath
   For her dying gasp.

Next morn, as the sun rose over the bay,
   Still floated our flag at the mainmast head.
Lord, how beautiful was Thy day!
     Every waft of the air
     Was a whisper of prayer,
   Or a dirge for the dead.

Ho! brave hearts that went down in the seas!
   Ye are at peace in the troubled stream;
Ho! brave land! with hearts like these,
     Thy flag, that is rent in twain,
     Shall be one again,
   And without a seam!

JOHN GREENLEAF WHITTIER 1807–1892

Proem to Edition of 1847

Written to introduce the first general collection of his poems

    I love the old melodious lays
Which softly melt the ages through,
      The songs of Spenser's golden days,
      Arcadian Sidney's silvery phrase,
Sprinkling our noon of time with freshest morning dew.

    Yet, vainly in my quiet hours
To breathe their marvellous notes I try;
      I feel them, as the leaves and flowers
      In silence feel the dewy showers,
And drink with glad still lips the blessing of the sky.

    The rigor of a frozen clime,
The harshness of an untaught ear,
      The jarring words of one whose rhyme
      Beats often Labor's hurried time,
Or Duty's rugged march through storm and strife, are here.

    Of mystic beauty, dreamy grace,
No rounded art the lack supplies;
      Unskilled the subtle lines to trace,
      Or softer shades of Nature's face,
I view her common forms with unanointed eyes.

Nor mine the seer-like power to show
The secrets of the heart and mind;
To drop the plummet-line below
Our common world of joy and woe,
A more intense despair or brighter hope to find.

Yet here at least an earnest sense
Of human right and weal is shown;
A hate of tyranny intense,
And hearty in its vehemence,
As if my brother's pain and sorrow were my own.

O Freedom! if to me belong
Nor mighty Milton's gift divine,
Nor Marvell's wit and graceful song,
Still with a love as deep and strong
As theirs, I lay, like them, my best gifts on thy shrine!

Randolph of Roanoke

O Mother Earth! upon thy lap
Thy weary ones receiving,
And o'er them, silent as a dream,
Thy grassy mantle weaving,
Fold softly in thy long embrace
That heart so worn and broken,
And cool its pulse of fire beneath
Thy shadows old and oaken.

JOHN GREENLEAF WHITTIER 1807–1892

Shut out from him the bitter word
    And serpent hiss of scorning;
Nor let the storms of yesterday
    Disturb his quiet morning.
Breathe over him forgetfulness
    Of all save deeds of kindness,
And, save to smiles of grateful eyes,
    Press down his lids in blindness.

There, where with living ear and eye
    He heard Potomac's flowing,
And, through his tall ancestral trees,
    Saw autumn's sunset glowing,
He sleeps,—still looking to the west,
    Beneath the dark wood shadow,
As if he still would see the sun
    Sink down on wave and meadow.

Bard, Sage, and Tribune!—in himself
    All moods of mind contrasting,—
The tenderest wail of human wo,
    The scorn-like lightning blasting;
The pathos which from rival eyes
    Unwilling tears could summon,
The stinging taunt, the fiery burst
    Of hatred scarcely human!

Mirth, sparkling like a diamond shower,
    From lips of life-long sadness;
Clear picturings of majestic thought
    Upon a ground of madness;

And over all Romance and Song
  A classic beauty throwing,
And laurelled Clio at his side
  Her storied pages showing.

All parties feared him: each in turn
  Beheld its schemes disjointed,
As right or left his fatal glance
  And spectral finger pointed.
Sworn foe of Cant, he smote it down
  With trenchant wit unsparing,
And, mocking, rent with ruthless hand
  The robe Pretence was wearing.

Too honest or too proud to feign
  A love he never cherished,
Beyond Virginia's border line
  His patriotism perished.
While others hailed in distant skies
  Our eagle's dusty pinion,
He only saw the mountain bird
  Stoop o'er his Old Dominion!

Still through each change of fortune strange,
  Racked nerve, and brain all burning,
His loving faith in Mother-land
  Knew never shade of turning;
By Britain's lakes, by Neva's wave,
  Whatever sky was o'er him,
He heard her rivers' rushing sound,
  Her blue peaks rose before him.

JOHN GREENLEAF WHITTIER 1807-1892

He held his slaves, yet made withal
    No false and vain pretences,
Nor paid a lying priest to seek
    For Scriptural defences.
His harshest words of proud rebuke,
    His bitterest taunt and scorning,
Fell fire-like on the Northern brow
    That bent to him in fawning.

He held his slaves: yet kept the while
    His reverence for the Human;
In the dark vassals of his will
    He saw but Man and Woman!
No hunter of God's outraged poor
    His Roanoke valley entered;
No trader in the souls of men
    Across his threshold ventured.

And when the old and wearied man
    Lay down for his last sleeping,
And at his side, a slave no more,
    His brother-man stood weeping,
His latest thought, his latest breath,
    To Freedom's duty giving,
With failing tongue and trembling hand
    The dying blest the living.

O, never bore his ancient State
    A truer son or braver!
None trampling with a calmer scorn
    On foreign hate or favor.

JOHN GREENLEAF WHITTIER 1807-1892

He knew her faults, yet never stooped
  His proud and manly feeling
To poor excuses of the wrong
  Or meanness of concealing.

But none beheld with clearer eye
  The plague-spot o'er her spreading,
None heard more sure the steps of Doom
  Along her future treading.
For her as for himself he spake,
  When, his gaunt frame upbracing,
He traced with dying hand "Remorse!"
  And perished in the tracing.

As from the grave where Henry sleeps,
  From Vernon's weeping willow,
And from the grassy pall which hides
  The Sage of Monticello,
So from the leaf-strewn burial-stone
  Of Randolph's lowly dwelling,
Virginia! o'er thy land of slaves
  A warning voice is swelling!

And hark! from thy deserted fields
  Are sadder warnings spoken,
From quenched hearths, where thy exiled sons
  Their household gods have broken.
The curse is on thee,—wolves for men,
  And briers for corn-sheaves giving!
O, more than all thy dead renown
  Were now one hero living!

JOHN GREENLEAF WHITTIER 1807–1892

Barclay of Ury

Up the streets of Aberdeen,
By the kirk and college green,
    Rode the Laird of Ury;
Close behind him, close beside,
Foul of mouth and evil-eyed,
    Pressed the mob in fury.

Flouted him the drunken churl,
Jeered at him the serving-girl,
    Prompt to please her master;
And the begging carlin, late
Fed and clothed at Ury's gate,
    Cursed him as he passed her.

Yet, with calm and stately mien,
Up the streets of Aberdeen
    Came he slowly riding;
And, to all he saw and heard,
Answering not with bitter word,
    Turning not for chiding.

Came a troop with broadswords swinging,
Bits and bridles sharply ringing,
    Loose and free and froward;
Quoth the foremost, "Ride him down!
Push him! prick him! through the town
    Drive the Quaker coward!"

But from out the thickening crowd
Cried a sudden voice and loud:
    "Barclay! Ho! a Barclay!"
And the old man at his side
Saw a comrade, battle tried,
    Scarred and sunburned darkly;

Who with ready weapon bare,
Fronting to the troopers there,
    Cried aloud: "God save us,
Call ye coward him who stood
Ankle deep in Lutzen's blood,
    With the brave Gustavus?"

"Nay, I do not need thy sword,
Comrade mine," said Ury's lord;
    "Put it up, I pray thee:
Passive to his holy will,
Trust I in my Master still,
    Even though he slay me."

"Pledges of thy love and faith,
Proved on many a field of death,
    Not by me are needed."
Marvelled much that henchman bold,
That his laird, so stout of old,
    Now so meekly pleaded.

JOHN GREENLEAF WHITTIER 1807–1892

"Wo's the day!" he sadly said,
With a slowly-shaking head,
    And a look of pity;
"Ury's honest lord reviled,
Mock of knave and sport of child,
    In his own good city!

"Speak the word, and, master mine,
As we charged on Tilly's line,
    And his Walloon lancers,
Smiting through their midst we'll teach
Civil look and decent speech
    To these boyish prancers!"

"Marvel not, mine ancient friend,
Like beginning, like the end:"
    Quoth the Laird of Ury,
"Is the sinful servant more
Than his gracious Lord who bore
    Bonds and stripes in Jewry?

"Give me joy that in his name
I can bear, with patient frame,
    All these vain ones offer;
While for them he suffereth long,
Shall I answer wrong with wrong,
    Scoffing with the scoffer?

JOHN GREENLEAF WHITTIER 1807–1892

"Happier I, with loss of all,
Hunted, outlawed, held in thrall,
    With few friends to greet me,
Than when reeve and squire were seen,
Riding out from Aberdeen,
    With bared heads to meet me.

"When each good wife, o'er and o'er,
Blessed me as I passed her door;
    And the snooded daughter,
Through her casement glancing down,
Smiled on him who bore renown
    From red fields of slaughter.

"Hard to feel the stranger's scoff,
Hard the old friend's falling off,
    Hard to learn forgiving:
But the Lord his own rewards,
And his love with theirs accords,
    Warm and fresh and living.

"Through this dark and stormy night
Faith beholds a feeble light
    Up the blackness streaking;
Knowing God's own time is best,
In a patient hope I rest
    For the full day-breaking!"

JOHN GREENLEAF WHITTIER 1807–1892

So the Laird of Ury said,
Turning slow his horse's head
    Towards the Tolbooth prison,
Where, through iron grates, he heard
Poor disciples of the Word
    Preach of Christ arisen!

Not in vain, Confessor old,
Unto us the tale is told
    Of thy day of trial;
Every age on him who strays
From its broad and beaten ways
    Pours its sevenfold vial.

Happy he whose inward ear
Angels comfortings can hear,
    O'er the rabble's laughter;
And, while Hatred's fagots burn,
Glimpses through the smoke discern
    Of the good hereafter.

Knowing this, that never yet
Share of Truth was vainly set
    In the world's wide fallow;
After hands shall sow the seed,
After hands from hill and mead
    Reap the harvests yellow.

Thus, with somewhat of the Seer,
Must the moral pioneer
    From the Future borrow;
Clothe the waste with dreams of grain,
And, on midnight's sky of rain,
    Paint the golden morrow!

Lines on the Death of S. O. Torrey, Secretary of the Boston Young Men's Anti-Slavery Society

Gone before us, O our brother,
    To the spirit-land!
Vainly look we for another
    In thy place to stand.
Who shall offer youth and beauty
    On the wasting shrine
Of a stern and lofty duty,
    With a faith like thine?

O, thy gentle smile of greeting
    Who again shall see?
Who amidst the solemn meeting
    Gaze again on thee?—
Who, when peril gathers o'er us,
    Wear so calm a brow?
Who, with evil men before us,
    So serene as thou?

JOHN GREENLEAF WHITTIER 1807–1892

Early hath the spoiler found thee,
    Brother of our love!
Autumn's faded earth around thee,
    And its storms above!
Evermore that turf lie lightly,
    And, with future showers,
O'er thy slumbers fresh and brightly
    Blow the summer flowers!

In the locks thy forehead gracing,
    Not a silvery streak;
Nor a line of sorrow's tracing
    On thy fair young cheek;
Eyes of light and lips of roses,
    Such as Hylas wore—
Over all that curtain closes,
    Which shall rise no more!

Will the vigil Love is keeping
    Round that grave of thine,
Mournfully, like Jazer weeping
    Over Sibmah's vine,—
Will the pleasant memories, swelling
    Gentle hearts, of thee,
In the spirit's distant dwelling
    All unheeded be?

If the spirit ever gazes,
    From its journeyings, back;
If the immortal ever traces
    O'er its mortal track;

Wilt thou not, O brother, meet us
    Sometimes on our way,
And, in hours of sadness, greet us
    As a spirit may?

Peace be with thee, O our brother,
    In the spirit-land!
Vainly look we for another
    In thy place to stand.
Unto Truth and Freedom giving
    All thy early powers,
Be thy virtues with the living,
    And thy spirit ours!

Ichabod

So fallen! so lost! the light withdrawn
    Which once he wore!
The glory from his gray hairs gone
    Forevermore!

Revile him not,—the Tempter hath
    A snare for all;
And pitying tears, not scorn and wrath,
    Befit his fall!

O, dumb be passion's stormy rage,
    When he who might
Have lighted up and led his age,
    Falls back in night.

JOHN GREENLEAF WHITTIER 1807–1892

Scorn! would the angels laugh, to mark
    A bright soul driven,
Fiend-goaded, down the endless dark,
    From hope and heaven!

Let not the land once proud of him
    Insult him now,
Nor brand with deeper shame his dim,
    Dishonored brow.

But let its humbled sons, instead,
    From sea to lake,
A long lament, as for the dead,
    In sadness make.

Of all we loved and honored, naught
    Save power remains,—
A fallen angel's pride of thought,
    Still strong in chains.

All else is gone; from those great eyes
    The soul has fled:
When faith is lost, when honor dies,
    The man is dead!

Then, pay the reverence of old days
    To his dead fame;
Walk backward, with averted gaze,
    And hide the shame!

JOHN GREENLEAF WHITTIER 1807–1892

Maud Muller

Maud Muller, on a summer's day,
Raked the meadow sweet with hay.

Beneath her torn hat glowed the wealth
Of simple beauty and rustic health.

Singing, she wrought, and her merry glee
The mock-bird echoed from his tree.

But when she glanced to the far-off town,
White from its hill-slope looking down,

The sweet song died, and a vague unrest
And a nameless longing filled her breast,—

A wish that she hardly dared to own,
For something better than she had known.

The Judge rode slowly down the lane,
Smoothing his horse's chestnut mane.

He drew his bridle in the shade
Of the apple-trees to greet the maid,

And ask a draught from the spring that flowed
Through the meadow across the road.

She stooped where the cool spring bubbled up,
And filled for him her small tin cup,

And blushed as she gave it, looking down
On her feet so bare, and her tattered gown.

JOHN GREENLEAF WHITTIER 1807–1892

"Thanks!" said the Judge; "a sweeter draught
From a fairer hand was never quaffed."

He spoke of the grass and flowers and trees,
Of the singing birds and the humming bees;

Then talked of the haying, and wondered whether
The cloud in the west would bring foul weather.

And Maud forgot her brier-torn gown
And her graceful ankles bare and brown;

And listened, while a pleased surprise
Looked from her long-lashed hazel eyes.

At last, like one who for delay
Seeks a vain excuse, he rode away.

Maud Muller looked and sighed: "Ah me!
That I the Judge's bride might be!

"He would dress me up in silks so fine,
And praise and toast me at his wine.

"My father should wear a broadcloth coat;
My brother should sail a painted boat.

"I'd dress my mother so grand and gay,
And the baby should have a new toy each day.

"And I'd feed the hungry and clothe the poor,
And all should bless me who left our door."

JOHN GREENLEAF WHITTIER 1807–1892

The Judge looked back as he climbed the hill,
And saw Maud Muller standing still.

"A form more fair, a face more sweet,
Ne'er hath it been my lot to meet.

"And her modest answer and graceful air
Show her wise and good as she is fair.

"Would she were mine, and I to-day,
Like her, a harvester of hay:

"No doubtful balance of rights and wrongs,
Nor weary lawyers with endless tongues,

"But low of cattle and song of birds,
And health and quiet and loving words."

But he thought of his sisters proud and cold,
And his mother vain of her rank and gold.

So, closing his heart, the Judge rode on,
And Maud was left in the field alone.

But the lawyers smiled that afternoon,
When he hummed in court an old love-tune;

And the young girl mused beside the well,
Till the rain on the unraked clover fell.

He wedded a wife of richest dower,
Who lived for fashion, as he for power.

JOHN GREENLEAF WHITTIER 1807–1892

Yet oft, in his marble hearth's bright glow,
He watched a picture come and go;

And sweet Maud Muller's hazel eyes
Looked out in their innocent surprise.

Oft, when the wine in his glass was red,
He longed for the wayside well instead;

And closed his eyes on his garnished rooms
To dream of meadows and clover-blooms.

And the proud man sighed, with a secret pain,
"Ah, that I were free again!

"Free as when I rode that day,
Where the barefoot maiden raked her hay."

She wedded a man unlearned and poor,
And many children played round her door.

But care and sorrow, and childbirth pain,
Left their traces on heart and brain.

And oft, when the summer sun shone hot
On the new-mown hay in the meadow lot,

And she heard the little spring brook fall
Over the roadside, through the wall,

In the shade of the apple-tree again
She saw a rider draw his rein.

And, gazing down with timid grace,
She felt his pleased eyes read her face.

Sometimes her narrow kitchen walls
Stretched away into stately halls;

The weary wheel to a spinet turned,
The tallow candle an astral burned,

And for him who sat by the chimney lug,
Dozing and grumbling o'er pipe and mug,

A manly form at her side she saw,
And joy was duty and love was law.

Then she took up her burden of life again,
Saying only, "It might have been."

Alas for maiden, alas for Judge,
For rich repiner and household drudge!

God pity them both! and pity us all,
Who vainly the dreams of youth recall.

For of all sad words of tongue or pen,
The saddest are these: "It might have been!"

Ah, well! for us all some sweet hope lies
Deeply buried from human eyes;

And, in the hereafter, angels may
Roll the stone from its grave away!

JOHN GREENLEAF WHITTIER 1807–1892

My Playmate

The pines were dark on Ramoth hill,
    Their song was soft and low;
The blossoms in the sweet May wind
    Were falling like the snow.

The blossoms drifted at our feet,
    The orchards birds sang clear;
The sweetest and the saddest day
    It seemed of all the year.

For, more to me than birds or flowers,
    My playmate left her home,
And took with her the laughing spring,
    The music and the bloom.

She kissed the lips of kith and kin,
    She laid her hand in mine:
What more could ask the bashful boy
    Who fed her father's kine?

She left us in the bloom of May:
    The constant years told o'er
Their seasons with as sweet May morns,
    But she came back no more.

I walk, with noiseless feet, the round
    Of uneventful years;
Still o'er and o'er I sow the spring
    And reap the autumn ears.

JOHN GREENLEAF WHITTIER 1807–1892

She lives where all the golden year
    Her summer roses blow;
The dusky children of the sun
    Before her come and go.

There haply with her jewelled hands
    She smooths her silken gown,—
No more the homespun lap wherein
    I shook the walnuts down.

The wild grapes wait us by the brook,
    The brown nuts on the hill,
And still the May-day flowers make sweet
    The woods of Follymill.

The lilies blossom in the pond,
    The bird builds in the tree,
The dark pines sing on Ramoth hill
    The slow song of the sea.

I wonder if she thinks of them,
    And how the old time seems,—
If ever the pines of Ramoth wood
    Are sounding in her dreams.

I see her face, I hear her voice:
    Does she remember mine?
And what to her is now the boy
    Who fed her father's kine?

What cares she that the orioles build
  For other eyes than ours,—
That other hands with nuts are filled,
  And other laps with flowers?

O playmate in the golden time!
  Our mossy seat is green,
Its fringing violets blossom yet,
  The old trees o'er it lean.

The winds so sweet with birch and fern
  A sweeter memory blow;
And there in spring the veeries sing
  The song of long ago.

And still the pines of Ramoth wood
  Are moaning like the sea,—
The moaning of the sea of change
  Between myself and thee!

The Old Burying-Ground

Our vales are sweet with fern and rose,
  Our hills are maple-crowned;
But not from them our fathers chose
  The village burying-ground.

The dreariest spot in all the land
  To Death they set apart;
With scanty grace from Nature's hand,
  And none from that of Art.

JOHN GREENLEAF WHITTIER 1807–1892

A winding wall of mossy stone,
    Frost-flung and broken, lines
A lonesome acre thinly grown
    With grass and wandering vines.

Without the wall a birch-tree shows
    Its drooped and tasselled head;
Within, a stag-horned sumach grows,
    Fern-leafed, with spikes of red.

There, sheep that graze the neighboring plain
    Like white ghosts come and go,
The farm-horse drags his fetlock chain,
    The cow-bell tinkles slow.

Low moans the river from its bed,
    The distant pines reply;
Like mourners shrinking from the dead,
    They stand apart and sigh.

Unshaded smites the summer sun,
    Unchecked the winter blast;
The school-girl learns the place to shun,
    With glances backward cast.

For thus our fathers testified,—
    That he might read who ran,—
The emptiness of human pride,
    The nothingness of man.

JOHN GREENLEAF WHITTIER 1807–1892

They dared not plant the grave with flowers,
    Nor dress the funeral sod,
Where, with a love as deep as ours,
    They left their dead with God.

The hard and thorny path they kept
    From beauty turned aside;
Nor missed they over those who slept
    The grace to life denied.

Yet still the wilding flowers would blow,
    The golden leaves would fall,
The seasons come, the seasons go,
    And God be good to all.

Above the graves the blackberry hung
    In bloom and green its wreath,
And harebells swung as if they rung
    The chimes of peace beneath.

The beauty Nature loves to share,
    The gifts she hath for all,
The common light, the common air,
    O'ercrept the graveyard's wall.

It knew the glow of eventide,
    The sunrise and the noon,
And glorified and sanctified
    It slept beneath the moon.

With flowers or snow-flakes for its sod,
   Around the seasons ran,
And evermore the love of God
   Rebuked the fear of man.

We dwell with fears on either hand,
   Within a daily strife,
And spectral problems waiting stand
   Before the gates of life.

The doubts we vainly seek to solve,
   The truths we know, are one;
The known and nameless stars revolve
   Around the Central Sun.

And if we reap as we have sown,
   And take the dole we deal,
The law of pain is love alone,
   The wounding is to heal.

Unharmed from change to change we glide,
   We fall as in our dreams;
The far-off terror at our side
   A smiling angel seems.

Secure on God's all-tender heart
   Alike rest great and small;
Why fear to lose our little part,
   When he is pledged for all?

JOHN GREENLEAF WHITTIER 1807–1892

O fearful heart and troubled brain!
   Take hope and strength from this,—
That Nature never hints in vain,
   Nor prophesies amiss.

Her wild birds sing the same sweet stave,
   Her lights and airs are given
Alike to playground and the grave;
   And over both is Heaven.

Dedication of "In War Time"

To Samuel E. Sewall and Harriet W. Sewall of Melrose

Olor Iscanus queries: "Why should we
Vex at the land's ridiculous miserie?"
So on his Usk banks, in the blood-red dawn
Of England's civil strife, did careless Vaughan
Bemock his times. O friends of many years!
Though faith and trust are stronger than our fears,
And the signs promise peace with liberty,
Not thus we trifle with our country's tears
And sweat of agony. The future's gain
Is certain as God's truth; but, meanwhile, pain
Is bitter and tears are salt: our voices take
A sober tone; our very household songs
Are heavy with a nation's griefs and wrongs;
And innocent mirth is chastened for the sake
Of the brave hearts that nevermore shall beat,
The eyes that smile no more, the unreturning feet!

JOHN GREENLEAF WHITTIER 1807–1892

The Watchers

Beside a stricken field I stood;
On the torn turf, on grass and wood,
Hung heavily the dew of blood.

Still in their fresh mounds lay the slain,
But all the air was quick with pain
And gusty sighs and tearful rain.

Two angels, each with drooping head
And folded wings and noiseless tread,
Watched by that valley of the dead.

The one, with forehead saintly bland
And lips of blessing, not command,
Leaned, weeping, on her olive wand.

The other's brows were scarred and knit,
His restless eyes were watch-fires lit,
His hands for battle-gauntlets fit.

"How long!"—I knew the voice of Peace,—
"Is there no respite?—no release?—
When shall the hopeless quarrel cease?

"O Lord, how long!—One human soul
Is more than any parchment scroll,
Or any flag thy winds unroll.

JOHN GREENLEAF WHITTIER 1807–1892

"What price was Ellsworth's, young and brave?
How weigh the gift that Lyon gave,
Or count the cost of Winthrop's grave?

"O brother! if thine eye can see,
Tell how and when the end shall be,
What hope remains for thee and me."

Then Freedom sternly said: "I shun
No strife nor pang beneath the sun,
When human rights are staked and won.

"I knelt with Ziska's hunted flock,
I watched in Toussaint's cell of rock,
I walked with Sidney to the block.

"The moor of Marston felt my tread,
Through Jersey snows the march I led,
My voice Magenta's charges sped.

"But now, through weary day and night,
I watch a vague and aimless fight
For leave to strike one blow aright.

"On either side my foe they own:
One guards through love his ghastly throne,
And one through fear to reverence grown.

"Why wait we longer, mocked, betrayed,
By open foes, or those afraid
To speed thy coming through my aid?

"Why watch to see who win or fall?—
I shake the dust against them all,
I leave them to their senseless brawl."

"Nay," Peace implored: "yet longer wait;
The doom is near, the stake is great:
God knoweth if it be too late.

"Still wait and watch; the way prepare
Where I with folded wings of prayer
May follow, weaponless and bare."

"Too late!" the stern, sad voice replied,
"Too late!" its mournful echo sighed,
In low lament the answer died.

A rustling as of wings in flight,
An upward gleam of lessening white,
So passed the vision, sound and sight.

But round me, like a silver bell
Rung down the listening sky to tell
Of holy help, a sweet voice fell.

"Still hope and trust," it sang; "the rod
Must fall, the wine-press must be trod,
But all is possible with God!"

JOHN GREENLEAF WHITTIER 1807–1892

Barbara Frietchie

Up from the meadows rich with corn,
Clear in the cool September morn,

The clustered spires of Frederick stand
Green-walled by the hills of Maryland.

Round about them orchards sweep,
Apple and peach tree fruited deep,

Fair as a garden of the Lord
To the eyes of the famished rebel horde,

On that pleasant morn of the early fall
When Lee marched over the mountain wall,—

Over the mountains winding down,
Horse and foot, into Frederick town.

Forty flags with their silver stars,
Forty flags with their crimson bars,

Flapped in the morning wind: the sun
Of noon looked down, and saw not one.

Up rose old Barbara Frietchie then,
Bowed with her fourscore years and ten;

Bravest of all in Frederick town,
She took up the flag the men hauled down;

JOHN GREENLEAF WHITTIER 1807–1892

In her attic-window the staff she set,
To show that one heart was loyal yet.

Up the street came the rebel tread,
Stonewall Jackson riding ahead.

Under his slouched hat left and right
He glanced: the old flag met his sight.

"Halt!"—the dust-brown ranks stood fast,
"Fire!"—out blazed the rifle-blast.

It shivered the window, pane and sash;
It rent the banner with seam and gash.

Quick, as it fell, from the broken staff
Dame Barbara snatched the silken scarf;

She leaned far out on the window-sill,
And shook it forth with a royal will.

"Shoot, if you must, this old gray head,
But spare your country's flag," she said.

A shade of sadness, a blush of shame,
Over the face of the leader came;

The nobler nature within him stirred
To life at that woman's deed and word:

JOHN GREENLEAF WHITTIER 1807–1892

"Who touches a hair of yon gray head
Dies like a dog! March on!" he said.

All day long through Frederick street
Sounded the tread of marching feet:

All day long that free flag tost
Over the heads of the rebel host.

Ever its torn folds rose and fell
On the loyal winds that loved it well;

And through the hill-gaps sunset light
Shone over it with a warm good-night.

Barbara Frietchie's work is o'er,
And the Rebel rides on his raids no more.

Honor to her! and let a tear
Fall, for her sake, on Stonewall's bier.

Over Barbara Frietchie's grave,
Flag of Freedom and Union, wave!

Peace and order and beauty draw
Round thy symbol of light and law;

And ever the stars above look down
On thy stars below in Frederick town!

JOHN GREENLEAF WHITTIER 1807–1892

What the Birds Said

The birds against the April wind
    Flew northward, singing as they flew;
They sang, "The land we leave behind
    Has swords for corn-blades, blood for dew."

"O wild-birds, flying from the South,
    What saw and heard ye, gazing down?"
"We saw the mortar's upturned mouth,
    The sickened camp, the blazing town!

"Beneath the bivouac's starry lamps,
    We saw your march-worn children die;
In shrouds of moss, in cypress swamps,
    We saw your dead uncoffined lie.

"We heard the starving prisoner's sighs,
    And saw, from line and trench, your sons
Follow our flight with home-sick eyes
    Beyond the battery's smoking guns."

"And heard and saw ye only wrong
    And pain," I cried, "O wing-worn flocks?"
"We heard," they sang, "the freedman's song,
    The crash of Slavery's broken locks!

"We saw from new, uprising States
    The treason-nursing mischief spurned,
As, crowding Freedom's ample gates,
    The long-estranged and lost returned.

JOHN GREENLEAF WHITTIER 1807–1892

"O'er dusky faces, seamed and old,
   And hands horn-hard with unpaid toil,
With hope in every rustling fold,
   We saw your star-dropt flag uncoil.

"And struggling up through sounds accursed,
   A grateful murmur clomb the air;
A whisper scarcely heard at first,
   It filled the listening heavens with prayer.

"And sweet and far, as from a star,
   Replied a voice which shall not cease,
Till, drowning all the noise of war,
   It sings the blessed song of peace!"

So to me, in a doubtful day
   Of chill and slowly greening spring,
Low stooping from the cloudy gray,
   The wild-birds sang or seemed to sing.

They vanished in the misty air,
   The song went with them in their flight;
But lo! they left the sunset fair,
   And in the evening there was light.

Faith

My faith looks up to Thee,
Thou Lamb of Calvary,
   Saviour divine!
Now hear me while I pray,
Take all my guilt away,
O let me from this day
   Be wholly Thine!

May Thy rich grace impart
Strength to my fainting heart,
   My zeal inspire;
As Thou hast died for me,
O may my love for Thee
Pure, warm, and changeless be,—
   A living fire!

While life's dark maze I tread,
And griefs around me spread,
   Be Thou my guide;
Bid darkness turn to day,
Wipe sorrow's tears away,
Nor let me ever stray
   From Thee aside.

RAY PALMER 1808–1887

When ends life's transient dream,
When death's cold, sullen stream
   Shall o'er me roll;
Blest Saviour, then, in love,
Fear and distrust remove;
O bear me safe above,
   A ransomed soul!

EDGAR ALLAN POE 1809–1849

The Raven

Once upon a midnight dreary, while I pondered, weak
    and weary,
Over many a quaint and curious volume of forgotten
    lore,—
While I nodded, nearly napping, suddenly there came
    a tapping,
As of some one gently rapping, rapping at my chamber
    door.
" 'T is some visitor," I muttered, "tapping at my chamber
    door;
    Only this and nothing more."

Ah, distinctly I remember it was in the bleak December
And each separate dying ember wrought its ghost upon
    the floor.
Eagerly I wished the morrow;—vainly I had sought to
    borrow
From my books surcease of sorrow—sorrow for the lost
    Lenore,
For the rare and radiant maiden whom the angels name
    Lenore:
    Nameless here for evermore.

And the silken sad uncertain rustling of each purple
    curtain
Thrilled me—filled me with fantastic terrors never felt
    before;

So that now, to still the beating of my heart, I stood repeating
" 'T is some visitor entreating entrance at my chamber door,
Some late visitor entreating entrance at my chamber door:
   This it is and nothing more."

Presently my soul grew stronger; hesitating then no longer,
"Sir," said I, "or Madam, truly your forgiveness I implore;
But the fact is I was napping, and so gently you came rapping,
And so faintly you came tapping, tapping at my chamber door,
That I scarce was sure I heard you"—here I opened wide the door:—
   Darkness there and nothing more.

Deep into that darkness peering, long I stood there wondering, fearing,
Doubting, dreaming dreams no mortals ever dared to dream before;
But the silence was unbroken, and the stillness gave no token,
And the only word there spoken was the whispered word, "Lenore?"

This I whispered, and an echo murmured back the word,
    "Lenore:"
      Merely this and nothing more.

Back into the chamber turning, all my soul within me
    burning,
Soon again I heard a tapping somewhat louder than
    before.
"Surely," said I, "surely that is something at my window
    lattice;
Let me see, then, what thereat is, and this mystery
    explore;
Let my heart be still a moment and this mystery explore:
      'T is the wind and nothing more."

Open here I flung the shutter, when, with many a flirt
    and flutter,
In there stepped a stately Raven of the saintly days of
    yore.
Not the least obeisance made he; not a minute stopped
    or stayed he;
But, with mien of lord or lady, perched above my chamber
    door,
Perched upon a bust of Pallas just above my chamber
    door:
      Perched, and sat, and nothing more.

Then this ebony bird beguiling my sad fancy into smiling
By the grave and stern decorum of the countenance it
    wore,—

"Though thy crest be shorn and shaven, thou," I said,
    "art sure no craven,
Ghastly grim and ancient Raven wandering from the
    Nightly shore:
Tell me what thy lordly name is on the Night's Plutonian
    shore!"
    Quoth the Raven, "Nevermore."

Much I marvelled this ungainly fowl to hear discourse
    so plainly,
Though its answer little meaning—little relevancy bore;
For we cannot help agreeing that no living human being
Ever yet was blessed with seeing bird above his chamber
    door,
Bird or beast upon the sculptured bust above his chamber
    door,
    With such name as "Nevermore."

But the Raven, sitting lonely on the placid bust, spoke
    only
That one word, as if his soul in that one word he did
    outpour.
Nothing further then he uttered, not a feather then he
    fluttered,
Till I scarcely more than muttered,—"Other friends have
    flown before;
On the morrow *he* will leave me, as my Hopes have flown
    before."
    Then the bird said, "Nevermore."

Startled at the stillness broken by reply so aptly spoken,
"Doubtless," said I, "what it utters is its only stock and
    store,
Caught from some unhappy master whom unmerciful
    Disaster
Followed fast and followed faster till his songs one
    burden bore:
Till the dirges of his Hope that melancholy burden bore
    Of 'Never—nevermore.'"

But the Raven still beguiling all my fancy into smiling,
Straight I wheeled a cushioned seat in front of bird and
    bust and door;
Then, upon the velvet sinking, I betook myself to linking
Fancy unto fancy, thinking what this ominous bird of
    yore,
What this grim, ungainly, ghastly, gaunt, and ominous
    bird of yore
    Meant in croaking "Nevermore."

This I sat engaged in guessing, but no syllable expressing
To the fowl whose fiery eyes now burned into my bosom's
    core;
This and more I sat divining, with my head at ease
    reclining
On the cushion's velvet lining that the lamplight gloated
    o'er,
But whose velvet violet lining with the lamp-light gloat-
    ing o'er
    She shall press, ah, nevermore!

Then, methought, the air grew denser, perfumed from an
    unseen censer
Swung by seraphim whose foot-falls tinkled on the tufted
    floor.
"Wretch," I cried, "thy God hath lent thee—by these
    angels he hath sent thee
Respite—respite and nepenthe from thy memories of
    Lenore!"
Quaff, oh quaff this kind nepenthe, and forget this lost
    Lenore."
    Quoth the Raven, "Nevermore."

"Prophet!" said I, "thing of evil! prophet still, if bird
    or devil!
Whether Tempter sent, or whether tempest tossed thee
    here ashore,
Desolate yet all undaunted, on this desert land en-
    chanted—
On this home by Horror haunted—tell me truly, I
    implore:
Is there—*is* there balm in Gilead?—tell me—tell me, I
    implore!"
    Quoth the Raven, "Nevermore."

"Prophet!" said I, "thing of evil—prophet still, if bird
    or devil!
By that Heaven that bends above us, by that God we
    both adore,
Tell this soul with sorrow laden if, within the distant
    Aidenn,

It shall clasp a sainted maiden whom the angels name
    Lenore:
Clasp a rare and radiant maiden whom the angels name
    Lenore!"
    Quoth the Raven, "Nevermore."

"Be that word our sign of parting, bird or fiend!" I
    shrieked, upstarting:
"Get thee back into the tempest and the Night's Plu-
    tonian shore!
Leave no black plume as a token of that lie thy soul hath
    spoken!
Leave my loneliness unbroken! quit the bust above my
    door!
Take thy beak from out my heart, and take thy form
    from off my door!"
    Quoth the Raven, "Nevermore."

And the Raven, never flitting, still is sitting, still is
    sitting
On the pallid bust of Pallas just above my chamber door;
And his eyes have all the seeming of a demon's that is
    dreaming,
And the lamp-light o'er him streaming throws his shadow
    on the floor:
And my soul from out that shadow that lies floating on
    the floor
    Shall be lifted—nevermore!

EDGAR ALLAN POE 1809–1849

To One in Paradise

Thou wast all that to me, love,
   For which my soul did pine:
A green isle in the sea, love,
   A fountain and a shrine
All wreathed with fairy fruits and flowers,
   And all the flowers were mine.

Ah, dream too bright to last!
   Ah, starry Hope, that didst arise
But to be overcast!
   A voice from out the Future cries,
"On! on!"—but o'er the Past
   (Dim gulf!) my spirit hovering lies
Mute, motionless, aghast.

For, alas! alas! with me
   The light of Life is o'er!
   No more—no more—no more—
(Such language holds the solemn sea
   To the sands upon the shore)
Shall bloom the thunder-blasted tree,
   Or the stricken eagle soar.

And all my days are trances,
   And all my nightly dreams
Are where thy gray eye glances,
   And where thy footstep gleams—
In what ethereal dances,
   By what eternal streams.

The Haunted Palace

In the greenest of our valleys
   By good angels tenanted,
Once a fair and stately palace—
   Radiant palace—reared its head.
In the monarch Thought's dominion,
   It stood there;
Never seraph spread a pinion
   Over fabric half so fair.

Banners yellow, glorious, golden,
   On its roof did float and flow
(This—all this—was in the olden
   Time long ago),
And every gentle air that dallied,
   In that sweet day,
Along the ramparts plumed and pallid,
   A wingèd odor went away.

Wanderers in that happy valley
   Through two luminous windows saw
Spirits moving musically,
   To a lute's well-tunèd law,
Round about a throne where, sitting,
   Porphyrogene,
In state his glory well befitting,
   The ruler of the realm was seen.

EDGAR ALLAN POE 1809–1849

And all with pearl and ruby glowing
    Was the fair palace door,
Through which came flowing, flowing, flowing,
    And sparkling evermore,
A troop of Echoes, whose sweet duty
    Was but to sing,
In voices of surpassing beauty,
    The wit and wisdom of their king.

But evil things, in robes of sorrow,
    Assailed the monarch's high estate;
(Ah, let us mourn, for never morrow
    Shall dawn upon him desolate!)
And round about his home the glory
    That blushed and bloomed,
Is but a dim-remembered story
    Of the old time entombed.

And travellers now within that valley
    Through the red-litten windows see
Vast forms that move fantastically
    To a discordant melody;
While, like a ghastly rapid river,
    Through the pale door
A hideous throng rush out forever,
    And laugh—but smile no more.

EDGAR ALLAN POE 1809–1849

The Conqueror Worm

Lo! 't is a gala night
   Within the lonesome latter years.
An angel throng, bewinged, bedight
   In veils, and drowned in tears,
Sit in a theatre to see
   A play of hopes and fears,
While the orchestra breathes fitfully
   The music of the spheres.

Mimes, in the form of God on high,
   Mutter and mumble low,
And hither and thither fly;
   Mere puppets they, who come and go
At bidding of vast formless things
   That shift the scenery to and fro,
Flapping from out their condor wings
   Invisible Woe.

That motley drama—oh, be sure
   It shall not be forgot!
With its Phantom chased for evermore
   By a crowd that seize it not,
Through a circle that ever returneth in
   To the self-same spot;
And much of Madness, and more of Sin,
   And Horror the soul of the plot.

EDGAR ALLAN POE 1809–1849

But see amid the mimic rout
   A crawling shape intrude:
A blood-red thing that writhes from out
   The scenic solitude!
It writhes—it writhes!—with mortal pangs
   The mimes become its food,
And the seraphs sob at vermin fangs
   In human gore imbued.

Out—out are the lights—out all!
   And over each quivering form
The curtain, a funeral pall,
   Comes down with the rush of a storm,
While the angels, all pallid and wan,
   Uprising, unveiling, affirm
That the play is the tragedy, "Man,"
   And its hero, the Conqueror Worm.

EDGAR ALLAN POE 1809–1849

The Bells

Hear the sledges with the bells,
      Silver bells!
What a world of merriment their melody foretells!
   How they tinkle, tinkle, tinkle,
     In the icy air of night!
  While the stars, that oversprinkle
  All the heavens, seem to twinkle
    With a crystalline delight;
   Keeping time, time, time,
   In a sort of Runic rhyme,
To the tintinnabulation that so musically wells
  From the bells, bells, bells, bells,
     Bells, bells, bells—
From the jingling and the tinkling of the bells.

 Hear the mellow wedding bells,
     Golden bells!
What a world of happiness their harmony foretells!
   Through the balmy air of night
   How they ring out their delight!
    From the molten-golden notes,
     And all in tune,
    What a liquid ditty floats
To the turtle-dove that listens, while she gloats
     On the moon!
  Oh, from out the sounding cells,

EDGAR ALLAN POE 1809–1849

What a gush of euphony voluminously wells!
      How it swells!
      How it dwells
    On the Future! how it tells
    Of the rapture that impels
  To the swinging and the ringing
    Of the bells, bells, bells,
Of the bells, bells, bells, bells,
      Bells, bells, bells—
To the rhyming and the chiming of the bells!

    Hear the loud alarum bells,
        Brazen bells!
What a tale of terror, now, their turbulency tells!
    In the startled ear of night
    How they scream out their affright!
      Too much horrified to speak,
      They can only shriek, shriek,
        Out of tune,
In a clamorous appealing to the mercy of the fire,
In a mad expostulation with the deaf and frantic fire,
     Leaping higher, higher, higher,
     With a desperate desire,
    And a resolute endeavor
    Now—now to sit or never,
  By the side of the pale-faced moon.
      Oh, the bells, bells, bells!
      What a tale their terror tells
        Of Despair!

EDGAR ALLAN POE 1809–1849

  How they clang, and clash, and roar!
  What a horror they outpour
On the bosom of the palpitating air!
  Yet the ear it fully knows,
    By the twanging
    And the clanging,
  How the danger ebbs and flows;
  Yet the ear distinctly tells,
    In the jangling
    And the wrangling,
  How the danger sinks and swells,—
By the sinking or the swelling in the anger of the bells,
    Of the bells,
  Of the bells, bells, bells, bells,
    Bells, bells, bells—
 In the clamor and the clangor of the bells!

  Hear the tolling of the bells,
    Iron bells!
What a world of solemn thought their monody compels!
  In the silence of the night
  How we shiver with affright
 At the melancholy menace of their tone!
  For every sound that floats
  From the rust within their throats
    Is a groan.
  And the people—ah, the people,
  They that dwell up in the steeple,
    All alone,

EDGAR ALLAN POE 1809–1849

And who tolling, tolling, tolling,
   In that muffled monotone,
Feel a glory in so rolling
   On the human heart a stone—
They are neither man nor woman,
They are neither brute nor human,
   They are Ghouls:
   And their king it is who tolls;
   And he rolls, rolls, rolls,
      Rolls
   A pæan from the bells;
And his merry bosom swells
   With the pæan of the bells,
And he dances, and he yells:
Keeping time, time, time,
In a sort of Runic rhyme,
   To the pæan of the bells,
     Of the bells:
Keeping time, time, time,
In a sort of Runic rhyme,
To the throbbing of the bells,
Of the bells, bells, bells—
   To the sobbing of the bells;
Keeping time, time, time,
   As he knells, knells, knells,
In a happy Runic rhyme,
To the rolling of the bells,
   Of the bells, bells, bells:
   To the tolling of the bells,

EDGAR ALLAN POE 1809–1849

Of the bells, bells, bells, bells,
    Bells, bells, bells—
To the moaning and the groaning of the bells.

Annabel Lee

It was many and many a year ago,
    In a kingdom by the sea,
That a maiden there lived whom you may know
    By the name of Annabel Lee;
And this maiden she lived with no other thought
    Than to love and be loved by me.

I was a child and she was a child,
    In this kingdom by the sea,
But we loved with a love that was more than love,
    I and my Annabel Lee;
With a love that the wingèd seraphs of heaven
    Coveted her and me.

And this was the reason that, long ago,
    In this kingdom by the sea,
A wind blew out of a cloud, chilling
    My beautiful Annabel Lee;
So that her highborn kinsmen came
    And bore her away from me,
To shut her up in a sepulchre
    In this kingdom by the sea.

The angels, not half so happy in heaven,
    Went envying her and me;
Yes! that was the reason (as all men know,
    In this kingdom by the sea)
That the wind came out of the cloud by night,
    Chilling and killing my Annabel Lee.

But our love it was stronger by far than the love
    Of those who were older than we,
    Of many far wiser than we;
And neither the angels in heaven above,
    Nor the demons down under the sea,
Can ever dissever my soul from the soul
    Of the beautiful Annabel Lee:

For the moon never beams, without bringing me dreams
    Of the beautiful Annabel Lee;
And the stars never rise, but I feel the bright eyes
    Of the beautiful Annabel Lee;
And so, all the night-tide, I lie down by the side
Of my darling—my darling—my life and my bride,
    In her sepulchre there by the sea,
    In her tomb by the sounding sea.

EDGAR ALLAN POE 1809–1849

Ulalume

The skies they were ashen and sober;
   The leaves they were crispèd and sere,
   The leaves they were withering and sere;
It was night in the lonesome October
   Of my most immemorial year;
It was hard by the dim lake of Auber,
   In the misty mid region of Weir:
It was down by the dank tarn of Auber,
   In the ghoul-haunted woodland of Weir.

Here once, through an alley Titanic
   Of cypress, I roamed with my Soul—
   Of cypress, with Psyche, my Soul.
These were days when my heart was volcanic
   As the scoriac rivers that roll,
   As the lavas that restlessly roll
Their sulphurous currents down Yaanek
   In the ultimate climes of the pole,
That groan as they roll down Mount Yaanek
   In the realms of the boreal pole.

Our talk had been serious and sober,
   But our thoughts they were palsied and sere,
   Our memories were treacherous and sere,
For we knew not the month was October,
   And we marked not the night of the year,
   (Ah, night of all nights in the year!)
We noted not the dim lake of Auber

(Though once we had journeyed down here),
Remembered not the dank tarn of Auber
   Nor the ghoul-haunted woodland of Weir.

And now, as the night was senescent
   And star-dials pointed to morn,
   As the star-dials hinted of morn,
At the end of our path a liquescent
   And nebulous lustre was born,
Out of which a miraculous crescent
   Arose with a duplicate horn,
Astarte's bediamonded crescent
   Distinct with its duplicate horn.

And I said—"She is warmer than Dian:
   She rolls through an ether of sighs,
   She revels in a region of sighs:
She has seen that the tears are not dry on
   These cheeks, where the worm never dies,
And has come past the stars of the Lion
   To point us the path to the skies,
   To the Lethean peace of the skies:
Come up, in despite of the Lion,
   To shine on us with her bright eyes:
Come up through the lair of the Lion,
   With love in her luminous eyes."

But Psyche, uplifting her finger,
   Said—"Sadly this star I mistrust,
   Her pallor I strangely mistrust:
Oh, hasten!—oh, let us not linger!

Oh, fly!—let us fly! for we must."
In terror she spoke, letting sink her
   Wings until they trailed in the dust,
In agony sobbed, letting sink her
   Plumes till they trailed in the dust,
   Till they sorrowfully trailed in the dust.

I replied—"This is nothing but dreaming:
   Let us on by this tremulous light!
   Let us bathe in this crystalline light!
Its sibyllic splendor is beaming
   With hope and in beauty to-night:
   See, it flickers up the sky through the night!
Ah, we safely may trust to its gleaming,
   And be sure it will lead us aright:
We safely may trust to a gleaming
   That cannot but guide us aright,
   Since it flickers up to Heaven through the night."

Thus I pacified Psyche and kissed her,
   And tempted her out of her gloom,
   And conquered her scruples and gloom;
And we passed to the end of the vista,
   But were stopped by the door of a tomb,
   By the door of a legended tomb;
And I said—"What is written, sweet sister,
   On the door of this legended tomb?"
   She replied—"Ulalume—Ulalume—
   'T is the vault of thy lost Ulalume!"

EDGAR ALLAN POE 1809–1849

Then my heart it grew ashen and sober
    As the leaves that were crispèd and sere,
    As the leaves that were withering and sere,
And I cried—"It was surely October
    On this very night of last year
      That I journeyed—I journeyed down here,
      That I brought a dread burden down here:
    On this night of all nights in the year,
    Ah, what demon has tempted me here?
Well I know, now, this dim lake of Auber,
    This misty mid region of Weir:
Well I know, now, this dank tarn of Auber,
    This ghoul-haunted woodland of Weir."

EDGAR ALLAN POE 1809-1849

To Helen

Helen, thy beauty is to me
   Like those Nicæan barks of yore,
That gently, o'er a perfumed sea,
   The weary, wayworn wanderer bore
   To his own native shore.

On desperate seas long wont to roam,
   Thy hyacinth hair, thy classic face,
Thy Naiad airs, have brought me home
   To the glory that was Greece
   And the grandeur that was Rome.

Lo! in yon brilliant window-niche
   How statue-like I see thee stand,
The agate lamp within thy hand!
   Ah, Psyche, from the regions which
   Are Holy Land!

OLIVER WENDELL HOLMES 1809–1894

The Last Leaf

I saw him once before,
As he passed by the door,
    And again
The pavement stones resound,
As he totters o'er the ground
    With his cane.

They say that in his prime,
Ere the pruning-knife of Time
    Cut him down,
Not a better man was found
By the Crier on his round
    Through the town.

But now he walks the streets,
And he looks at all he meets
    Sad and wan,
And he shakes his feeble head,
That it seems as if he said,
    "They are gone."

The mossy marbles rest
On the lips that he has prest
    In their bloom,
And the names he loved to hear
Have been carved for many a year
    On the tomb.

OLIVER WENDELL HOLMES 1809–1894

My grandmamma has said—
Poor old lady, she is dead
    Long ago—
That he had a Roman nose,
And his cheek was like a rose
    In the snow.

But now his nose is thin,
And it rests upon his chin
    Like a staff,
And a crook is in his back,
And a melancholy crack
    In his laugh.

I know it is a sin
For me to sit and grin
    At him here;
But the old three-cornered hat,
And the breeches, and all that,
    Are so queer!

And if I should live to be
The last leaf upon the tree
    In the spring,—
Let them smile, as I do now,
At the old forsaken bough
    Where I cling.

OLIVER WENDELL HOLMES 1809–1894

The Dilemma

Now, by the blessed Paphian queen,
Who heaves the breast of sweet sixteen;
By every name I cut on bark
Before my morning star grew dark;
By Hymen's torch, by Cupid's dart,
By all that thrills the beating heart;
The bright black eye, the melting blue,—
I cannot choose between the two.

I had a vision in my dreams;—
I saw a row of twenty beams;
From every beam a rope was hung,
In every rope a lover swung;
I asked the hue of every eye,
That bade each luckless lover die;
Ten shadowy lips said, heavenly blue,
And ten accused the darker hue.

I asked a matron which she deemed
With fairest light of beauty beamed;
She answered, some thought both were fair,—
Give her blue eyes and golden hair.
I might have liked her judgment well,
But, as she spoke, she rung the bell,
And all her girls, nor small nor few,
Came marching in,—their eyes were blue.

OLIVER WENDELL HOLMES 1809–1894

I asked a maiden; back she flung
The locks that round her forehead hung,
And turned her eye, a glorious one,
Bright as a diamond in the sun,
On me, until beneath its rays
I felt as if my hair would blaze;
She liked all eyes but eyes of green;
She looked at me; what could she mean?

Ah! many lids Love lurks between,
Nor heeds the coloring of his screen;
And when his random arrows fly,
The victim falls, but knows not why.
Gaze not upon his shield of jet,
The shaft upon the string is set;
Look not beneath his azure veil,
Though every limb were cased in mail.

Well, both might make a martyr break
The chain that bound him to the stake;
And both, with but a single ray,
Can melt our very hearts away;
And both, when balanced, hardly seem
To stir the scales, or rock the beam;
But that is dearest, all the while,
That wears for us the sweetest smile.

OLIVER WENDELL HOLMES 1809–1894

My Aunt

My aunt! my dear unmarried aunt!
    Long years have o'er her flown;
Yet still she strains the aching clasp
    That binds her virgin zone;
I know it hurts her,—though she looks
    As cheerful as she can;
Her waist is ampler than her life,
    For life is but a span.

My aunt! my poor deluded aunt!
    Her hair is almost gray;
Why will she train that winter curl
    In such a springlike way?
How can she lay her glasses down,
    And say she reads as well,
When, through a double convex lens,
    She just makes out to spell?

Her father—grandpapa! forgive
    This erring lip its smiles—
Vowed she should make the finest girl
    Within a hundred miles;
He sent her to a stylish school;
    'T was in her thirteenth June;
And with her, as the rules required,
    "Two towels and a spoon."

They braced my aunt against a board,
   To make her straight and tall;
They laced her up, they starved her down,
   To make her light and small;
They pinched her feet, they singed her hair,
   They screwed it up with pins;—
O never mortal suffered more
   In penance for her sins.

So, when my precious aunt was done,
   My grandsire brought her back;
(By daylight, lest some rabid youth
   Might follow on the track;)
"Ah!" said my grandsire, as he shook
   Some powder in his pan,
"What could this lovely creature do
   Against a desperate man!"

Alas! nor chariot, nor barouche,
   Nor bandit cavalcade,
Tore from the trembling father's arms
   His all-accomplished maid.
For her how happy had it been!
   And Heaven had spared to me
To see one sad, ungathered rose
   On my ancestral tree.

OLIVER WENDELL HOLMES 1809–1894

To the Portrait of "A Lady"
In the Athenæum Gallery.

Well, Miss, I wonder where you live,
    I wonder what's your name,
I wonder how you came to be
    In such a stylish frame;
Perhaps you were a favorite child,
    Perhaps an only one;
Perhaps your friends were not aware
    You had your portrait done!

Yet you must be a harmless soul;
    I cannot think that Sin
Would care to throw his loaded dice,
    With such a stake to win;
I cannot think you would provoke
    The poet's wicked pen,
Or make young women bite their lips,
    Or ruin fine young men.

Pray, did you ever hear, my love,
    Of boys that go about,
Who, for a very trifling sum,
    Will snip one's picture out?
I'm not averse to red and white,
    But all things have their place,
I think a profile cut in black
    Would suit your style of face!

OLIVER WENDELL HOLMES 1809–1894

I love sweet features; I will own
  That I should like myself
To see my portrait on a wall,
  Or bust upon a shelf;
But nature sometimes makes one up
  Of such sad odds and ends,
It really might be quite as well
  Hushed up among one's friends!

The Music-Grinders

There are three ways in which men take
  One's money from his purse,
And very hard it is to tell
  Which of the three is worse;
But all of them are bad enough
  To make a body curse.

You 're riding out some pleasant day,
  And counting up your gains;
A fellow jumps from out a bush,
  And takes your horse's reins,
Another hints some words about
  A bullet in your brains.

OLIVER WENDELL HOLMES 1809–1894

It's hard to meet such pressing friends
   In such a lonely spot;
It's very hard to lose your cash,
   But harder to be shot;
And so you take your wallet out,
   Though you would rather not.

Perhaps you're going out to dine,—
   Some odious creature begs
You'll hear about the cannon-ball
   That carried off his pegs,
And says it is a dreadful thing
   For men to lose their legs.

He tells you of his starving wife,
   His children to be fed,
Poor little, lovely innocents,
   All clamorous for bread,—
And so you kindly help to put
   A bachelor to bed.

You're sitting on your window-seat,
   Beneath a cloudless moon;
You hear a sound, that seems to wear
   The semblance of a tune,
As if a broken fife should strive
   To drown a cracked bassoon.

And nearer, nearer still, the tide
   Of music seems to come,
There's something like a human voice,
   And something like a drum;

OLIVER WENDELL HOLMES 1809–1894

You sit in speechless agony,
   Until your ear is numb.

Poor "home, sweet home" should seem to be
   A very dismal place;
Your "auld acquaintance" all at once
   Is altered in the face;
Their discords sting through Burns and Moore,
   Like hedgehogs dressed in lace.

You think they are crusaders, sent
   From some infernal clime,
To pluck the eyes of Sentiment,
   And dock the tail of Rhyme,
To crack the voice of Melody,
   And break the legs of Time.

But hark! the air again is still,
   The music all is ground,
And silence, like a poultice, comes
   To heal the blows of sound;
It cannot be,—it is,—it is,—
   A hat is going round!

No! Pay the dentist when he leaves
   A fracture in your jaw,
And pay the owner of the bear
   That stunned you with his paw,
And buy the lobster that has had
   Your knuckles in his claw;

But if you are a portly man,
    Put on your fiercest frown,
And talk about a constable
    To turn them out of town;
Then close your sentence with an oath,
    And shut the window down!

And if you are a slender man,
    Not big enough for that,
Or, if you cannot make a speech,
    Because you are a flat,
Go very quietly and drop
    A button in the hat!

Lexington

Slowly the mist o'er the meadow was creeping,
    Bright on the dewy buds glistened the sun,
When from his couch, while his children were sleeping,
    Rose the bold rebel and shouldered his gun.
        Waving her golden veil
        Over the silent dale,
Blithe looked the morning on cottage and spire;
        Hushed was his parting sigh,
        While from his noble eye
Flashed the last sparkle of liberty's fire.

OLIVER WENDELL HOLMES 1809–1894

On the smooth green where the fresh leaf is springing
   Calmly the first-born of glory have met;
Hark! the death-volley around them is ringing!
   Look! with their life-blood the young grass is wet!
      Faint is the feeble breath,
      Murmuring low in death,
"Tell to our sons how their fathers have died";
      Nerveless the iron hand,
      Raised for its native land,
Lies by the weapon that gleams at its side.

Over the hillsides the wild knell is tolling,
   From their far hamlets the yeomanry come;
As through the storm-clouds the thunder-burst rolling,
   Circles the beat of the mustering drum.
      Fast on the soldier's path
      Darken the waves of wrath,
Long have they gathered and loud shall they fall;
      Red glares the musket's flash,
      Sharp rings the rifle's crash,
Blazing and clanging from thicket and wall.

Gayly the plume of the horseman was dancing,
   Never to shadow his cold brow again;
Proudly at morning the war-steed was prancing,
   Reeking and panting he droops on the rein;
      Pale is the lip of scorn,
      Voiceless the trumpet horn,

OLIVER WENDELL HOLMES 1809–1894

Torn is the silken-fringed red cross on high;
      Many a belted breast
      Low on the turf shall rest,
Ere the dark hunters the herd have passed by.

Snow-girdled crags where the hoarse wind is raving,
   Rocks where the weary floods murmur and wail,
Wilds where the fern by the furrow is waving,
   Reeled with the echoes that rode on the gale;
      Far as the tempest thrills
      Over the darkened hills,
Far as the sunshine streams over the plain,
      Roused by the tyrant band,
      Woke all the mighty land,
Girded for battle, from mountain to main.

Green be the graves where her martyrs are lying!
   Shroudless and tombless they sunk to their rest,—
While o'er their ashes the starry fold flying
   Wraps the proud eagle they roused from his nest.
      Borne on her Northern pine,
      Long o'er the foaming brine
Spread her broad banner to storm and to sun;
      Heaven keep her ever free
      Wide as o'er land and sea
Floats the fair emblem her heroes have won!

On Lending a Punch-Bowl

This ancient silver bowl of mine,—it tells of good old times,
Of joyous days, and jolly nights, and merry Christmas chimes;
They were a free and jovial race, but honest, brave, and true,
That dipped their ladle in the punch when this old bowl was new.

A Spanish galleon brought the bar,—so runs the ancient tale;
'T was hammered by an Antwerp smith, whose arm was like a flail;
And now and then between the strokes, for fear his strength should fail,
He wiped his brow, and quaffed a cup of good old Flemish ale.

'T was purchased by an English squire to please his loving dame,
Who saw the cherubs, and conceived a longing for the same;
And oft as on the ancient stock another twig was found,
'T was filled with caudle spiced and hot, and handed smoking round.

But, changing hands, it reached at length a Puritan divine,
Who used to follow Timothy, and take a little wine,
But hated punch and prelacy; and so it was, perhaps,
He went to Leyden, where he found conventicles and schnaps.

And then, of course, you know what's next,—it left the Dutchman's shore
With those that in the Mayflower came,—a hundred souls and more,—
Along with all the furniture, to fill their new abodes,
To judge by what is still on hand, at least a hundred loads.

'T was on a dreary winter's eve, the night was closing dim,
When brave Miles Standish took the bowl, and filled it to the brim;
The little Captain stood and stirred the posset with his sword,
And all his sturdy men-at-arms were ranged about the board.

He poured the fiery Hollands in,—the man that never feared,—
He took a long and solemn draught, and wiped his yellow beard;

And one by one the musketeers—the men that fought
    and prayed—
All drank as 't were their mother's milk, and not a man
    afraid.

That night, affrighted from his nest, the screaming eagle
    flew,
He heard the Pequot's ringing whoop, the soldier's wild
    halloo;
And there the sachem learned the rule he taught to kith
    and kin,
"Run from the white man when you find he smells of
    Hollands gin!"

A hundred years, and fifty more, had spread their leaves
    and snows,
A thousand rubs had flattened down each little cherub's
    nose,
When once again the bowl was filled, but not in mirth
    or joy,
'T was mingled by a mother's hand to cheer her parting
    boy.

Drink, John, she said, 't will do you good,—poor child,
    you 'll never bear
This working in the dismal trench, out in the midnight
    air;

And if—God bless me!—you were hurt, 't would keep
 away the chill;
So John *did* drink,—and well he wrought that night at
 Bunker's Hill!

I tell you, there was generous warmth in good old Eng-
 lish cheer;
I tell you, 't was a pleasant thought to bring its symbol
 here.
'T is but the fool that loves excess;—hast thou a drunken
 soul?
Thy bane is in thy shallow skull, not in my silver bowl!

I love the memory of the past,—its pressed yet fragrant
 flowers,—
The moss that clothes its broken walls,—the ivy on its
 towers;—
Nay, this poor bawble it bequeathed,—my eyes grow
 moist and dim,
To think of all the vanished joys that danced around its
 brim.

Then fill a fair and honest cup, and bear it straight to
 me;
The goblet hallows all it holds, whate'er the liquid be;
And may the cherubs on its face protect me from the sin
That dooms one to those dreadful words,—"My dear,
 where *have* you been?"

OLIVER WENDELL HOLMES 1809–1894

The Parting Word

I must leave thee, lady sweet!
Months shall waste before we meet;
Winds are fair, and sails are spread,
Anchors leave their ocean bed;
Ere this shining day grow dark,
Skies shall gird my shoreless bark;
Through thy tears, O lady mine,
Read thy lover's parting line.

When the first sad sun shall set,
Thou shalt tear thy locks of jet;
When the morning star shall rise,
Thou shalt wake with weeping eyes;
When the second sun goes down,
Thou more tranquil shalt be grown,
Taught too well that wild despair
Dims thine eyes, and spoils thy hair.

All the first unquiet week
Thou shalt wear a smileless cheek;
In the first month's second half
Thou shalt once attempt to laugh;
Then in Pickwick thou shalt dip,
Slightly puckering round the lip,
Till at last, in sorrow's spite,
Samuel makes thee laugh outright.

OLIVER WENDELL HOLMES 1809–1894

While the first seven mornings last,
Round thy chamber bolted fast,
Many a youth shall fume and pout,
"Hang the girl, she 's always out!"
While the second week goes round,
Vainly shall they ring and pound;
When the third week shall begin,
"Martha, let the creature in."

Now once more the flattering throng
Round thee flock with smile and song,
But thy lips, unweaned as yet,
Lisp, "O, how can I forget!"
Men and devils both contrive
Traps for catching girls alive;
Eve was duped, and Helen kissed,—
How, O how can you resist?

First be careful of your fan,
Trust it not to youth or man;
Love has filled a pirate's sail
Often with its perfumed gale.
Mind your kerchief most of all,
Fingers touch when kerchiefs fall;
Shorter ell than mercers clip
Is the space from hand to lip.

OLIVER WENDELL HOLMES 1809–1894

Trust not such as talk in tropes,
Full of pistols, daggers, ropes;
All the hemp that Russia bears
Scarce would answer lovers' prayers;
Never thread was spun so fine,
Never spider stretched the line,
Would not hold the lovers true
That would really swing for you.

Fiercely some shall storm and swear,
Beating breasts in black despair;
Others murmur with a sigh,
You must melt, or they will die;
Painted words on empty lies,
Grubs with wings like butterflies;
Let them die, and welcome, too;
Pray what better could they do?

Fare thee well, if years efface
From thy heart love's burning trace,
Keep, O keep that hallowed seat
From the tread of vulgar feet;
If the blue lips of the sea
Wait with icy kiss for me,
Let not thine forget the vow,
Sealed how often, Love, as now.

OLIVER WENDELL HOLMES 1809–1894

The Star and the Water-Lily

The sun stepped down from his golden throne,
    And lay in the silent sea,
And the Lily had folded her satin leaves,
    For a sleepy thing was she;
What is the Lily dreaming of?
    Why crisp the waters blue?
See, see, she is lifting her varnished lid!
    Her white leaves are glistening through!

The Rose is cooling his burning cheek
    In the lap of the breathless tide;—
The Lily hath sisters fresh and fair,
    That would lie by the Rose's side;
He would love her better than all the rest,
    And he would be fond and true;—
But the Lily unfolded her weary lids,
    And looked at the sky so blue.

Remember, remember, thou silly one,
    How fast will thy summer glide,
And wilt thou wither a virgin pale,
    Or flourish a blooming bride?
"O the rose is old, and thorny, and cold,
    And he lives on earth," said she;
"But the Star is fair and he lives in the air,
    And he shall my bridegroom be."

But what if the stormy cloud should come,
   And ruffle the silver sea?
Would he turn his eye from the distant sky,
   To smile on a thing like thee?
O no, fair Lily, he will not send
   One ray from his far-off throne;
The winds shall blow and the waves shall flow,
   And thou wilt be left alone.

There is not a leaf on the mountain-top
   Nor a drop of evening dew,
Nor a golden sand on the sparkling shore,
   Nor a pearl in the waters blue,
That he has not cheered with his fickle smile,
   And warmed with his faithless beam,—
And will he be true to a pallid flower,
   That floats on the quiet stream?

Alas for the Lily! she would not heed,
   But turned to the skies afar,
And bared her breast to the trembling ray
   That shot from the rising star;
The cloud came over the darkened sky,
   And over the waters wide:
She looked in vain through the beating rain,
   And sank in the stormy tide.

OLIVER WENDELL HOLMES 1809–1894

The Philosopher to His Love

Dearest, a look is but a ray
Reflected in a certain way;
A word, whatever tone it wear,
Is but a trembling wave of air;
A touch, obedience to a clause
In nature's pure material laws.

The very flowers that bend and meet,
In sweetening others, grow more sweet;
The clouds by day, the stars by night,
Inweave their floating locks of light;
The rainbow, Heaven's own forehead's braid,
Is but the embrace of sun and shade.

How few that love us have we found!
How wide the world that girds them round!
Like mountain streams we meet and part,
Each living in the other's heart,
Our course unknown, our hope to be
Yet mingled in the distant sea.

But Ocean coils and heaves in vain,
Bound in the subtle moonbeam's chain;
And love and hope do but obey
Some cold, capricious planet's ray,
Which lights and leads the tide it charms
To Death's dark caves and icy arms.

OLIVER WENDELL HOLMES 1809–1894

Alas! one narrow line is drawn,
That links our sunset with our dawn;
In mist and shade life's morning rose,
And clouds are round it at its close;
But ah! no twilight beam ascends
To whisper where that evening ends.

Oh! in the hour when I shall feel
Those shadows round my senses steal,
When gentle eyes are weeping o'er
The clay that feels their tears no more,
Then let thy spirit with me be,
Or some sweet angel, likest thee!

The Ballad of the Oysterman

It was a tall young oysterman lived by the river-side,
His shop was just upon the bank, his boat was on the tide;
The daughter of a fisherman, that was so straight and slim,
Lived over on the other bank, right opposite to him.

It was the pensive oysterman that saw a lovely maid,
Upon a moonlight evening, a sitting in the shade;
He saw her wave her handkerchief as much as if to say,
"I'm wide awake, young oysterman, and all the folks away."

OLIVER WENDELL HOLMES 1809–1894

Then up arose the oysterman, and to himself said he,
"I guess I 'll leave the skiff at home, for fear that folks should see;
I read it in the story-book, that, for to kiss his dear,
Leander swam the Hellespont,—and I will swim this here."

And he has leaped into the waves, and crossed the shining stream,
And he has clambered up the bank, all in the moonlight gleam;
O there were kisses sweet as dew, and words as soft as rain,—
But they have heard her father's step, and in he leaps again!

Out spoke the ancient fisherman,—"O what was that, my daughter?"
"'T was nothing but a pebble, sir, I threw into the water."
"And what is that, pray tell me, love, that paddles off so fast?"
"It 's nothing but a porpoise, sir, that 's been a swimming past."

Out spoke the ancient fisherman,—"Now bring me my harpoon!
I 'll get into my fishing-boat, and fix the fellow soon."

Down fell that pretty innocent, as falls a snow-white
    lamb,
Her hair drooped round her pallid cheeks, like seaweed
    on a clam.

Alas for those two loving ones! she waked not from her
    swound,
And he was taken with the cramp, and in the waves was
    drowned;
But Fate has metamorphosed them, in pity of their woe,
And now they keep an oyster-shop for mermaids down
    below.

The Deacon's Masterpiece:
or The Wonderful "One-Hoss Shay"

A LOGICAL STORY

Have you heard of the wonderful one-hoss shay,
That was built in such a logical way
It ran a hundred years to a day,
And then of a sudden, it—ah, but stay,
I'll tell you what happened without delay,
Scaring the parson into fits,
Frightening people out of their wits,—
Have you ever heard of that, I say?

OLIVER WENDELL HOLMES 1809–1894

Seventeen hundred and fifty-five.
Georgius Secundus was then alive,—
Snuffy old drone from the German hive.
That was the year when Lisbon-town
Saw the earth open and gulp her down,
And Braddock's army was done so brown,
Left without a scalp to its crown.
It was on the terrible Earthquake-day
That the Deacon finished the one-hoss shay.

Now in building of chaises, I tell you what,
There is always *somewhere* a weakest spot,—
In hub, tire, felloe, in spring or thill,
In panel, or crossbar, or floor, or sill,
In screw, bolt, thoroughbrace,—lurking still,
Find it somewhere, you must and will,—
Above or below, or within or without,—
And that's the reason, beyond a doubt,
A chaise *breaks down,* but doesn't *wear out.*

But the Deacon swore (as Deacons do,
With an "I dew vum," or an "I tell *yeou,*")
He would build one shay to beat the taown
'n' the keounty 'n' all the kentry raoun';
It should be so built that it *could n'* break daown;
—"Fur," said the Deacon, " 't 's mighty plain
Thut the weakes' place mus' stan' the strain;
'n' the way t' fix it, uz I maintain,
    Is only jest
T' make that place uz strong uz the rest."

OLIVER WENDELL HOLMES 1809–1894

So the Deacon inquired of the village folk
Where he could find the strongest oak,
That could n't be split nor bent nor broke,—
That was for spokes and floor and sills;
He sent for lancewood to make the thills;
The crossbars were ash, from the straightest trees;
The panels of whitewood, that cuts like cheese,
But lasts like iron for things like these;
The hubs of logs from the "Settler's ellum,"—
Last of its timber,—they could n't sell 'em,
Never an axe had seen their chips,
And the wedges flew from between their lips,
Their blunt ends frizzled like celery-tips;
Step and prop-iron, bolt and screw,
Spring, tire, axle, and linchpin too,
Steel of the finest, bright and blue;
Thoroughbrace bison-skin, thick and wide;
Boot, top, dasher, from tough old hide
Found in the pit when the tanner died.
That was the way he "put her through."—
"There!" said the Deacon, "naow she 'll dew!"

Do! I tell you, I rather guess
She was a wonder, and nothing less!
Colts grew horses, beards turned gray,
Deacon and deaconess dropped away,
Children and grandchildren,—where were they?
But there stood the stout old one-hoss shay
As fresh as on Lisbon-earthquake-day!

OLIVER WENDELL HOLMES 1809–1894

EIGHTEEN HUNDRED;—it came and found
The Deacon's masterpiece strong and sound.
Eighteen hundred increased by ten;—
"Hahnsum kerridge" they called it then.
Eighteen hundred and twenty came;—
Running as usual; much the same.
Thirty and forty at last arrive,
And then came fifty, and FIFTY-FIVE.

Little of all we value here
Wakes on the morn of its hundredth year
Without both feeling and looking queer.
In fact, there's nothing that keeps its youth,
So far as I know, but a tree and truth.
(This is a moral that runs at large;
Take it.—You're welcome.—No extra charge.)

FIRST OF NOVEMBER,—the Earthquake-day.—
There are traces of age in the one-hoss shay,
A general flavor of mild decay,
But nothing local as one may say.
There could n't be,—for the Deacon's art
Had made it so like in every part
That there was n't a chance for one to start.
For the wheels were just as strong as the thills,
And the floor was just as strong as the sills,
And the panels just as strong as the floor,
And the whippletree neither less nor more,
And the back-crossbar as strong as the fore,
And spring and axle and hub *encore*.

And yet, *as a whole,* it is past a doubt
In another hour it will be *worn out!*

First of November, 'Fifty-five!
This morning the parson takes a drive.
Now, small boys, get out of the way!
Here comes the wonderful one-hoss shay,
Drawn by a rat-tailed, ewe-necked bay.
"Huddup!" said the parson.—Off went they.
The parson was working his Sunday's text,—
Had got to *fifthly,* and stopped perplexed
At what the—Moses—was coming next.
All at once the horse stood still,
Close by the meet'n'-house on the hill.
—First a shiver, and then a thrill,
Then something decidedly like a spill,—
And the parson was sitting upon a rock,
At half past nine by the meet'n'-house clock,—
Just the hour of the Earthquake shock!
—What do you think the parson found,
When he got up and stared around?
The poor old chaise in a heap or mound,
As if it had been to the mill and ground!
You see, of course, if you're not a dunce,
How it went to pieces all at once,—
All at once, and nothing first,—
Just as bubbles do when they burst.

End of the wonderful one-hoss shay.
Logic is logic. That's all I say.

OLIVER WENDELL HOLMES 1809–1894

"Qui Vive"

"Qui vive!" The sentry's musket rings,
   The channelled bayonet gleams;
High o'er him, like a raven's wings
The broad tri-colored banner flings
Its shadow, rustling as it swings
   Pale in the moonlight beams;
Pass on! while steel-clad sentries keep
Their vigil o'er the monarch's sleep,
   Thy bare, unguarded breast
Asks not the unbroken, bristling zone
That girds yon sceptred trembler's throne;—
   Pass on, and take thy rest!

"Qui vive!" How oft the midnight air
   That startling cry has borne!
How oft the evening breeze has fanned
The banner of this haughty land,
O'er mountain snow and desert sand,
   Ere yet its folds were torn!
Through Jena's carnage flying red,
Or tossing o'er Marengo's dead,
   Or curling on the towers
Where Austria's eagle quivers yet,
And suns the ruffled plumage, wet
   With battle's crimson showers!

"Qui vive!" And is the sentry's cry,—
  The sleepless soldier's hand,—
Are these—the painted folds that fly
And lift their emblems, printed high
On morning mist and sunset sky—
  The guardians of a land?
No! If the patriot's pulses sleep,
How vain the watch that hirelings keep,—
  The idle flag that waves,
When Conquest, with his iron heel,
Treads down the standards and the steel
  That belt the soil of slaves!

The Voiceless

We count the broken lyres that rest
  Where the sweet wailing singers slumber,
But o'er their silent sister's breast
  The wild-flowers who will stoop to number?
A few can touch the magic string,
  And noisy Fame is proud to win them:—
Alas for those that never sing,
  But die with all their music in them!

Nay, grieve not for the dead alone
  Whose song has told their hearts' sad story,—
Weep for the voiceless, who have known
  The cross without the crown of glory!

OLIVER WENDELL HOLMES 1809–1894

Not where Leucadian breezes sweep
   O'er Sappho's memory-haunted billow,
But where the glistening night-dews weep
   On nameless sorrow's churchyard pillow.

O hearts that break and give no sign
   Save whitening lip and fading tresses,
Till Death pours out his cordial wine
   Slow-dropped from Misery's crushing presses,—
If singing breath or echoing chord
   To every hidden pang were given,
What endless melodies were poured,
   As sad as earth, as sweet as heaven!

Under the Washington Elm, Cambridge
April 27, 1861

   Eighty years have passed, and more,
     Since under the brave old tree
Our fathers gathered in arms, and swore
They would follow the sign their banners bore,
     And fight till the land was free.

   Half of their work was done,
     Half is left to do,—
Cambridge, and Concord, and Lexington!
When the battle is fought and won,
     What shall be told of you?

OLIVER WENDELL HOLMES 1809–1894

    Hark!—'t is the south-wind moans,—
      Who are the martyrs down?
Ah, the marrow was true in your children's bones
That sprinkled with blood the cursed stones
      Of the murder-haunted town!

    What if the storm-clouds blow?
      What if the green leaves fall?
Better the crashing tempest's throe
Than the army of worms that gnawed below;
      Trample them one and all!

    Then, when the battle is won,
      And the land from traitors free,
Our children shall tell of the strife begun
When Liberty's second April sun
      Was bright on our brave old tree!

The Chambered Nautilus

This is the ship of pearl, which, poets feign,
    Sails the unshadowed main,—
    The venturous bark that flings
On the sweet summer wind its purpled wings
In gulfs enchanted, where the Siren sings,
    And coral reefs lie bare,
Where the cold sea-maids rise to sun their streaming hair.

OLIVER WENDELL HOLMES 1809–1894

Its webs of living gauze no more unfurl;
    Wrecked is the ship of pearl!
    And every chambered cell,
Where its dim dreaming life was wont to dwell,
As the frail tenant shaped his growing shell,
    Before thee lies revealed,—
Its irised ceiling rent, its sunless crypt unsealed!

Year after year beheld the silent toil
    That spread his lustrous coil;
    Still, as the spiral grew,
He left the past year's dwelling for the new,
Stole with soft step its shining archway through,
    Built up its idle door,
Stretched in his last-found home, and knew the old no more.

Thanks for the heavenly message brought by thee,
    Child of the wandering sea,
    Cast from her lap, forlorn!
From thy dead lips a clearer note is born
Than ever Triton blew from wreathèd horn!
    While on mine ear it rings,
Through the deep caves of thought I hear a voice that sings:—

Build thee more stately mansions, O my soul,
    As the swift seasons roll!
    Leave thy low-vaulted past!
Let each new temple, nobler than the last,

Shut thee from heaven with a dome more vast,
    Till thou at length art free,
Leaving thine outgrown shell by life's unresting sea!

A Voice of the Loyal North
National Fast, January 4, 1861

We sing "Our Country's" song to-night
    With saddened voice and eye;
Her banner droops in clouded light
    Beneath the wintry sky.
We'll pledge her once in golden wine
    Before her stars have set:
Though dim one reddening orb may shine,
    We have a Country yet.

'T were vain to sigh o'er errors past,
    The fault of sires or sons;
Our soldier heard the threatening blast,
    And spiked his useless guns;
He saw the star-wreathed ensign fall,
    By mad invaders torn;
But saw it from the bastioned wall
    That laughed their rage to scorn!

What though their angry cry is flung
    Across the howling wave,—
They smite the air with idle tongue
    The gathering storm who brave;

OLIVER WENDELL HOLMES 1809–1894

Enough of speech! the trumpet rings;
   Be silent, patient, calm,—
God help them if the tempest swings
   The pine against the palm!

Our toilsome years have made us tame;
   Our strength has slept unfelt;
The furnace-fire is slow to flame
   That bids our ploughshares melt;
'T is hard to lose the bread they win
   In spite of Nature's frowns,—
To drop the iron threads we spin
   That weave our web of towns,

To see the rusting turbines stand
   Before the emptied flumes,
To fold the arms that flood the land
   With rivers from their looms,—
But harder still for those who learn
   The truth forgot so long;
When once their slumbering passions burn,
   The peaceful are the strong!

The Lord have mercy on the weak,
   And calm their frenzied ire,
And save our brothers ere they shriek,
   "We played with Northern fire!"
The eagle hold his mountain height,—
   The tiger pace his den!
Give all their country, each his right!
   God keep us all! Amen!

ALBERT PIKE 1809–1891

Dixie

Southrons, hear your Country call you!
Up, lest worse than death befall you!
To arms! To arms! To arms, in Dixie!
Lo! all the beacon-fires are lighted,
Let all hearts be now united!
    To arms! To arms! To arms! in Dixie!
        Advance the flag of Dixie!
            Hurrah! hurrah!
For Dixie's land we'll take our stand,
    To live or die for Dixie!
        To arms! To arms!
    And conquer peace for Dixie!
        To arms! To arms!
    And conquer peace for Dixie!

Hear the Northern thunders mutter!
Northern flags in South winds flutter!
Send them back your fierce defiance!
Stamp upon the accursed alliance!

Fear no danger! Shun no labor!
Lift up rifle, pike, and sabre!
Shoulder pressing close to shoulder,
Let the odds make each heart bolder!

How the South's great heart rejoices
At your cannons' ringing voices!
For faith betrayed and pledges broken,
Wrongs inflicted, insults spoken.

ALBERT PIKE 1809–1891

Strong as lions, swift as eagles,
Back to their kennels hunt these beagles!
Cut the unequal bonds asunder!
Let them hence each other plunder!

Swear upon your Country's altar
Never to submit or falter,
Till the spoilers are defeated,
Till the Lord's work is completed.

Halt not till our Federation
Secures among earth's Powers its station!
Then at peace, and crowned with glory,
Hear your children tell the story!

If the loved ones weep in sadness,
Victory soon shall bring them gladness;
   To arms!
Exultant pride soon banish sorrow,
Smiles chase tears away to-morrow.
  To arms! To arms! To arms, in Dixie!
   Advance the flag of Dixie!
    Hurrah! hurrah!
For Dixie's land we take our stand,
   And live or die for Dixie!
    To arms! To arms!
   And conquer peace for Dixie!
    To arms! To arms!
   And conquer peace for Dixie!

ELIZABETH (LLOYD) HOWELL 1811–1896

Milton's Prayer of Patience

I am old and blind!
Men point at me as smitten by God's frown;
Afflicted and deserted of my kind,
    Yet am I not cast down.

I am weak, yet strong;
I murmur not that I no longer see;
Poor, old, and helpless, I the more belong,
    Father Supreme! to Thee.

All-merciful One!
When men are furthest, then art Thou most near,
When friends pass by, my weaknesses to shun,
    Thy chariot I hear.

Thy glorious face
Is leaning toward me, and its holy light
Shines in upon my lonely dwelling-place,—
    And there is no more night.

On my bended knee
I recognize Thy purpose clearly shown;
My vision Thou hast dimmed, that I may see
    Thyself—Thyself alone.

I have naught to fear:
This darkness is the shadow of Thy wing;
Beneath it I am almost sacred—here
    Can come no evil thing.

ELIZABETH (LLOYD) HOWELL 1811–1896

     Oh, I seem to stand
Trembling, where foot of mortal ne'er hath been,
Wrapped in that radiance from the sinless land,
     Which eye hath never seen!

     Visions come and go:
Shapes of resplendent beauty round me throng;
From angel lips I seem to hear the flow
     Of soft and holy song.

     It is nothing now,
When heaven is opening on my sightless eyes,
When airs from Paradise refresh my brow,
     That earth in darkness lies.

     In a purer clime
My being fills with rapture,—waves of thought
Roll in upon my spirit,—strains sublime
     Break over me unsought.

     Give me now my lyre!
I feel the stirrings of a gift divine:
Within my bosom glows unearthly fire
     Lit by no skill of mine.

ROBERT HINCKLEY MESSINGER 1811–1874

A Winter Wish

 Old wine to drink!
  Ay, give the slippery juice
That drippeth from the grape thrown loose
  Within the tun;
Plucked from beneath the cliff
Of sunny-sided Teneriffe,
 And ripened 'neath the blink
  Of India's sun!
  Peat whiskey hot,
Tempered with well-boiled water!
These make the long night shorter,—
  Forgetting not
Good stout old English porter.

 Old wood to burn!
Ay, bring the hillside beech
From where the owlets meet and screech,
  And ravens croak;
The crackling pine, and cedar sweet;
Bring too a clump of fragrant peat,
 Dug 'neath the fern;
  The knotted oak,
  A fagot too, perhap,
Whose bright flame, dancing, winking,
Shall light us at our drinking;
  While the oozing sap
Shall make sweet music to our thinking.

ROBERT HINCKLEY MESSINGER 1811–1874

Old books to read!
Ay, bring those nodes of wit,
The brazen-clasped, the vellum writ,
   Time-honored tomes!
The same my sire scanned before,
The same my grandsire thumbèd o'er,
The same his sire from college bore,
  The well-earned meed
    Of Oxford's domes:
    Old Homer blind,
Old Horace, rake Anacreon, by
Old Tully, Plautus, Terence lie;
Mort Arthur's olden minstrelsie,
Quaint Burton, quainter Spenser, ay!
And Gervase Markham's venerie—
   Nor leave behind
The holye Book by which we live and die.

  Old friends to talk!
Ay, bring those chosen few,
The wise, the courtly, and the true,
   So rarely found;
Him for my wine, him for my stud,
Him for my easel, distich, bud
  In mountain walk!
   Bring Walter good,
With soulful Fred, and learned Will,
And thee, my alter ego (dearer still
   For every mood).

ROBERT HINCKLEY MESSINGER 1811–1874

These add a bouquet to my wine!
These add a sparkle to my pine!
   If these I tine,
Can books, or fire, or wine be good?

CHARLES DAWSON SHANLY 1811–1875

The Fancy Shot

"Rifleman, shoot me a fancy shot
   Straight at the heart of yon prowling vidette;
Ring me a ball in the glittering spot
   That shines on his breast like an amulet!"

"Ah, Captain! here goes for a fine-drawn bead;
   There's music around when my barrel's in tune!"
Crack! went the rifle, the messenger sped,
   And dead from his horse fell the ringing dragoon.

"Now, Rifleman, steal through the bushes and snatch
   From your victim some trinket to hansel first blood—
A button, a loop, or that luminous patch
   That gleams in the moon like a diamond stud."

"Oh, Captain! I staggered, and sunk on my track,
   When I gazed on the face of that fallen vidette;
For he looked so like you as he lay on his back
   That my heart rose upon me, and masters me yet.

"But I snatched off the trinket—this locket of gold;
   An inch from the centre my lead broke its way,
Scarce grazing the picture, so fair to behold,
   Of a beautiful lady in bridal array."

"Ha! Rifleman, fling me the locket—'t is she,
   My brother's young bride, and the fallen dragoon
Was her husband—Hush! soldier, 't was Heaven's decree;
   We must bury him here, by the light of the moon!

CHARLES DAWSON SHANLY 1811–1875

"But, hark! the far bugles their warnings unite;
   War is a virtue—weakness a sin;
There's lurking and loping around us to-night;
   Load again, Rifleman, keep your hand in!"

EPES SARGENT   1813–1880

A Life on the Ocean Wave

A life on the ocean wave,
   A home on the rolling deep,
Where the scattered waters rave,
   And the winds their revels keep:
Like an eagle caged, I pine
   On this dull, unchanging shore:
Oh! give me the flashing brine,
   The spray and the tempest's roar!

Once more on the deck I stand
   Of my own swift-gliding craft:
Set sail! farewell to the land!
   The gale follows fair abaft.
We shoot through the sparkling foam
   Like an ocean bird set free;—
Like the ocean bird, our home
   We'll find far out on the sea.

The land is no longer in view,
   The clouds have begun to frown;
But with a stout vessel and crew,
   We'll say, Let the storm come down!
And the song of our hearts shall be,
   While the winds and the waters rave,
A home on the rolling sea!
   A life on the ocean wave!

JOHN GODFREY SAXE 1816–1887

Early Rising

"God bless the man who first invented sleep!"
   So Sancho Panza said, and so say I:
And bless him, also, that he did n't keep
   His great discovery to himself; nor try
To make it—as the lucky fellow might—
A close monopoly by patent-right!

Yes; bless the man who first invented sleep
   (I really can't avoid the iteration),
But blast the man, with curses loud and deep,
   Whate'er the rascal's name, or age, or station,
Who first invented, and went round advising,
That artificial cut-off, Early Rising!

"Rise with the lark, and with the lark to bed,"
   Observes some solemn, sentimental owl;
Maxims like these are very cheaply said;
   But, ere you make yourself a fool or fowl,
Pray just inquire about his rise and fall,
And whether larks have any beds at all!

The time for honest folks to be a-bed
   Is in the morning, if I reason right;
And he who cannot keep his precious head
   Upon his pillow till it's fairly light,
And so enjoy his forty morning winks,
Is up to knavery; or else—he drinks!

JOHN GODFREY SAXE 1816–1887

Thomson, who sung about the "Seasons," said
   It was a glorious thing to *rise* in season;
But then he said it—lying—in his bed,
   At ten o'clock A.M.,—the very reason
He wrote so charmingly. The simple fact is,
His preaching was n't sanctioned by his practice.

'T is, doubtless, well to be sometimes awake,—
   Awake to duty, and awake to truth,—
But when, alas! a nice review we take
   Of our best deeds and days, we find, in sooth,
The hours that leave the slightest cause to weep
Are those we passed in childhood or asleep!

'T is beautiful to leave the world awhile
   For the soft visions of the gentle night;
And free, at last, from mortal care or guile,
   To live as only in the angels' sight,
In sleep's sweet realm so cosily shut in,
Where, at the worst, we only *dream* of sin!

So let us sleep, and give the Maker praise.
   I like the lad who, when his father thought
To clip his morning nap by hackneyed phrase
   Of vagrant worm by early songster caught,
Cried, "Served him right!—it 's not at all surprising;
The worm was punished, sir, for early rising!"

JOHN GODFREY SAXE 1816–1887

Polyphemus and Ulysses

A very remarkable history this is
Of one POLYPHEMUS and CAPTAIN ULYSSES:
The latter a hero accomplished and bold,
The former a knave, and a fright to behold,—
A horrid big giant who lived in a den,
And dined every day on a couple of men,
Ate a woman for breakfast, and (dreadful to see!)
Had a nice little baby served up with his tea!
Indeed, if there's truth in the sprightly narration
Of HOMER, a poet of some reputation,
Or VIRGIL, a writer but little inferior,
And in some things, perhaps, the other's superior,—
POLYPHEMUS was truly a terrible creature,
In manners and morals, in form and in feature;
For law and religion he cared not a copper,
And, in short, led a life that was very improper:—
What made him a very remarkable guy,
Like the late MR. THOMPSON, he'd only one eye;
But that was a whopper,—a terrible one,—
"As large" (VIRGIL says) "as the disk of the sun!"
A brilliant, but rather extravagant figure,
Which means, I suppose, that his eye was much bigger
Than yours,—or even the orb of your sly
Old bachelor-friend "who's a wife in his eye."

ULYSSES, the hero I mentioned before,
Was shipwrecked, one day, on the pestilent shore
Where the CYCLOPS resided, along with their chief,

JOHN GODFREY SAXE 1816–1887

POLYPHEMUS, the terrible man-eating thief,
Whose manners they copied, and laws they obeyed,
While driving their horrible cannibal trade.

With many expressions of civil regret
That ULYSSES had got so unpleasantly wet,
With many expressions of pleasure profound
That all had escaped being thoroughly drowned,
The rascal declared he was "fond of the brave,"
And invited the strangers all home to his cave.

Here the cannibal king, with as little remorse
As an omnibus feels for the death of a horse,
Seized, crushed, and devoured a brace of the Greeks,
As a Welshman would swallow a couple of leeks,
Or a Frenchman, supplied with his usual prog,
Would punish the hams of a favorite frog.
Dashed and smashed against the stones,
He broke their bodies and cracked their bones,
Minding no more their moans and groans,
Than the grinder heeds his organ's tones!
With purple gore the pavement swims,
While the giant crushes their crackling limbs,
And poor ULYSSES trembles with fright
At the horrid sound, and the horrid sight,—
Trembles lest the monster grim
Should make his "nuts and raisins" of him!
  And, really, since
  The man was a Prince,
It's not very odd that his Highness should wince,

JOHN GODFREY SAXE 1816–1887

(Especially after such very strong hints,)
At the cannibal's manner, as rather more free
Than his Highness at court was accustomed to see!

But the crafty Greek, to the tyrant's hurt,
(Though he did n't deserve so fine a dessert),
Took a dozen of wine from his leather trunk,
And plied the giant until he was drunk!—
Drunker than any one you or *I* know,
Who buys his "Rhenish" with ready rhino,—
Exceedingly drunk,—*sepultus vino!*

Gazing a moment upon the sleeper,
Ulysses cried, "Let's spoil his peeper!—
'T will put him, boys, in a pretty trim,
If we can manage to douse his glim!"
So, taking a spar that was lying in sight,
They poked it into his "forward light,"
And gouged away with furious spite,
Ramming and jamming with all their might!

In vain the giant began to roar,
      And even swore
      That he never before
Had met, in his life, such a terrible bore:
They only plied the auger the more
And mocked his grief with a bantering cry,
"Don't talk of pain,—*it's all in your eye!*"
Until, alas for the wretched Cyclops!
He gives a groan, and out his eye pops!

JOHN GODFREY SAXE 1816–1887

Leaving the knave, one need n't be told,
As blind as a puppy of three days old.

The rest of the tale I can't tell now,—
Except that Ulysses got out of the row,
With the rest of his crew—it's no matter how;
While old Polyphemus, until he was dead,—
Which was n't till many years after, 't is said,—
Had a grief in his heart and a hole in his head!

Moral

Don't use strong drink,—pray let me advise,—
It 's bad for the stomach, and ruins the eyes;
Don't impose upon sailors with land-lubber tricks,
Or you 'll catch it some day like a thousand of bricks!

Orpheus and Eurydice

Sir Orpheus, whom the poets have sung
In every metre and every tongue,
Was, you may remember, a famous musician,—
At least for a youth in his pagan condition,—
For historians tell he played on his shell
From morning till night, so remarkably well
That his music created a regular spell
On trees and stones in forest and dell!
What sort of an instrument his could be
Is really more than is known to me,—

JOHN GODFREY SAXE 1816–1887

For none of the books have told, d' ye see!
It's very certain those heathen "swells"
Knew nothing at all of oyster-shells,
And it's clear Sir Orpheus never could own a
Shell like those they make in Cremona;
But whatever it was, to "move the stones"
It must have shelled out some powerful tones,
And entitled the player to rank in my rhyme
As the very *Vieuxtemps* of the very old time!

But alas for the joys of this mutable life!
Sir Orpheus lost his beautiful wife—
Eurydice, who vanished one day
From Earth, in a very unpleasant way!
It chanced, as near as I can determine,
Through one of those vertebrated vermin
That lie in the grass so prettily curled,
Waiting to "snake" you out of the world!
And the poets tell she went to—well—
A place where Greeks and Romans dwell
After they burst their mortal shell;
A region that in deepest shade is,
And known by the classical name of Hades,—
A different place from the terrible furnace
Of Tartarus, down below Avernus.

Now, having a heart uncommonly stout,
Sir Orpheus did n't go whining about,
Nor marry another, as *you* would, no doubt,
But made up his mind to fiddle her out!

JOHN GODFREY SAXE 1816–1887

But near the gate he had to wait,
For there in state old Cerberus sate,
A three-headed dog, as cruel as Fate,
Guarding the entrance early and late;
A beast so sagacious, and very voracious,
So uncommonly sharp and extremely rapacious,
That it really may be doubted whether
He'd have his match, should a common tether
Unite three aldermen's heads together!

But Orpheus, not in the least afraid,
Tuned up his shell, and quickly essayed
What could be done with a serenade,
In short, so charming an air he played,
He quite succeeded in overreaching
The cunning cur, by musical teaching,
And put him to sleep as fast as preaching!

And now our musical champion, Orpheus,
Having given the janitor over to Morpheus,
Went groping around among the ladies
Who throng the dismal halls of Hades,
      Calling aloud
      To the shady crowd,
In a voice as shrill as a martial fife,
"O, tell me where in hell is my wife!"
(A natural question, 't is very plain,
Although it may sound a little profane.)
      "Eurydice! Eu-ryd-i-ce!"
He cried as loud as loud could be,

(A singular sound, and funny withal,
In a place where nobody *rides* at all!)
     "Eurydice!—Eurydice!
O, come, my dear, along with me!"
And then he played so remarkably fine,
That it really might be called divine,—
     For who can show,
     On earth or below,
Such wonderful feats in the musical line?

  E'en Tantalus ceased from trying to sip
The cup that flies from his arid lip;
Ixion, too, the magic could feel,
And, for a moment, blocked his wheel;
  Poor Sisyphus, doomed to tumble and toss
The notable stone that gathers no moss,
Let go his burden, and turned to hear
The charming sounds that ravished his ear;
And even the Furies—those terrible shrews
Whom no one before could ever amuse,
Those strong-bodied ladies with strong-minded views
Whom even the Devil would doubtless refuse,
Were his Majesty only permitted to choose,
Each felt for a moment her nature desert her,
And wept like a girl o'er the "Sorrows of Werther."

  And still Sir Orpheus chanted his song,
Sweet and clear and strong and long,
     "Eurydice!—Eurydice!"
He cried as loud as loud could be;

JOHN GODFREY SAXE 1816–1887

And Echo, taking up the word,
Kept it up till the lady heard,
And came with joy to meet her lord.
And he led her along the infernal route,
Until he had got her almost out,
When, suddenly turning his head about,
(To take a peep at his wife, no doubt,)
      He gave a groan,
      For the lady was gone,
And had left him standing there all alone!
For by an oath the gods had bound
Sir Orpheus not to look around
Till he was clear of the sacred ground,
If he'd have Eurydice safe and sound;
For the moment he did an act so rash
His wife would vanish as quick as a flash!

Moral

Young women! beware, for goodness' sake,
Of every sort of "sarpent snake";
Remember the rogue is apt to deceive,
And played the deuce with grandmother Eve!

Young men! it's a critical thing to go
Exactly right with a lady in tow;
But when you are in the proper track,
Just go ahead, and never look back!

JOHN GODFREY SAXE 1816–1887

Bereavement

Nay, weep not, dearest, though the child be dead;
   He lives again in Heaven's unclouded life,
With other angels that have early fled
   From these dark scenes of sorrow, sin, and strife.
Nay, weep not, dearest, though thy yearning love
   Would fondly keep for earth its fairest flowers,
And e'en deny to brighter realms above
   The few that deck this dreary world of ours:
Though much it seems a wonder and a woe
   That one so loved should be so early lost,
And hallowed tears may unforbidden flow
   To mourn the blossom that we cherished most,
Yet all is well; God's good design I see,
That where our treasure is, our hearts may be!

PHILIP PENDLETON COOKE 1816–1850

Florence Vane

I loved thee long and dearly,
    Florence Vane;
My life's bright dream, and early,
    Hath come again;
I renew, in my fond vision,
    My heart's dear pain,
My hope, and thy derision,
    Florence Vane.

The ruin lone and hoary,
    The ruin old,
Where thou didst hark my story,
    At even told,—
That spot—the hues Elysian
    Of sky and plain—
I treasure in my vision,
    Florence Vane.

Thou wast lovelier than the roses
    In their prime;
Thy voice excelled the closes
    Of sweetest rhyme;
Thy heart was as a river
    Without a main.
Would I had loved thee never,
    Florence Vane!

PHILIP PENDLETON COOKE 1816–1850

But, fairest, coldest wonder!
 Thy glorious clay
Lieth the green sod under—
 Alas the day!
And it boots not to remember
 Thy disdain—
To quicken love's pale ember,
 Florence Vane.

The lilies of the valley
 By young graves weep,
The pansies love to dally
 Where maidens sleep;
May their bloom, in beauty vying,
 Never wane
Where thine earthly part is lying,
 Florence Vane!

WILLIAM WETMORE STORY 1819–1895

Cleopatra

Here, Charmian, take my bracelets,
 They bar with a purple stain
My arms; turn over my pillows—
 They are hot where I have lain:
Open the lattice wider,
 A gauze on my bosom throw,
And let me inhale the odors
 That over the garden blow.

I dreamed I was with my Antony,
 And in his arms I lay;
Ah, me! the vision has vanished—
 The music has died away.
The flame and the perfume have perished—
 As this spiced aromatic pastille
That wound the blue smoke of its odor
 Is now but an ashy hill.

Scatter upon me rose-leaves,
 They cool me after my sleep,
And with sandal odors fan me
 Till into my veins they creep;
Reach down the lute, and play me
 A melancholy tune,
To rhyme with the dream that has vanished,
 And the slumbering afternoon.

WILLIAM WETMORE STORY 1819–1895

There, drowsing in golden sunlight,
   Loiters the slow, smooth Nile,
Through slender papyri, that cover
   The wary crocodile.
The lotus lolls on the water,
   And opens its heart of gold,
And over its broad leaf-pavement
   Never a ripple is rolled.
The twilight breeze is too lazy
   Those feathery palms to wave,
And yon little cloud is as motionless
   As a stone above a grave.

Ah, me! this lifeless nature
   Oppresses my heart and brain!
Oh! for a storm and thunder—
   For lightning and wild, fierce rain!
Fling down that lute—I hate it!
   Take rather his buckler and sword,
And crash them and clash them together
   Till this sleeping world is stirred.

Hark! to my Indian beauty—
   My cockatoo, creamy white,
With roses under his feathers—
   That flashes across the light.
Look! listen! as backward and forward
   To his hoop of gold he clings,
How he trembles, with crest uplifted,
   And shrieks as he madly swings!

WILLIAM WETMORE STORY 1819–1895

Oh, cockatoo, shriek for Antony!
   Cry, "Come, my love, come home!"
Shriek, "Antony! Antony! Antony!"
   Till he hears you even in Rome.

There—leave me, and take from my chamber
   That stupid little gazelle,
With its bright black eyes so meaningless,
   And its silly tinkling bell!
Take him,—my nerves he vexes,—
   The thing without blood or brain,—
Or, by the body of Isis,
   I'll snap his thin neck in twain!

Leave me to gaze at the landscape
   Mistily stretching away,
Where the afternoon's opaline tremors
   O'er the mountains quivering play;
Till the fiercer splendor of sunset
   Pours from the west its fire,
And melted, as in a crucible,
   Their earthy forms expire;
And the bald, blear skull of the desert
   With glowing mountains is crowned,
That burning like molten jewels
   Circle its temples round.

I will lie and dream of the past time,
   Æons of thought away,
And through the jungle of memory
   Loosen my fancy to play;

WILLIAM WETMORE STORY 1819–1895

When, a smooth and velvety tiger,
   Ribbed with yellow and black,
Supple and cushion-footed
   I wandered, where never the track
Of a human creature had rustled
   The silence of mighty woods,
And, fierce in a tyrannous freedom,
   I knew but the law of my moods.
The elephant, trumpeting, started,
   When he heard my footstep near,
And the spotted giraffes fled wildly
   In a yellow cloud of fear.
I sucked in the noontide splendor,
   Quivering along the glade,
Or yawning, panting, and dreaming,
   Basked in the tamarisk shade,
Till I heard my wild mate roaring,
   As the shadows of night came on,
To brood in the trees' thick branches
   And the shadow of sleep was gone;
Then I roused, and roared in answer,
   And unsheathed from my cushioned feet
My curving claws, and stretched me,
   And wandered my mate to greet.
We toyed in the amber moonlight,
   Upon the warm, flat sand,
And struck at each other our massive arms—
   How powerful he was and grand!
His yellow eyes flashed fiercely

WILLIAM WETMORE STORY 1819–1895

    As he crouched and gazed at me,
And his quivering tail, like a serpent,
    Twitched curving nervously.
Then like a storm he seized me,
    With a wild, triumphant cry,
And we met, as two clouds in heaven
    When the thunders before them fly.
We grappled and struggled together,
    For his love like his rage was rude;
And his teeth in the swelling folds of my neck
    At times, in our play, drew blood.

Often another suitor—
    For I was flexile and fair—
Fought for me in the moonlight,
    While I lay couching there,
Till his blood was drained by the desert;
    And, ruffled with triumph and power,
He licked me and lay beside me
    To breathe him a vast half-hour.
Then down to the fountain we loitered,
    Where the antelopes came to drink;
Like a bolt we sprang upon them,
    Ere they had time to shrink,
We drank their blood and crushed them,
    And tore them limb from limb,
And the hungriest lion doubted
    Ere he disputed with him.
That was a life to live for!
    Not this weak human life,

With its frivolous bloodless passions,
   Its poor and petty strife!

Come to my arms, my hero,
   The shadows of twilight grow,
And the tiger's ancient fierceness
   In my veins begins to flow.
Come not cringing to sue me!
   Take me with triumph and power,
As a warrior storms a fortress!
   I will not shrink or cower.
Come, as you came in the desert,
   Ere we were women and men,
When the tiger passions were in us,
   And love as you loved me then!

Praxiteles and Phryne

A thousand silent years ago,
   The twilight faint and pale
Was drawing o'er the sunset glow
   Its soft and shadowy veil;

When from his work the Sculptor stayed
   His hand, and turned to one
Who stood beside him, half in shade,
   Said, with a sigh, " 'T is done.

WILLIAM WETMORE STORY 1819–1895

"Thus much is saved from chance and change,
   That waits for me and thee;
Thus much—how little!—from the range
   Of Death and Destiny.

"Phryne, thy human lips shall pale,
   Thy rounded limbs decay,—
Nor love nor prayers can aught avail
   To bid thy beauty stay;

"But there thy smile for centuries
   On marble lips shall live,—
For Art can grant what Love denies,
   And fix the fugitive.

"Sad thought! nor age nor death shall fade
   The youth of this cold bust;
When this quick brain and hand that made,
   And thou and I art dust!

"When all our hopes and fears are dead,
   And both our hearts are cold,
And love is like a tune that's played,
   And life a tale that's told,

"This senseless stone, so coldly fair,
   That love nor life can warm,
The same enchanting look shall wear,
   The same enchanting form.

"Its peace no sorrow shall destroy;
   Its beauty age shall spare
The bitterness of vanished joy,
   The wearing waste of care.

"And there upon that silent face
   Shall unborn ages see
Perennial youth, perennial grace,
   And sealed serenity.

"And strangers, when we sleep in peace,
   Shall say, not quite unmoved,
'So smiled upon Praxiteles
   The Phryne whom he loved!'"

L'Abbate

Were it not for that singular smell
   That seems to the genus priest to belong,
Where snuff and incense are mingled well
   With a natural odor quite as strong:
Were it not for those little ways
   Of clasped and deprecating hands;
And raising and lowering his eyes always
   As if he only waited commands—

WILLIAM WETMORE STORY 1819–1895

Little there is in him of the priest,
   With only the slightest touch of cant,
With a simple, guileless heart in his breast,
   And a mind as honest as ignorant.
Half a child and half a man,
   Ripe in the Fathers and green in thought,
In his little circle of half a span
   He thinks that he thinks what he was taught.

His duty he does to the scruple's weight;
   Recites his prayers, and mumbles his mass,
And without his litanies, early and late,
   Never permits a day to pass.
Look at him there in the garden-plots
   Repeating his office, as to and fro
He paces around the orange-pots,
   Looking about while his quick lips go.

His simple pleasure in simple things,
   His willing spirit that never tires,
His trivial jokes and wonderings,
   His peaceful temper that never fires,
His joy over trifles of every day,
   The feeble poems he loves to quote,—
Are just like a child, with his heart in his play,
   While his duty and lessons are drill and rote.

WILLIAM WETMORE STORY 1819–1895

What life means he does not think;
   Reason and thought he has been told
Only lead to a perilous brink,
   Away from Christ and the Church's fold.
Therefore he humbly and blindly obeys;
   Does what he's ordered and reasons not;
Performs his prayers, and thinks he prays,
   And asks not how, or why, or what.

Happy in this, why stir his mind,
   Stagnant in thought although it be?
Leave him alone—he is gentle and kind,
   And blest with a child's simplicity.
Thinking would only give him unrest,
   Struggle, and toil, and inward strain;
His heart is right in his thoughtless breast,
   Why should one wish to torment his brain?

Yet out of pastime one evil day
   I unfolded to him Pythagoras' plan—
How step by step the soul made its way
   From sea-anemone up to man,—
How onward to higher grades it went,
   If its human life had been fair and pure;
Or if not, to the lower scale was sent,
   Again to ascend to man, and endure.

WILLIAM WETMORE STORY 1819–1895

And so the soul had gleams of the past,
   And felt in itself dim sympathies
With nature, that ended in us at last,
   And each of whose forms within us lies.
He smiled at first, and then by degrees
   Grew silent and sad, and confessed 't was true,
But with spirit so pained and ill at ease,
   That my foolish work I strove to undo.

This thinking 's the spawn of Satan, I said,
   That tempts us into the sea of doubt;
And Satan has endless snares to spread,
   If once with our reason we venture out.
Here you are in your Church like a port,
   Anchored secure, where never a gale
Can break your moorings,—nor even in sport
   Should you weigh your anchor or spread your sail.

So I got him back to his anchor again,
   And there in the stagnant harbor he lies;
And he looks upon me with a sense of pain
   As a wild freebooter; for to his eyes
Free thinking, free sailing seems to be,
   A sort of a godless, dangerous thing,
Like a pirate's life on a stormy sea—
   And sure at the last damnation to bring.

Black Eyes

Those black eyes I once so praised
  Now are hard and sharp and cold;
Where's the love that through them blazed?
  Where's the tenderness of old?
All is gone—how utterly—
  From its stem the flower has dropped.
Ah! how ugly Life can be
  After Love from it is lopped!

Do we hate each other now,
  While we call each other dear?
On that faultless mouth and brow
  To the world does change appear?
No! your smile is just as sweet,
  Just as fair your outward grace;
But I look in vain to greet
  The dear ghost behind the face.

That is gone! I look on you
  As a corpse from which has fled
All that once I loved and knew,
  All that once I thought to wed.
'T is not your fault, 't is not mine;
  Yet I still recall a dream
Of a joy almost divine—
  'T was an image in a stream.

WILLIAM WETMORE STORY 1819–1895

Nothing can be sour and sharp
  As a love that has decayed—
On the loose strings of the harp
  Only discord can be made.
Cold this common friendship seems
  After love's auroral glow;
On the broken stem of dreams
  Only disappointments grow.

Do I hate you? No! Not hate?
  Hate's a word far too intense,
Too alive, to speak a state
  Of supreme indifference.
Once, behind your eyes I thought
  Worlds of love and life to see;
Now I see behind them nought
  But a soulless vacancy.

Out and out I know you now;
  There's no issue of your heart
Where my soul with you may go
  To a beauty all apart,
Where the world can never come.
  'T is a little narrow place—
Friendship there might find a home;
  Love would die—for want of space.

So we live! The world still says,
   "What expression in her eyes!
What sweet manners—graceful ways!"
   How it would the world surprise
If I said, "This woman's soul
   Made for love you think, but try;
Plunge therein—how clear and shoal!—
   You might drown there—so can't I?"

In the Rain

I stand in the cold gray weather,
   In the white and silvery rain;
The great trees huddle together,
   And sway with the windy strain.
I dream of the purple glory
   Of the roseate mountain-height
And the sweet-to-remember story
   Of a distant and clear delight.

The rain keeps constantly raining,
   And the sky is cold and gray,
And the wind in the trees keeps complaining
   That summer has passed away;—
But the gray and the cold are haunted
   By a beauty akin to pain,—
By a sense of a something wanted,
   That never will come again.

WILLIAM WETMORE STORY 1819–1895

Snowdrop

When, full of warm and eager love,
   I clasp you in my fond embrace,
You gently push me back and say,
   "Take care, my dear, you'll spoil my lace."

You kiss me just as you would kiss
   Some woman friend you chanced to see;
You call me "dearest." All love's forms
   Are yours, not its reality.

Oh, Annie! cry, and storm, and rave!
   Do anything with passion in it!
Hate me an hour, and then turn round
   And love me truly, just one minute.

JAMES RUSSELL LOWELL 1819–1891

What Mr. Robinson Thinks

Guvener B. is a sensible man;
  He stays to his home an' looks arter his folks;
He draws his furrer ez straight ez he can,
  An' into nobody's tater-patch pokes;
      But John P.
      Robinson he
  Sez he wunt vote fer Guvener B.

My! aint it terrible? Wut shall we du?
  We can't never choose him o' course,—thet's flat;
Guess we shall hev to come round, (don't you?)
  An' go in fer thunder an' guns, an' all that;
      Fer John P.
      Robinson he
  Sez he wunt vote fer Guvener B.

Gineral C. is a dreffle smart man:
  He's ben on all sides thet give places or pelf;
But consistency still wuz a part of his plan,—
  He's ben true to *one* party,—an' thet is himself;—
      So John P.
      Robinson he
  Sez he shall vote fer Gineral C.

Gineral C. he goes in fer the war;
  He don't vally princerple more 'n an old cud;
Wut did God make us raytional creeturs fer,

JAMES RUSSELL LOWELL 1819–1891

But glory an' gunpowder, plunder an' blood?
    So John P.
    Robinson he
Sez he shall vote fer Gineral C.

We were gittin' on nicely up here to our village,
  With good old idees o' wut 's right an' wut aint,
We kind o' thought Christ went agin war an' pillage,
  An' thet eppyletts worn't the best mark of a saint;
    But John P.
    Robinson he
Sez this kind o' thing 's an exploded idee.

The side of our country must ollers be took,
  An' Presidunt Polk, you know, *he* is our country.
An' the angel thet writes all our sins in a book
  Puts the *debit* to him, an' to us the *per contry;*
    An' John P.
    Robinson he
Sez this is his view o' the thing to a T.

Parson Wilbur he calls all these argimunts lies;
  Sez they 're nothin' on airth but jest *fee, faw, fum;*
An' thet all this big talk of our destinies
  Is half on it ign'ance, an' t' other half rum;
    But John P.
    Robinson he
Sez it aint no sech thing; an', of course, so must
    we.

Parson Wilbur sez *he* never heerd in his life
    Thet th' Apostles rigged out in their swaller-tail
        coats,
An' marched round in front of a drum an' a fife,
    To git some on 'em office, an' some on 'em votes;
        But John P.
        Robinson he
Sez they did n't know everythin' down in Judee.

Wal, it 's a marcy we 've gut folks to tell us
    The rights an' the wrongs o' these matters, I vow,—
God sends country lawyers, an' other wise fellers,
    To start the world's team wen it gits in a slough;
        Fer John P.
        Robinson he
Sez the world 'll go right, ef he hollers out Gee!

The Courtin'

God makes sech nights, all white an' still
    Fur 'z you can look or listen,
Moonshine an' snow on field an' hill,
    All silence an' all glisten.

Zekle crep' up quite unbeknown
    An' peeked in thru' the winder,
An' there sot Huldy all alone,
    'ith no one nigh to hender.

JAMES RUSSELL LOWELL 1819–1891

A fireplace filled the room's one side
    With half a cord o' wood in—
There warn't no stoves (tell comfort died)
    To bake ye to a puddin'.

The wa'nut logs shot sparkles out
    Towards the pootiest, bless her,
An' leetle flames danced all about
    The chiny on the dresser.

Agin the chimbley crook-necks hung,
    An' in amongst 'em rusted
The ole queen's-arm thet gran'ther Young
    Fetched back f'om Concord busted.

The very room, coz she was in,
    Seemed warm f'om floor to ceilin',
An' she looked full ez rosy agin
    Ez the apples she was peelin'.

'T was kin' o' kingdom-come to look
    On sech a blessed cretur,
A dogrose blushin' to a brook
    Ain't modester nor sweeter.

He was six foot o' man, A 1,
    Clear grit an' human natur';
None could n't quicker pitch a ton
    Nor dror a furrer straighter.

JAMES RUSSELL LOWELL 1819–1891

He 'd sparked it with full twenty gals,
   He 'd squired 'em, danced 'em, druv 'em,
Fust this one, an' then thet, by spells—
   All is, he could n't love 'em.

But long o' her his veins 'ould run
   All crinkly like curled maple,
The side she breshed felt full o' sun
   Ez a south slope in Ap'il.

She thought no v'ice hed sech a swing
   Ez hisn in the choir;
My! when he made Ole Hunderd ring,
   She *knowed* the Lord was nigher.

An' she 'd blush scarlit, right in prayer,
   When her new meetin'-bunnet
Felt somehow thru' its crown a pair
   O' blue eyes sot upun it.

Thet night, I tell ye, she looked *some!*
   She seemed to 've gut a new soul,
For she felt sartin-sure he 'd come,
   Down to her very shoe-sole.

She heered a foot, an' knowed it tu,
   A-raspin' on the scraper,—
All ways to once her feelin's flew
   Like sparks in burnt-up paper.

JAMES RUSSELL LOWELL 1819–1891

He kin' o' l'itered on the mat,
    Some doubtfle o' the sekle,
His heart kep' goin' pity-pat,
    But hern went pity Zekle.

An' yit she gin her cheer a jerk
    Ez though she wished him furder,
An' on her apples kep' to work,
    Parin' away like murder.

"You want to see my Pa, I s'pose?"
    "Wal . . . . no . . . . I come dasignin' "—
"To see my Ma? She 's sprinklin' clo'es
    Agin to-morrer's i'nin'."

To say why gals acts so or so,
    Or don't, 'ould be presumin';
Mebby to mean *yes* an' say *no*
    Comes nateral to women.

He stood a spell on one foot fust,
    Then stood a spell on t' other,
An' on which one he felt the wust
    He could n't ha' told ye nuther.

Says he, "I 'd better call agin";
    Says she, "Think likely, Mister":
Thet last word pricked him like a pin,
    An' . . . . Wal, he up an' kist her.

When Ma bimeby upon 'em slips,
   Huldy sot pale ez ashes,
All kin' o' smily roun' the lips
   An' teary roun' the lashes.

For she was jes' the quiet kind
   Whose naturs never vary,
Like streams that keep a summer mind
   Snowhid in Jenooary.

The blood clost roun' her heart felt glued
   Too tight for all expressin',
Tell mother see how metters stood,
   An' gin 'em both her blessin'.

Then her red come back like the tide
   Down to the Bay o' Fundy,
An' all I know is they was cried
   In meetin' come nex' Sunday.

Song

O, moonlight deep and tender,
   A year and more agone,
Your mist of golden splendor
   Round my betrothal shone!

O, elm-leaves dark and dewy,
   The very same ye seem,
The low wind trembles through ye,
   Ye murmur in my dream!

JAMES RUSSELL LOWELL 1819–1891

O, river, dim with distance,
    Flow thus forever by,
A part of my existence
    Within your heart doth lie!

O, stars, ye saw our meeting,
    Two beings and one soul,
Two hearts so madly beating
    To mingle and be whole!

O, happy night, deliver
    Her kisses back to me,
Or keep them all, and give her
    A blissful dream of me!

The Present Crisis

When a deed is done for Freedom, through the broad earth's aching breast
Runs a thrill of joy prophetic, trembling on from east to west,
And the slave, where'er he cowers, feels the soul within him climb
To the awful verge of manhood, as the energy sublime
Of a century bursts full-blossomed on the thorny stem of Time.

JAMES RUSSELL LOWELL 1819–1891

Through the walls of hut and palace shoots the instantaneous throe,
When the travail of the Ages wrings earth's systems to and fro;
At the birth of each new Era, with a recognizing start,
Nation wildly looks at nation, standing with mute lips apart,
And glad Truth's yet mightier man-child leaps beneath the Future's heart.

So the Evil's triumph sendeth, with a terror and a chill,
Under continent to continent, the sense of coming ill,
And the slave, where'er he cowers, feels his sympathies with God
In hot tear-drops ebbing earthward, to be drunk up by the sod,
Till a corpse crawls round unburied, delving in the nobler clod.

For mankind are one in spirit, and an instinct bears along,
Round the earth's electric circle, the swift flash of right or wrong;
Whether conscious or unconscious, yet Humanity's vast frame
Through its ocean-sundered fibres feels the gush of joy or shame;—
In the gain or loss of one race all the rest have equal claim.

JAMES RUSSELL LOWELL 1819–1891

Once to every man and nation comes the moment to
    decide,
In the strife of Truth with Falsehood, for the good or
    evil side;
Some great cause, God's new Messiah, offering each the
    bloom or blight,
Parts the goats upon the left hand, and the sheep upon
    the right,
And the choice goes by forever 'twixt that darkness and
    that light.

Hast thou chosen, O my people, on whose party thou
    shalt stand,
Ere the Doom from its worn sandals shakes the dust
    against our land?
Though the cause of Evil prosper, yet 't is Truth alone
    is strong,
And, albeit she wander outcast now, I see around her
    throng
Troops of beautiful, tall angels, to enshield her from all
    wrong.

Backward look across the ages and the beacon-moments
    see,
That, like peaks of some sunk continent, jut through
    Oblivion's sea;
Not an ear in court or market for the low, foreboding cry
Of those Crises, God's stern winnowers, from whose feet
    earth's chaff must fly;

Never shows the choice momentous till the judgment hath
    passed by.

Careless seems the great Avenger; history's pages but
    record
One death-grapple in the darkness 'twixt old systems and
    the Word;
Truth forever on the scaffold, Wrong forever on the
    throne,—
Yet that scaffold sways the future, and, behind the dim
    unknown,
Standeth God within the shadow, keeping watch above
    his own.

We see dimly in the Present what is small and what is
    great,
Slow of faith how weak an arm may turn the iron helm
    of fate,
But the soul is still oracular; amid the market's din,
List the ominous stern whisper from the Delphic cave
    within,—
"They enslave their children's children who make com-
    promise with sin."

Slavery, the earth-born Cyclops, fellest of the giant
    brood,
Sons of brutish Force and Darkness, who have drenched
    the earth with blood,
Famished in his self-made desert, blinded by our purer
    day,

Gropes in yet unblasted regions for his miserable prey;—
Shall we guide his gory fingers where our helpless children play?

Then to side with Truth is noble when we share her wretched crust,
Ere her cause bring fame and profit, and 't is prosperous to be just;
Then it is the brave man chooses, while the coward stands aside,
Doubting in his abject spirit, till his Lord is crucified,
And the multitude make virtue of the faith they had denied.

Count me o'er earth's chosen heroes,—they were souls that stood alone,
While the men they agonized for hurled the contumelious stone,
Stood serene, and down the future saw the golden beam incline
To the side of perfect justice, mastered by their faith divine,
By one man's plain truth to manhood and to God's supreme design.

By the light of burning heretics Christ's bleeding feet I track,
Toiling up new Calvaries ever with the cross that turns not back,

And these mounts of anguish number how each generation
    learned
One new word of that grand *Credo* which in prophet-
    hearts hath burned
Since the first man stood God-conquered with his face
    to heaven upturned.

For Humanity sweeps onward: where to-day the martyr
    stands,
On the morrow crouches Judas with the silver in his
    hands;
Far in front the cross stands ready and the crackling
    fagots burn,
While the hooting mob of yesterday in silent awe return
To glean up the scattered ashes into History's golden
    urn.

'T is as easy to be heroes as to sit the idle slaves
Of a legendary virtue carved upon our fathers' graves,
Worshippers of light ancestral make the present light a
    crime;—
Was the Mayflower launched by cowards, steered by men
    behind their time?
Turn those tracks toward Past or Future, that made
    Plymouth Rock sublime?

They were men of present valor, stalwart old iconoclasts,
Unconvinced by axe or gibbet that all virtue was the
    Past's;

But we make their truth our falsehood, thinking that hath made us free,
Hoarding it in mouldy parchments, while our tender spirits flee
The rude grasp of that great Impulse which drove them across the sea.

They have rights who dare maintain them; we are traitors to our sires,
Smothering in their holy ashes Freedom's new-lit altar-fires;
Shall we make their creed our jailer? Shall we, in our haste to slay,
From the tombs of the old prophets steal the funeral lamps away
To light up the martyr-fagots round the prophets of to-day?

New occasions teach new duties; Time makes ancient good uncouth;
They must upward still, and onward, who would keep abreast of Truth;
Lo, before us gleam her camp-fires! we ourselves must Pilgrims be,
Launch our Mayflower, and steer boldly through the desperate winter sea,
Nor attempt the Future's portal with the Past's blood-rusted key.

JAMES RUSSELL LOWELL 1819–1891

The Washers of the Shroud

October, 1861

Along a river-side, I know not where,
I walked one night in mystery of dream;
A chill creeps curdling yet beneath my hair,
To think what chanced me by the pallid gleam
Of a moon-wraith that waned through haunted air.

Pale fireflies pulsed within the meadow-mist
Their halos, wavering thistledowns of light;
The loon, that seemed to mock some goblin tryst,
Laughed; and the echoes, huddling in affright,
Like Odin's hounds, fled baying down the night.

Then all was silent, till there smote my ear
A movement in the stream that checked my breath:
Was it the slow plash of a wading deer?
But something said, "This water is of Death!
The Sisters wash a shroud,—ill thing to hear!"

I, looking then, beheld the ancient Three
Known to the Greek's and to the Northman's creed,
That sit in shadow of the mystic Tree,
Still crooning, as they weave their endless brede,
One song: "Time was, Time is, and Time shall be."

JAMES RUSSELL LOWELL 1819–1891

No wrinkled crones were they as I had deemed,
But fair as yesterday, to-day, to-morrow,
To mourner, lover, poet, ever seemed;
Something too high for joy, too deep for sorrow,
Thrilled in their tones, and from their faces gleamed.

"Still men and nations reap as they have strawn,"
So sang they, working at their task the while;
"The fatal raiment must be cleansed ere dawn:
For Austria? Italy? the Sea-Queen's isle?
O'er what quenched grandeur must our shroud be drawn?

"What make we, murmur'st thou? and what are we?
When empires must be wound, we bring the shroud,
The time-old web of the implacable Three:
Is it too coarse for him, the young and proud?
Earth's mightiest deigned to wear it,—why not he?"

"Is there no hope?" I moaned, "so strong, so fair!
Our Fowler whose proud bird would brook erewhile
No rival's swoop in all our western air!
Gather the ravens, then, in funeral file
For him, life's morn yet golden in his hair?

"Leave me not hopeless, ye unpitying dames!
I see, half seeing. Tell me, ye who scanned
The stars, Earth's elders, still must noblest aims
Be traced upon oblivious ocean-sands?
Must Hesper join the wailing ghosts of names?"

JAMES RUSSELL LOWELL 1819–1891

"When grass-blades stiffen with red battle-dew,
Ye deem we choose the victor and the slain:
Say, choose we them that shall be leal and true
To the heart's longing, the high faith of brain?
Yet there the victory lies, if ye but knew.

"Three roots bear up Dominion: Knowledge, Will,—
These twain are strong, but stronger yet the third,—
Obedience,—'t is the great tap-root that still,
Knit round to rock of Duty, is not stirred,
Though Heaven-loosed tempests spend their utmost skill.

"Is the doom sealed for Hesper? 'T is not we
Denounce it, but the Law before all time:
The brave makes danger opportunity;
The waverer, paltering with the chance sublime,
Dwarfs it to peril: which shall Hesper be?

"Hath he let vultures climb his eagle's seat
To make Jove's bolts purveyors of their maw?
Hath he the Many's plaudits found more sweet
Than Wisdom? held Opinion's wind for Law?
Then let him hearken for the doomster's feet!

"Rough are the steps, slow-hewn in flintiest rock,
States climb to power by; slippery those with gold
Down which they stumble to eternal mock:
No chafferer's hand shall long the sceptre hold,
Who, given a Fate to shape, would sell the block.

JAMES RUSSELL LOWELL 1819–1891

"We sing old Sagas, songs of weal and woe,
Mystic because cheaply understood;
Dark sayings are not ours; men hear and know,
See Evil weak, see strength alone in Good,
Yet hope to stem God's fire with walls of tow.

"Time Was unlocks the riddle of Time Is,
That offers choice of glory or of gloom;
The solver makes Time Shall Be surely his.
But hasten, Sisters! for even now the tomb
Grates its slow hinges and calls from the abyss."

"But not for him," I cried, "not yet for him,
Whose large horizon, westering, star by star
Wins from the void to where on Ocean's rim
The sunset shuts the world with golden bar,
Not yet his thews shall fail, his eyes grow dim!

"His shall be larger manhood, save for those
That walk unblenching through the trial-fires;
Not suffering, but faint heart, is worst of woes,
And he no base-born son of craven sires,
Whose eye need blench confronted with his foes.

"Tears may be ours, but proud, for those who win
Death's royal purple in the foeman's lines;
Peace, too, brings tears; and mid the battle-din,
The wiser ear some text of God divines,
For the sheathed blade may rust with darker sin.

"God, give us peace! not such as lulls to sleep,
But sword on thigh, and brow with purpose knit!
And let our Ship of State to harbor sweep,
Her ports all up, her battle-lanterns lit,
And her leashed thunders gathering for their leap!"

So cried I with clenched hands and passionate pain,
Thinking of dear ones by Potomac's side;
Again the loon laughed mocking, and again
The echoes bayed far down the night and died,
While waking I recalled my wandering brain.

Ode Recited at the Harvard Commemoration
July 21, 1865

I

Weak-winged is song,
Nor aims at that clear-ethered height
Whither the brave deeds climb for light:
    We seem to do them wrong,
Bringing our robin's-leaf to deck their hearse
Who in warm life-blood wrote their nobler verse,
Our trivial song to honor those who come
With ears attuned to strenuous trump and drum,
And shaped in squadron-strophes their desire,
Live battle-odes whose lines were steel and fire:
    Yet sometimes feathered words are strong,

JAMES RUSSELL LOWELL 1819–1891

A gracious memory to buoy up and save
From Lethe's dreamless ooze, the common grave
   Of the unventurous throng.

II

To-day our Reverend Mother welcomes back
  Her wisest Scholars, those who understood
The deeper teaching of her mystic tome,
    And offered their fresh lives to make it good:
      No lore of Greece or Rome,
No science peddling with the names of things,
Or reading stars to find inglorious fates,
      Can lift our life with wings
Far from Death's idle gulf that for the many waits,
      And lengthen out our dates
With that clear fame whose memory sings
In manly hearts to come, and nerves them and dilates:
Nor such thy teaching, Mother of us all!
      Not such the trumpet-call
      Of thy diviner mood,
      That could thy sons entice
From happy homes and toils, the fruitful nest
Of those half-virtues which the world calls best,
      Into War's tumult rude;
      But rather far that stern device
The sponsors chose that round thy cradle stood
      In the dim, unventured wood,
      The Veritas that lurks beneath
      The letter's unprolific sheath,

Life of whate'er makes life worth living,
Seed-grain of high emprise, immortal food,
  One heavenly thing whereof earth hath the giving.

III

Many loved Truth, and lavished life's best oil
  Amid the dust of books to find her,
Content at last, for guerdon of their toil,
  With the cast mantle she hath left behind her.
    Many in sad faith sought for her,
    Many with crossed hands sighed for her;
    But these, our brothers, fought for her,
    At life's dear peril wrought for her,
    So loved her that they died for her,
    Tasting the raptured fleetness
    Of her divine completeness:
    Their higher instinct knew
Those love her best who to themselves are true,
And what they dare to dream of, dare to do;
  They followed her and found her
  Where all may hope to find,
Not in the ashes of the burnt-out mind,
But beautiful, with danger's sweetness round her.
  Where faith made whole with deed
  Breathes its awakening breath
  Into the lifeless creed,
  They saw her plumed and mailed,
  With sweet, stern face unveiled,
And all-repaying eyes, looked proud on them in death.

IV

Our slender life runs rippling by, and glides
   Into the silent hollow of the past;
      What is there that abides
   To make the next age better for the last?
      Is earth too poor to give us
  Something to live for here that shall outlive us?
      Some more substantial boon
Than such as flows and ebbs with Fortune's fickle moon?
      The little that we see
      From doubt is never free;
      The little that we do
      Is but half-nobly true;
      With our laborious hiving
What men call treasure, and the gods call dross,
   Life seems a jest of Fate's contriving,
   Only secure in every one's conniving,
A long account of nothings paid with loss,
Where we poor puppets, jerked by unseen wires,
   After our little hour of strut and rave,
With all our pasteboard passions and desires,
Loves, hates, ambitions, and immortal fires,
   Are tossed pell-mell together in the grave.
   But stay! no age was e'er degenerate,
   Unless men held it at too cheap a rate,
   For in our likeness still we shape our fate.
      Ah, there is something here
   Unfathomed by the cynic's sneer,
   Something that gives our feeble light

A high immunity from Night,
  Something that leaps life's narrow bars
To claim its birthright with the hosts of heaven;
  A seed of sunshine that can leaven
  Our earthly dulness with the beams of stars,
      And glorify our clay
With light from fountains elder than the Day;
    A conscience more divine than we,
    A gladness fed with secret tears,
    A vexing, forward-reaching sense
    Of some more noble permanence;
      A light across the sea,
Which haunts the soul and will not let it be,
Still beaconing from the heights of undegenerate years.

V

    Whither leads the path
    To ampler fates that leads?
    Not down through flowery meads,
    To reap an aftermath
  Of youth's vainglorious weeds,
    But up the steep, amid the wrath
  And shock of deadly-hostile creeds,
    Where the world's best hope and stay
By battle's flashes gropes a desperate way,
And every turf the fierce foot clings to bleeds.
    Peace hath her not ignoble wreath,
    Ere yet the sharp, decisive word
Light the black lips of cannon, and the sword

JAMES RUSSELL LOWELL 1819–1891

Dreams in its easeful sheath;
But some day the live coal behind the thought,
    Whether from Baäl's stone obscene,
    Or from the shrine serene
    Of God's pure altar brought,
Bursts up in flame; the war of tongue and pen
Learns with what deadly purpose it was fraught,
And, helpless in the fiery passion caught,
Shakes all the pillared state with shock of men:
Some day the soft Ideal that we wooed
Confronts us fiercely, foe-beset, pursued,
And cries reproachful: "Was it, then, my praise,
And not myself was loved? Prove now thy truth;
I claim of thee the promise of thy youth;
Give me thy life, or cower in empty phrase,
The victim of thy genius, not its mate!"
  Life may be given in many ways,
  And loyalty to Truth be sealed
As bravely in the closet as the field,
    So bountiful is Fate:
    But then to stand beside her,
    When craven churls deride her,
To front a lie in arms and not to yield,
    This shows, methinks, God's plan
    And measure of a stalwart man,
    Limbed like the old heroic breeds,
    Who stands self-poised on manhood's solid earth,
  Not forced to frame excuses for his birth,
Fed from within with all the strength he needs.

JAMES RUSSELL LOWELL 1819–1891

VI

Such was he, our Martyr-Chief,
    Whom late the Nation he had led,
    With ashes on her head,
Wept with the passion of an angry grief:
Forgive me, if from present things I turn
To speak what in my heart will beat and burn,
And hang my wreath on his world-honored urn.
        Nature, they say, doth dote,
        And cannot make a man
        Save on some worn-out plan,
        Repeating us by rote:
For him her Old-World moulds aside she threw,
    And, choosing sweet clay from the breast
        Of the unexhausted West,
With stuff untainted shaped a hero new,
Wise, stedfast in the strength of God, and true.
        How beautiful to see
Once more a shepherd of mankind indeed,
Who loved his charge, but never loved to lead;
One whose meek flock the people joyed to be,
    Not lured by any cheat of birth,
    But by his clear-grained human worth,
And brave old wisdom of sincerity!
    They knew that outward grace is dust;
    They could not choose but trust
In that sure-footed mind's unfaltering skill,
    And supple-tempered will
That bent like perfect steel to spring again and thrust.

JAMES RUSSELL LOWELL 1819-1891

His was no lonely mountain-peak of mind,
Thrusting to thin air o'er our cloudy bars,
A sea-mark now, now lost in vapors blind;
Broad prairie rather, genial, level-lined,
  Fruitful and friendly for all human kind,
Yet also nigh to heaven and loved of loftiest stars.
    Nothing of Europe here,
Or, then, of Europe fronting mornward still,
    Ere any names of Serf and Peer
    Could Nature's equal scheme deface
    And thwart her genial will;
Here was a type of the true elder race,
And one of Plutarch's men talked with us face to face.
    I praise him not; it were too late;
And some innative weakness there must be
In him who condescends to victory
Such as the Present gives, and cannot wait,
    Safe in himself as in a fate.
      So always firmly he:
      He knew to bide his time,
      And can his fame abide,
Still patient in his simple faith sublime,
    Till the wise years decide.
    Great captains, with their guns and drums,
    Disturb our judgment for the hour,
      But at last silence comes;
  These are all gone, and, standing like a tower,
  Our children shall behold his fame,
    The kindly-earnest, brave, foreseeing man,

Sagacious, patient, dreading praise, not blame,
　New birth of our new soil, the first American.

VII

　Long as man's hope insatiate can discern
　　Or only guess some more inspiring goal
　　Outside of Self, enduring as the pole,
　Along whose course the flying axles burn
　Of spirits bravely-pitched, earth's manlier brood;
　　Long as below we cannot find
　The meed that stills the inexorable mind;
　So long this faith to some ideal Good,
　　Under whatever mortal names it masks,
　　Freedom, Law, Country, this ethereal mood
That thanks the Fates for their severer tasks,
　　Feeling its challenged pulses leap,
　　While others skulk in subterfuges cheap,
And, set in Danger's van, has all the boon it asks,
　　Shall win man's praise and woman's love,
　　Shall be a wisdom that we set above
All other skills and gifts to culture dear,
　　A virtue round whose forehead we inwreathe
　　Laurels that with a living passion breathe
When other crowns grow, while we twine them, sear.
　　What brings us thronging these high rites to pay,
　　And seal these hours the noblest of our year,
　Save that our brothers found this better way?

VIII

We sit here in the Promised Land
  That flows with Freedom's honey and milk;
  But 't was they won it, sword in hand,
Making the nettle danger soft for us as silk.
  We welcome back our bravest and our best;—
  Ah, me! not all! some come not with the rest,
Who went forth brave and bright as any here!
I strive to mix some gladness with my strain,
        But the sad strings complain,
        And will not please the ear:
I sweep them for a pæan, but they wane
        Again and yet again
Into a dirge, and die away in pain.
In these brave ranks I only see the gaps,
Thinking of dear ones whom the dumb turf wraps,
Dark to the triumph which they died to gain:
  Fitlier may others greet the living,
  For me the past is unforgiving;
    I with uncovered head
    Salute the sacred dead,
Who went, and who return not.—Say not so!
'T is not the grapes of Canaan that repay,
But the high faith that failed not by the way;
Virtue treads paths that end not in the grave;
No bar of endless night exiles the brave;
        And to the saner mind
We rather seem the dead that stayed behind.
Blow, trumpets, all your exultations blow!

For never shall their aureoled presence lack:
I see them muster in a gleaming row,
With ever-youthful brows that nobler show;
We find in our dull road their shining track;
    In every nobler mood
We feel the orient of their spirit glow,
Part of our life's unalterable good,
Of all our saintlier aspiration;
    They come transfigured back,
Secure from change in their high-hearted ways,
Beautiful evermore, and with the rays
Of morn on their white Shields of Expectation!

IX

    But is there hope to save
  Even this ethereal essence from the grave?
  What ever 'scaped Oblivion's subtle wrong
Save a few clarion names, or golden threads of song?
    Before my musing eye
  The mighty ones of old sweep by,
Disvoiced now and insubstantial things,
As noisy once as we; poor ghosts of kings,
Shadows of empire wholly gone to dust,
And many races, nameless long ago,
To darkness driven by that imperious gust
Of ever-rushing Time that here doth blow:
O visionary world, condition strange,
Where naught abiding is but only Change,

JAMES RUSSELL LOWELL 1819-1891

Where the deep-bolted stars themselves still shift and
        range!
  Shall we to more continuance make pretence?
Renown builds tombs; a life-estate is Wit;
        And, bit by bit,
The cunning years steal all from us but woe;
  Leaves are we, whose decays no harvest sow.
        But, when we vanish hence,
  Shall they lie forceless in the dark below,
  Save to make green their little length of sods,
  Or deepen pansies for a year or two,
  Who now to us are shining-sweet as gods?
  Was dying all they had the skill to do?
  That were not fruitless: but the Soul resents
Such short lived service, as if blind events
  Ruled without her, or earth could so endure:
  She claims a more divine investiture
  Of longer tenure than Fame's airy rents;
  Whate'er she touches doth her nature share;
  Her inspiration haunts the ennobled air,
        Gives eyes to mountains blind,
  Ears to the deaf earth, voices to the wind,
  And her clear trump sings succor everywhere
  By lonely bivouacs to the wakeful mind;
  For soul inherits all that soul could dare:
    Yea, Manhood hath a wider span
  And larger privilege of life than man.
  The single deed, the private sacrifice,
  So radiant now through proudly-hidden tears,

Is covered up erelong from mortal eyes
With thoughtless drift of the deciduous years;
But that high privilege that makes all men peers,
That leap of heart whereby a people rise
  Up to a noble anger's height,
And, flamed on by the Fates, not shrink, but grow more bright,
 That swift validity in noble veins,
 Of choosing danger and disdaining shame,
  Of being set on flame
By the pure fire that flies all contact base,
But wraps its chosen with angelic might,
  These are imperishable gains,
 Sure as the sun, medicinal as light,
 These hold great futures in their lusty reins
And certify to earth a new imperial race.

X

  Who now shall sneer?
 Who dare again to say we trace
 Our lines to a plebeian race?
  Roundhead and Cavalier!
Dumb are those names erewhile in battle loud;
Dream-footed as the shadow of a cloud,
  They flit across the ear:
That is best blood that hath most iron in 't
To edge resolve with, pouring without stint
  For what makes manhood dear.
 Tell us not of Plantagenets,

Hapsburgs, and Guelfs, whose thin bloods crawl
Down from some victor in a border-brawl!
    How poor their outworn coronets,
Matched with one leaf of that plain civic wreath
Our brave for honor's blazon shall bequeath,
  Through whose desert a rescued Nation sets
Her heel on treason, and the trumpet hears
Shout victory, tingling Europe's sullen ears
    With vain resentments and more vain regrets!

XI

    Not in anger, not in pride,
    Pure from passion's mixture rude
    Ever to base earth allied,
    But with far-heard gratitude,
    Still with heart and voice renewed,
To heroes living and dear martyrs dead,
The strain should close that consecrates our brave.
  Lift the heart and lift the head!
    Lofty be its mood and grave,
    Not without a martial ring,
    Not without a prouder tread
    And a peal of exultation:
    Little right has he to sing
    Through whose heart in such an hour
    Beats no march of conscious power,
    Sweeps no tumult of elation!
    'T is no Man we celebrate,
    By his country's victories great,

JAMES RUSSELL LOWELL 1819–1891

A hero half, and half the whim of Fate,
    But the pith and marrow of a Nation
    Drawing force from all her men,
    Highest, humblest, weakest, all,
    For her time of need, and then
    Pulsing it again through them,
Till the basest can no longer cower,
Feeling his soul spring up divinely tall,
Touched but in passing by her mantle-hem.
Come back, then, noble pride, for 't is her dower!
    How could poet ever tower,
    If his passions, hopes, and fears,
    If his triumphs and his tears,
    Kept not measure with his people?
Boom, cannon, boom to all the winds and waves!
Clash out, glad bells, from every rocking steeple!
Banners, a-dance with triumph, bend your staves!
    And from every mountain-peak
    Let beacon-fire to answering beacon speak,
    Katahdin tell Monadnock, Whiteface he,
And so leap on in light from sea to sea,
    Till the glad news be sent
    Across a kindling continent,
Making earth feel more firm and air breathe braver:
  "Be proud! for she is saved, and all have helped to
    save her!
  She that lifts up the manhood of the poor,
  She of the open soul and open door,
  With room about her hearth for all mankind!

JAMES RUSSELL LOWELL 1819–1891

The fire is dreadful in her eyes no more;
From her bold front the helm she doth unbind,
Sends all her handmaid armies back to spin,
    And bids her navies, that so lately hurled
    Their crashing battle, hold their thunders in;
    Swimming like birds of calm along the unharmful
        shore.
    No challenge sends she to the elder world,
    That looked askance and hated; a light scorn
    Plays o'er her mouth, as round her mighty knees
    She calls her children back, and waits the morn
Of nobler day, enthroned between her subject seas."

XII

Bow down, dear Land, for thou hast found release!
    Thy God, in these distempered days,
    Hath taught thee the sure wisdom of His ways,
And through thine enemies hath wrought thy peace!
        Bow down in prayer and praise!
No poorest in thy borders but may now
Lift to the juster skies a man's enfranchised brow.
O Beautiful! my Country! ours once more!
Smoothing thy gold of war-dishevelled hair
O'er such sweet brows as never other wore,
        And letting thy set lips,
        Freed from wrath's pale eclipse,
The rosy edges of their smile lay bare,
What words divine of lover or of poet

Could tell our love and make thee know it,
Among the Nations bright beyond compare?
    What were our lives without thee?
    What all our lives to save thee?
    We reck not what we gave thee:
    We will not dare to doubt thee,
But ask whatever else, and we will dare!

Auf Wiedersehen

Summer

The little gate was reached at last,
    Half hid in lilacs down the lane;
She pushed it wide, and, as she past,
A wistful look she backward cast,
    And said,—*"Auf wiedersehen!"*

With hand on latch, a vision white
    Lingered reluctant, and again
Half doubting if she did aright,
Soft as the dews that fell that night,
    She said,—*"Auf wiedersehen!"*

The lamp's clear gleam flits up the stair;
    I lingered in delicious pain;
Ah, in that chamber, whose rich air
To breathe in thought I scarcely dare,
    Thinks she,—*"Auf wiedersehen!"*

JAMES RUSSELL LOWELL 1819–1891

'T is thirteen years; once more I press
   The turf that silences the lane;
I hear the rustle of her dress,
I smell the lilacs, and—ah, yes,
   I hear, *"Auf wiedersehen!"*

Sweet piece of bashful maiden art!
   The English words had seemed too fain,
But these—they drew us heart to heart,
Yet held us tenderly apart;
   She said, *"Auf wiedersehen!"*

Palinode

Autumn

Still thirteen years: 't is autumn now
   On field and hill, in heart and brain;
The naked trees at evening sough;
The leaf to the forsaken bough
   Sighs not,—*"Auf wiedersehen!"*

Two watched yon oriole's pendent dome,
   That now is void, and dank with rain,
And one,—O, hope more frail than foam!
The bird to his deserted home
   Sings not,—*"Auf wiedersehen!"*

JAMES RUSSELL LOWELL 1819–1891

The loath gate swings with rusty creak;
   Once, parting there, we played at pain;
There came a parting, when the weak
And fading lips essayed to speak
   Vainly,—"*Auf wiedersehen!*"

Somewhere is comfort, somewhere faith,
   Though thou in outer dark remain;
One sweet sad voice ennobles death,
And still, for eighteen centuries saith
   Softly,—"*Auf wiedersehen!*"

If earth another grave must bear,
   Yet heaven hath won a sweeter strain,
And something whispers my despair,
That, from an orient chamber there,
   Floats down,—"*Auf wiedersehen!*"

Without and Within

My coachman, in the moonlight there,
   Looks through the side light of the door;
I hear him with his brethren swear,
   As I could do,—but only more.

Flattening his nose against the pane,
   He envies me my brilliant lot,
Breathes on his aching fists in vain,
   And dooms me to a place more hot.

JAMES RUSSELL LOWELL 1819–1891

He sees me in to supper go,
   A silken wonder by my side.
Bare arms, bare shoulders, and a row
   Of flounces, for the door too wide.

He thinks how happy is my arm
   'Neath its white-gloved and jewelled load;
And wishes me some dreadful harm,
   Hearing the merry corks explode.

Meanwhile I inly curse the bore
   Of hunting still the same old coon,
And envy him, outside the door,
   In golden quiets of the moon.

The winter wind is not so cold
   As the bright smile he sees me win,
Nor the host's oldest wine so old
   As our poor gabble sour and thin.

I envy him the ungyved prance
   With which his freezing feet he warms,
And drag my lady's-chains and dance
   The galley-slave of dreary forms.

Oh, could he have my share of din,
   And I his quiet!—past a doubt
'T would still be one man bored within,
   And just another bored without.

JAMES RUSSELL LOWELL 1819–1891

Nay, when, once paid my mortal fee,
   Some idler on my headstone grim
Traces the moss-blurred name, will he
   Think me the happier, or I him?

The Petition

Oh, tell me less or tell me more,
Soft eyes with mystery at the core,
That always seem to meet my own
Frankly as pansies fully grown,
Yet waver still 'tween no and yes!

So swift to cavil and deny,
Then parley with concessions shy,
Dear eyes, that make their youth be mine
And through my inmost shadows shine,
Oh, tell me more or tell me less!

Telepathy

"And how could you dream of meeting?"
   Nay, how can you ask me, sweet?
All day my pulse had been beating
   The tune of your coming feet.

JAMES RUSSELL LOWELL 1819–1891

And as nearer and ever nearer
   I felt the throb of your tread,
To be in the world grew dearer,
   And my blood ran rosier red.

Love called, and I could not linger,
   But sought the forbidden tryst,
As music follows the finger
   Of the dreaming lutanist.

And though you had said it and said it,
   "We must not be happy to-day,"
Was I not wiser to credit
   The fire in my feet than your Nay?

Credidimus Jovem Regnare

O days endeared to every Muse,
When nobody had any Views,
Nor, while the cloudscape of his mind
By every breeze was new designed,
Insisted all the world should see
Camels or whales where none there be!
O happy days, when men received
From sire to son what all believed,
And left the other world in bliss,
Too busy with bedevilling this!

JAMES RUSSELL LOWELL 1819–1891

Beset by doubts of every breed
In the last bastion of my creed,
With shot and shell for Sabbath-chime,
I watch the storming-party climb,
Panting (their prey in easy reach),
To pour triumphant through the breach
In wall that shed like snowflakes tons
Of missiles from old-fashioned guns,
But crumble 'neath the storm that pours
All day and night from bigger bores.
There, as I hopeless watch and wait
The last life-crushing coil of Fate,
Despair finds solace in the praise
Of those serene dawn-rosy days
Ere microscopes had made us heirs
To large estates of doubts and snares,
By proving that the title-deeds,
Once all-sufficient for men's needs,
Are palimpsests that scarce disguise
The tracings of still earlier lies,
Themselves as surely written o'er
An older fib erased before.

So from these days I fly to those
That in the landlocked Past repose,
Where no rude wind of doctrine shakes
From bloom-flushed boughs untimely flakes;
Where morning's eyes see nothing strange,
No crude perplexity of change,

JAMES RUSSELL LOWELL 1819–1891

And morrows trip along their ways
Secure as happy yesterdays.
Then there were rulers who could trace
Through heroes up to gods their race,
Pledged to fair fame and noble use
By veins from Odin filled or Zeus,
And under bonds to keep divine
The praise of a celestial line.
Then priests could pile the altar's sods,
With whom gods spake as they with gods,
And everywhere from haunted earth
Broke springs of wonder, that had birth
In depths divine beyond the ken
And fatal scrutiny of men;
Then hills and groves and streams and seas
Thrilled with immortal presences,
Not too ethereal for the scope
Of human passion's dream or hope.

Now Pan at last is surely dead,
And King No-Credit reigns instead,
Whose officers, morosely strict,
Poor Fancy's tenantry evict,
Chase the last Genius from the door,
And nothing dances any more.
Nothing? Ah, yes, our tables do,
Drumming the Old One's own tattoo,
And, if the oracles are dumb,
Have we not mediums? Why be glum?

JAMES RUSSELL LOWELL 1819–1891

Fly thither? Why, the very air
Is full of hindrance and despair!
Fly thither? But I cannot fly;
My doubts enmesh me if I try,—
Each lilliputian, but, combined,
Potent a giant's limbs to bind.
This world and that are growing dark;
A huge interrogation mark,
The Devil's crook episcopal,
Still borne before him since the Fall,
Blackens with its ill-omened sign
The old blue heaven of faith benign.

Whence? Whither? Wherefore? How?
  Which? Why?
All ask at once, all wait reply.
Men feel old systems cracking under 'em;
Life saddens to a mere conundrum
Which once Religion solved, but she
Has lost—has Science found?—the key.

What was snow-bearded Odin, trow,
The mighty hunter long ago,
Whose horn and hounds the peasant hears
Still when the Northlights shake their spears?
Science hath answers twain, I 've heard;
Choose which you will, nor hope a third;
Whichever box the truth be stowed in,
There 's not a sliver left of Odin.
Either he was a pinchbrowed thing,

JAMES RUSSELL LOWELL 1819–1891

With scarcely wit a stone to fling,
A creature both in size and shape
Nearer than we are to the ape,
Who hung sublime with brat and spouse
By tail prehensile from the boughs,
And, happier than his maimed descendants,
The culture-curtailed *in*dependents,
Could pluck his cherries with both paws,
And stuff with both his big-boned jaws;
Or else the core his name enveloped
Was from a solar myth developed,
Which, hunted to its primal shoot,
Takes refuge in a Sanskrit root,
Thereby to instant death explaining
The little poetry remaining.

Try it with Zeus, 't is just the same;
The thing evades, we hug a name;
Nay, scarcely that,—perhaps a vapor
Born of some atmospheric caper.
All Lempriere's fables blur together
In cloudy symbols of the weather,
And Aphrodite rose from frothy seas
But to illustrate such hypotheses.
With years enough behind his back,
Lincoln will take the selfsame track,
And prove, hulled fairly to the cob,
A mere vagary of Old Prob.
Give the right man a solar myth,
And he 'll confute the sun therewith.

JAMES RUSSELL LOWELL 1819–1891

They make things admirably plain,
But one hard question *will* remain:
If one hypothesis you lose,
Another in its place you choose,
But, your faith gone, O man and brother,
Whose shop shall furnish you another?
One that will wash, I mean, and wear,
And wrap us warmly from despair?
While they are clearing up our puzzles,
And clapping prophylactic muzzles
On the Actæon's hounds that sniff
Our devious track through But and If,
Would they 'd explain away the Devil
And other facts that won't keep level,
But rise beneath our feet or fail,
A reeling ship's deck in a gale!
God vanished long ago, iwis,
A mere subjective synthesis;
A doll, stuffed out with hopes and fears,
Too homely for us pretty dears,
Who want one that conviction carries,
Last make of London or of Paris.
He gone, I felt a moment's spasm,
But calmed myself with Protoplasm,
A finer name, and, what is more,
As enigmatic as before;
Greek, too, and sure to fill with ease
Minds caught in the Symplegades
Of soul and sense, life's two conditions,

JAMES RUSSELL LOWELL 1819-1891

Each baffled with its own omniscience.
The men who labor to revise
Our Bibles will, I hope, be wise,
And print it without foolish qualms
Instead of God in David's psalms:
Noll had been more effective far
Could he have shouted at Dunbar,
"Rise, Protoplasm!" No dourest Scot
Had waited for another shot.

And yet I frankly must confess
A secret unforgivingness,
And shudder at the saving chrism
Whose best New Birth is Pessimism;
My soul—I mean the bit of phosphorus
That fills the place of what that was for us—
Can't bid its inward bores defiance
With the new nursery-tales of science.
What profits me, though doubt by doubt,
As nail by nail, be driven out,
When every new one, like the last,
Still holds my coffin-lid as fast?
Would I find thought a moment's truce,
Give me the young world's Mother Goose
With life and joy in every limb,
The chimney-corner tales of Grimm!

Our dear and admirable Huxley
Cannot explain to me why ducks lay,
Or, rather, how into their eggs

JAMES RUSSELL LOWELL 1819–1891

Blunder potential wings and legs
With will to move them and decide
Whether in air or lymph to glide.
Who gets a hair's-breadth on by showing
That Something Else set all agoing?
Farther and farther back we push
From Moses and his burning bush;
Cry, "Art Thou there?" Above, below,
All Nature mutters *yes* and *no!*
'T is the old answer: we 're agreed
Being from Being must proceed,
Life be Life's source. I might as well
Obey the meeting-house's bell,
And listen while Old Hundred pours
Forth through the summer-opened doors,
From old and young. I hear it yet,
Swelled by bass-viol and clarinet,
While the gray minister, with face
Radiant, let loose his noble bass.

If Heaven it reached not, yet its roll
Waked all the echoes of the soul,
And in it many a life found wings
To soar away from sordid things.
Church gone and singers too, the song
Sings to me voiceless all night long,
Till my soul beckons me afar,
Glowing and trembling like a star.
Will any scientific touch
With my worn strings achieve as much?

JAMES RUSSELL LOWELL 1819–1891

I don't object, not I, to know
My sires were monkeys, if 't was so;
I touch my ear's collusive tip
And own the poor-relationship.
That apes of various shapes and sizes
Contained their germs that all the prizes
Of senate, pulpit, camp, and bar win
May give us hopes that sweeten Darwin.
Who knows but from our loins may spring
(Long hence) some winged sweet-throated thing
As much superior to us
As we to Cynocephalus?

This is consoling, but, alas,
It wipes no dimness from the glass
Where I am flattening my poor nose,
In hope to see beyond my toes.
Though I accept my pedigree,
Yet where, pray tell me, is the key
That should unlock a private door
To the Great Mystery, such no more?
Each offers his, but one nor all
Are much persuasive with the wall
That rises now, as long ago,
Between I wonder and I know,
Nor will vouchsafe a pin-hole peep
At the veiled Isis in its keep.
Where is no door, I but produce
My key to find it of no use.

JAMES RUSSELL LOWELL 1819–1891

Yet better keep it, after all,
Since Nature's economical,
And who can tell but some fine day
(If it occur to her) she may,
In her good-will to you and me,
Make door and lock to match the key?

JULIA WARD HOWE 1819–1911

Battle-Hymn of the Republic

Mine eyes have seen the glory of the coming of the Lord:
He is trampling out the vintage where the grapes of wrath are stored;
He hath loosed the fateful lightning of his terrible swift sword:
    His truth is marching on.

I have seen Him in the watch-fires of a hundred circling camps;
They have builded Him an altar in the evening dews and damps;
I can read his righteous sentence by the dim and flaring lamps:
    His day is marching on.

I have read a fiery gospel, writ in burnished rows of steel:
"As ye deal with my contemners, so with you my grace shall deal;
Let the Hero, born of woman, crush the serpent with his heel,
    Since God is marching on."

He has sounded forth the trumpet that shall never call retreat;
He is sifting out the hearts of men before his judgment-seat:
O, be swift, my soul, to answer Him! be jubilant, my feet!
    Our God is marching on.

JULIA WARD HOWE 1819–1911

In the beauty of the lilies Christ was born across the sea,
With a glory in His bosom that transfigures you and me:
As He died to make men holy, let us die to make men free,
   While God is marching on.

Our Orders

Weave no more silks, ye Lyons looms,
   To deck our girls for gay delights!
The crimson flower of battle blooms,
   And solemn marches fill the night.

Weave but the flag whose bars to-day
   Drooped heavy o'er our early dead,
And homely garments, coarse and gray,
   For orphans that must earn their bread!

Keep back your tunes, ye viols sweet,
   That poured delight from other lands!
Rouse there the dancer's restless feet:
   The trumpet leads our warrior bands.

And ye that wage the war of words
   With mystic fame and subtle power,
Go, chatter to the idle birds,
   Or teach the lesson of the hour!

JULIA WARD HOWE 1819–1911

Ye Sibyl Arts, in one stern knot
   Be all your offices combined!
Stand close, while Courage draws the lot,
   The destiny of human kind.

And if that destiny could fail,
   The sun should darken in the sky,
The eternal bloom of Nature pale,
   And God, and Truth, and Freedom die!

The Summons

I expect you in September
With the glory of the year:
You shall make the Autumn precious,
And the death of Summer dear;
You shall help the days that shorten,
With a lengthening of delight;
You shall whisper long-drawn blisses
Through the gathering screen of night.

I will lead you, dream-enchanted,
Where the fairest grasses grow;
I will hear your murmured music
Where the fresh winds pipe and blow.
On the brown heath, weird-encircled,
Shall our noiseless footsteps fall,—
We, communing with twin counsel,
Each to other all in all.

JULIA WARD HOWE 1819–1911

Leave the titles that men owe thee;
Like the first pair let us meet;
Name the world all over to me,
New-created at thy feet;
Gentle task and duteous learning,
I will hang upon thy breath
With the tender zeal of childhood,
With the constancy of death.

What shall be the gods declare not,—
They who stamp Love's burning coin
Into spangles of a moment,
Into stars that deathless shine.
Oh! the foolish music lingers;
For the theme is heavenly dear:
I expect you in September,
With the glories of the year.

WALT WHITMAN 1819-1892

O Captain! My Captain!

O Captain! my Captain! our fearful trip is done,
The ship has weather'd every rack, the prize we sought is won,
The port is near, the bells I hear, the people all exulting,
While follow eyes the steady keel, the vessel grim and daring;
   But O heart! heart! heart!
     O the bleeding drops of red,
       Where on the deck my Captain lies,
         Fallen cold and dead.

O Captain! my Captain! rise up and hear the bells;
Rise up—for you the flag is flung—for you the bugle trills,
For you bouquets and ribbon'd wreaths—for you the shores a-crowding,
For you they call, the swaying mass, their eager faces turning;
   Here Captain! dear father!
     This arm beneath your head!
       It is some dream that on the deck,
         You 've fallen cold and dead.

My Captain does not answer, his lips are pale and still,
My father does not feel my arm, he has no pulse nor will,

The ship is anchor'd safe and sound, its voyage closed
  and done,
From fearful trip the victor ship comes in with object
  won;
  Exult, O shores, and ring, O bells!
   But I, with mournful tread,
    Walk the deck my Captain lies,
     Fallen cold and dead.

THOMAS WILLIAM PARSONS 1819–1892

On a Bust of Dante

See, from this counterfeit of him
   Whom Arno shall remember long,
How stern of lineament, how grim,
   The father was of Tuscan song:
There but the burning sense of wrong,
   Perpetual care and scorn, abide;
Small friendship for the lordly throng;
   Distrust of all the world beside.

Faithful if this wan image be,
   No dream his life was,—but a fight;
Could any Beatrice see
   A lover in that anchorite?
To that cold Ghibelline's gloomy sight
   Who could have guessed the visions came
Of Beauty, veiled with heavenly light,
   In circles of eternal flame?

The lips as Cumæ's cavern close,
   The cheeks with fast and sorrow thin,
The rigid front, almost morose,
   But for the patient hope within,
Declare a life whose course hath been
   Unsullied still, though still severe,
Which, through the wavering days of sin,
   Kept itself icy-chaste and clear.

THOMAS WILLIAM PARSONS 1819–1892

Not wholly such his haggard look
   When wandering once, forlorn, he strayed,
With no companion save his book,
   To Corvo's hushed monastic shade;
Where, as the Benedictine laid
   His palm upon the convent's guest,
The single boon for which he prayed
   Was peace, that pilgrim's one request.

Peace dwells not here,—this rugged face
   Betrays no spirit of repose;
The sullen warrior sole we trace,
   The marble man of many woes.
Such was his mien when first arose
   The thought of that strange tale divine,
When hell he peopled with his foes,
   The scourge of many a guilty line.

War to the last he waged with all
   The tyrant canker-worms of earth;
Baron and duke, in hold and hall,
   Cursed the dark hour that gave him birth;
He used Rome's harlot for his mirth;
   Plucked bare hypocrisy and crime;
But valiant souls of knightly worth
   Transmitted to the rolls of Time.

O Time! whose verdicts mock our own,
   The only righteous judge art thou;
That poor old exile, sad and lone,
   Is Latium's other Virgil now:

THOMAS WILLIAM PARSONS 1819–1892

Before his name the nations bow; —
  His words are parcel for mankind,
Deep in whose hearts, as on his brow,
  The marks have sunk of Dante's mind.

Mary Booth

What shall we do now, Mary being dead,
  Or say or write that shall express the half?
What can we do but pillow that fair head,
  And let the Spring-time write her epitaph?—

As it will soon, in snowdrop, violet,
  Wind-flower and columbine and maiden's tear;
Each letter of that pretty alphabet,
  That spells in flowers the pageant of the year.

She was a maiden for a man to love;
  She was a woman for a husband's life;
One that had learned to value, far above
  The name of love, the sacred name of wife.

Her little life-dream, rounded so with sleep,
  Had all there is of life, except gray hairs,—
Hope, love, trust, passion and devotion deep;
  And that mysterious tie a Mother bears.

She hath fulfilled her promise and hath passed;
  Set her down gently at the iron door!
Eyes look on that loved image for the last:
  Now cover it in earth,—her earth no more.

THOMAS WILLIAM PARSONS 1819–1892

Her Epitaph

The handful here, that once was Mary's earth,
    Held, while it breathed, so beautiful a soul,
That, when she died, all recognized her birth,
    And had their sorrow in serene control.

"Not here! not here!" to every mourner's heart
    The wintry wind seemed whispering round her bier;
And when the tomb-door opened, with a start
    We heard it echoed from within,—"Not here!"

Shouldst thou, sad pilgrim, who mayst hither pass,
    Note in these flowers a delicater hue,
Should spring come earlier to this hallowed grass,
    Or the bee later linger on the dew,—

Know that her spirit to her body lent
    Such sweetness, grace, as only goodness can;
That even her dust, and this her monument,
    Have yet a spell to stay one lonely man,—

Lonely through life, but looking for the day
    When what is mortal of himself shall sleep,
When human passion shall have passed away,
    And Love no longer be a thing to weep.

THOMAS WILLIAM PARSONS 1819–1892

Obituary

Finding Francesca full of tears, I said,
"Tell me thy trouble." "Oh, my dog is dead!
Murdered by poison!—no one knows for what—
Was ever dog born capable of that?"
"Child,"—I began to say, but checked my thought,—
"A better dog can easily be bought."
For no—what animal could him replace?
Those loving eyes! That fond, confiding face!
Those dear, dumb touches! Therefore I was dumb.
From word of mine could any comfort come?
A bitter sorrow 't is to lose a brute
Friend, dog or horse, for grief must then be mute,—
So many smile to see the rivers shed
Of tears for one poor, speechless creature dead.
When parents die there 's many a word to say—
Kind words, consoling—one can always pray;
When children die 't is natural to tell
Their mother, "Certainly, with them 't is well!"
But for a dog, 't was all the life he had,
Since death is end of dogs, or good or bad.
This was his world; he was contented here;
Imagined nothing better, naught more dear,
Than his young mistress; sought no brighter sphere;
Having no sin, asked not to be forgiven;
Ne'er guessed at God nor ever dreamed of heaven.

Now he has passed away, so much of love
Goes from our life, without one hope above!
When a dog dies there's nothing to be said
But—kiss me, darling!—dear old Smiler's dead.

Paradisi Gloria

"*O frate mio! ciascuna e cittadina
D' una vera città*" . . . .

There is a city, builded by no hand,
   And unapproachable by sea or shore,
And unassailable by any band
   Of storming soldiery for evermore.

There we no longer shall divide our time
   By acts or pleasures,—doing petty things
Of work or warfare, merchandise or rhyme;
   But we shall sit beside the silver springs

That flow from God's own footstool, and behold
   Sages and martyrs, and those blessèd few
Who loved us once and were beloved of old,
   To dwell with them and walk with them anew,

In alternations of sublime repose,
   Musical motion, the perpetual play
Of every faculty that Heaven bestows
   Through the bright, busy, and eternal day.

THOMAS WILLIAM PARSONS 1819–1892

Saint Peray

When to any saint I pray,
It shall be to Saint Peray.
He alone, of all the brood,
Ever did me any good:
Many I have tried that are
Humbugs in the calendar.

On the Atlantic, faint and sick,
Once I prayed Saint Dominick:
He was holy, sure, and wise;—
Was 't not he that did devise
Auto da Fès and rosaries?—
But for one in my condition
This good saint was no physician.

Next, in pleasant Normandie,
I made a prayer to Saint Denis,
In the great cathedral, where
   All the ancient kings repose;
But, how I was swindled there
   At the "Golden Fleece,"—he knows!

In my wanderings, vague and various,
   Reaching Naples—as I lay
   Watching Vesuvius from the bay,
I besought Saint Januarius.
But I was a fool to try him;
Naught I said could liquefy him;

THOMAS WILLIAM PARSONS 1819–1892

And I swear he did me wrong,
Keeping me shut up so long
In that pest-house, with obscene
Jews and Greeks and things unclean—
What need had I of quarantine?

In Sicily at least a score,—
In Spain about as many more,—
And in Rome almost as many
As the loves of Don Giovanni,
Did I pray to—sans reply;
Devil take the tribe!—said I.

Worn with travel, tired and lame,
To Assisi's walls I came:
Sad and full of homesick fancies,
I addressed me to Saint Francis:
But the beggar never did
Anything as he was bid,
Never gave me aught—but fleas,—
Plenty had I at Assise.

But in Pròvence, near Vaucluse,
   Hard by the Rhone, I found a Saint
Gifted with a wondrous juice,
   Potent for the worst complaint.

'T was at Avignon that first—
In the witching time of thirst—
To my brain the knowledge came

THOMAS WILLIAM PARSONS 1819–1892

Of this blessed Catholic's name;
Forty miles of dust that day
Made me welcome Saint Peray.

Though till then I had not heard
Aught about him, ere a third
Of a litre passed my lips,
All saints else were in eclipse.
For his gentle spirit glided
  With such magic into mine,
That methought such bliss as I did
    Poet never drew from wine.

Rest he gave me and refection,—
Chastened hopes, calm retrospection,—
Softened images of sorrow,
Bright forebodings for the morrow,—
Charity for what is past,—
Faith in something good at last.

Now, why should any almanack
The name of this good creature lack?
Or wherefore should the breviary
Omit a saint so sage and merry?
The Pope himself should grant a day
Especially to Saint Peray.
But, since no day hath been appointed,
On purpose, by the Lord's anointed,
Let us not wait—we'll do him right;
Send round your bottles, Hal—and set your night.

THEODORE O'HARA 1820–1867

The Bivouac of the Dead

The muffled drum's sad roll has beat
   The soldier's last tattoo;
No more on Life's parade shall meet
   That brave and fallen few.
On Fame's eternal camping-ground
   Their silent tents are spread,
And Glory guards, with solemn round,
   The bivouac of the dead.

No rumor of the foe's advance
   Now swells upon the wind;
No troubled thought at midnight haunts
   Of loved ones left behind;
No vision of the morrow's strife
   The warrior's dream alarms;
No braying horn nor screaming fife
   At dawn shall call to arms.

Their shivered swords are red with rust,
   Their plumèd heads are bowed;
Their haughty banner, trailed in dust,
   Is now their martial shroud.
And plenteous funeral tears have washed
   The red stains from each brow,
And the proud forms, by battle gashed,
   Are free from anguish now.

THEODORE O'HARA 1820–1867

The neighing troop, the flashing blade,
   The bugle's stirring blast,
The charge, the dreadful cannonade,
   The din and shout, are past;
Nor war's wild note nor glory's peal
   Shall thrill with fierce delight
Those breasts that nevermore may feel
   The rapture of the fight.

Like the fierce northern hurricane
   That sweeps his great plateau,
Flushed with the triumph yet to gain,
   Came down the serried foe.
Who heard the thunder of the fray
   Break o'er the field beneath,
Knew well the watchword of that day
   Was "Victory or Death."

Long had the doubtful conflict raged
   O'er all that stricken plain,
For never fiercer fight had waged
   The vengeful blood of Spain;
And still the storm of battle blew,
   Still swelled the gory tide;
Not long, our stout old chieftain knew,
   Such odds his strength could bide.

THEODORE O'HARA 1820–1867

'T was in that hour his stern command
   Called to a martyr's grave
The flower of his beloved land,
   The nation's flag to save.
By rivers of their fathers' gore
   His first-born laurels grew,
And well he deemed the sons would pour
   Their lives for glory too.

Full many a norther's breath has swept
   O'er Angostura's plain,
And long the pitying sky has wept
   Above its mouldered slain.
The raven's scream, or eagle's flight,
   Or shepherd's pensive lay,
Alone awakes each sullen height
   That frowned o'er that dread fray.

Sons of the Dark and Bloody Ground,
   Ye must not slumber there,
Where stranger steps and tongues resound
   Along the heedless air.
Your own proud land's heroic soil
   Shall be your fitter grave:
She claims from war his richest spoil—
   The ashes of her brave.

THEODORE O'HARA 1820–1867

Thus 'neath their parent turf they rest
   Far from the gory field,
Borne to a Spartan mother's breast
   On many a bloody shield;
The sunshine of their native sky
   Smiles sadly on them here,
And kindred eyes and hearts watch by
   The heroes' sepulchre.

Rest on, embalmed and sainted dead!
   Dear as the blood ye gave;
No impious footstep here shall tread
   The herbage of your grave;
Nor shall your glory be forgot
   While Fame her record keeps,
Or Honor points the hallowed spot
   Where Valor proudly sleeps.

Yon marble minstrel's voiceless stone
   In deathless song shall tell,
When many a vanished age hath flown,
   The story how ye fell;
Nor wreck, nor change, nor winter's blight,
   Nor Time's remorseless doom,
Shall dim one ray of glory's light
   That gilds your deathless tomb.

THOMAS BUCHANAN READ 1822–1872

Some Things Love Me

All within and all without me
   Feel a melancholy thrill;
And the darkness hangs about me,
   Oh, how still;
To my feet, the river glideth
   Through the shadow, sullen, dark;
On the stream the white moon rideth,
   Like a barque—
And the linden leans above me,
   .Till I think some things there be
In the dreary world that love me,
   Even me!

Gentle buds are blooming near me,
   Shedding sweetest breath around;
Countless voices rise, to cheer me,
   From the ground;
And the lone bird comes—I hear it
   In the tall and windy pine
Pour the sadness of its spirit
   Into mine;
There it swings and sings above me,
   Till I think some things there be
In this dreary world that love me,
   Even me!

Now the moon hath floated to me,
   On the stream I see it sway,
Swinging, boat-like, as 't would woo me
   Far away—
And the stars bend from the azure,
   I could reach them where I lie,
And they whisper all the pleasure
   Of the sky.
There they hang and smile above me,
   Till I think some things there be
In the very heavens that love me,
   Even me!

The Celestial Army

I stood by the open casement
   And looked upon the night,
And saw the westward-going stars
   Pass slowly out of sight.

Slowly the bright procession
   Went down the gleaming arch,
And my soul discerned the music
   Of their long triumphal march;

Till the great celestial army,
   Stretching far beyond the poles,
Became the eternal symbol
   Of the mighty march of souls.

THOMAS BUCHANAN READ 1822–1872

Onward, forever onward,
   Red Mars led down his clan;
And the Moon, like a mailèd maiden,
   Was riding in the van.

And some were bright in beauty,
   And some were faint and small,
But these might be in their great height
   The noblest of them all.

Downward, forever downward,
   Behind Earth's dusky shore
They passed into the unknown night,
   They passed and were no more.

No more! Oh, say not so!
   And downward is not just;
For the sight is weak and the sense is dim
   That looks through heated dust.

The stars and the mailèd moon,
   Though they seem to fall and die,
Still sweep with their embattled lines
   An endless reach of sky.

And though the hills of Death
   May hide the bright array,
The marshalled brotherhood of souls
   Still keeps its upward way.

THOMAS BUCHANAN READ 1822–1872

Upward, forever upward,
  I see their march sublime,
And hear the glorious music
  Of the conquerors of Time.

And long let me remember,
  That the palest, fainting one
May to diviner vision be
  A bright and blazing sun.

Sheridan's Ride

Up from the South at break of day,
Bringing to Winchester fresh dismay,
The affrighted air with a shudder bore,
Like a herald in haste, to the chieftain's door,
The terrible grumble, and rumble, and roar,
Telling the battle was on once more,
And Sheridan twenty miles away.

And wider still those billows of war,
Thundered along the horizon's bar;
And louder yet into Winchester rolled
The roar of that red sea uncontrolled,
Making the blood of the listener cold,
As he thought of the stake in that fiery fray,
And Sheridan twenty miles away.

THOMAS BUCHANAN READ 1822–1872

But there is a road from Winchester town,
A good, broad highway leading down;
And there, through the flush of the morning light,
A steed as black as the steeds of night,
Was seen to pass, as with eagle flight,
As if he knew the terrible need;
He stretched away with his utmost speed;
Hills rose and fell; but his heart was gay,
With Sheridan fifteen miles away.

Still sprung from those swift hoofs, thundering South,
The dust, like smoke from the cannon's mouth;
Or the trail of a comet, sweeping faster and faster,
Foreboding to traitors the doom of disaster.
The heart of the steed, and the heart of the master
Were beating like prisoners assaulting their walls,
Impatient to be where the battle-field calls;
Every nerve of the charger was strained to full play,
With Sheridan only ten miles away.

Under his spurning feet the road
Like an arrowy Alpine river flowed,
And the landscape sped away behind
Like an ocean flying before the wind,
And the steed, like a barque fed with furnace ire,
Swept on, with his wild eyes full of fire.
But lo! he is nearing his heart's desire;
He is snuffing the smoke of the roaring fray,
With Sheridan only five miles away.

THOMAS BUCHANAN READ 1822–1872

The first that the general saw were the groups
Of stragglers, and then the retreating troops;
What was done? what to do? a glance told him both,
Then, striking his spurs, with a terrible oath,
He dashed down the line 'mid a storm of huzzas,
And the wave of retreat checked its course there, because
The sight of the master compelled it to pause.
With foam and with dust the black charger was gray;
By the flash of his eye, and the red nostril's play,
He seemed to the whole great army to say,
"I have brought you Sheridan all the way
From Winchester, down to save the day!"

Hurrah! hurrah for Sheridan!
Hurrah! hurrah for horse and man!
And when their statues are placed on high,
Under the dome of the Union sky,
The American soldier's Temple of Fame;
There with the glorious general's name,
Be it said, in letters both bold and bright,
  "Here is the steed that saved the day,
By carrying Sheridan into the fight,
  From Winchester, twenty miles away!"

GEORGE WILLIAM CURTIS 1824–1892

O listen to the sounding sea
  That beats on the remorseless shore,
O listen! for that sound will be
  When our wild hearts shall beat no more.

O listen well and listen long!
  For sitting folded close to me,
You could not hear a sweeter song
  Than that hoarse murmur of the sea.

Spring Song

A bird sang sweet and strong
  In the top of the highest tree,
He said, "I pour out my heart in song
  For the summer that soon shall be."

But deep in the shady wood,
  Another bird sang, "I pour
My heart on the solemn solitude
  For the springs that return no more."

GEORGE WILLIAM CURTIS 1824–1892

Egyptian Serenade

Sing again the song you sung
When we were together young—
When there were but you and I
Underneath the summer sky.

Sing the song, and o'er and o'er
Though I know that nevermore
Will it seem the song you sung
When we were together young.

PHOEBE CARY 1824–1871

Nearer Home

One sweetly solemn thought
   Comes to me o'er and o'er;
I am nearer home to-day
   Than I ever have been before;

Nearer my Father's house,
   Where the many mansions be;
Nearer the great white throne,
   Nearer the crystal sea;

Nearer the bound of life,
   Where we lay our burdens down;
Nearer leaving the cross,
   Nearer gaining the crown!

But lying darkly between,
   Winding down through the night,
Is the silent, unknown stream,
   That leads at last to the light.

Closer and closer my steps
   Come to the dread abysm:
Closer Death to my lips
   Presses the awful chrism.

Oh, if my mortal feet
   Have almost gained the brink;
If it be I am nearer home
   Even to-day than I think;

PHOEBE CARY 1824–1871

Father, perfect my trust;
  Let my spirit feel in death,
That her feet are firmly set
  On the rock of a living faith!

Alas!

Since, if you stood by my side to-day,
  Only our hands could meet,
What matter that half the weary world
  Lies between our feet;

That I am here by the lonesome sea,
  You by the pleasant Rhine?—
Our hearts were just as far apart
  If I held your hand in mine!

Therefore, with never a backward glance,
  I leave the past behind;
And standing here by the sea alone,
  I give it to the wind.

I give it all to the cruel wind,
  And I have no word to say;
Yet, alas! to be as we have been,
  And to be as we are to-day!

WILLIAM ALLEN BUTLER 1825–1902

The Incognita of Raphael

Long has the summer sunlight shone
   On the fair form, the quaint costume;
Yet, nameless still, she sits, unknown,
   A lady in her youthful bloom.

Fairer for this! no shadows cast
   Their blight upon her perfect lot,
Whate'er her future or her past,
   In this bright moment matters not.

No record of her high descent
   There needs, nor memory of her name;
Enough that Raphael's colors blent
   To give her features deathless fame!

'T was his anointing hand that set
   The crown of beauty on her brow;
Still lives its early radiance yet,
   As at the earliest, even now.

'T is not the ecstasy that glows
   In all the rapt Cecilia's grace;
Nor yet the holy, calm repose
   He painted on the Virgin's face.

Less of the heavens, and more of earth,
   There lurk within these earnest eyes
The passions that have had their birth
   And grown beneath Italian skies.

WILLIAM ALLEN BUTLER 1825–1902

What mortal thoughts, and cares, and dreams,
   What hopes, and fears, and longings rest
Where falls the folded veil, or gleams
   The golden necklace on her breast!

What mockery of painted glow
   May shade the secret soul within;
What griefs from passion's overflow,
   What shame that follows after sin!

Yet calm as heaven's serenest deeps
   Are those pure eyes, those glances pure;
And queenly is the state she keeps,
   In beauty's lofty trust secure.

And who has strayed, by happy chance,
   Through all those grand and pictured halls,
Nor felt the magic of her glance,
   As when a voice of music calls?

Not soon shall I forget the day,
   Sweet day, in spring's unclouded time,
While on the glowing canvas lay
   The light of that delicious clime;

I marked the matchless colors wreathed
   On the fair brow, the peerless cheek;
The lips, I fancied, almost breathed
   The blessings that they could not speak.

WILLIAM ALLEN BUTLER 1825–1902

Fair were the eyes with mine that bent
    Upon the picture their mild gaze,
And dear the voice that gave consent
    To all the utterance of my praise.

O fit companionship of thought;
    O happy memories shrined apart;
The rapture that the painter wrought,
    The kindred rapture of the heart!

Nothing to Wear

Miss Flora M'Flimsey, of Madison Square,
    Has made three separate journeys to Paris,
And her father assures me, each time she was there,
    That she and her friend Mrs. Harris
(Not the lady whose name is so famous in history,
But plain Mrs. H., without romance or mystery)
Spent six consecutive weeks, without stopping,
In one continuous round of shopping—
Shopping alone, and shopping together,
At all hours of the day, and in all sorts of weather,
For all manner of things that a woman can put
On the crown of her head, or the sole of her foot,
Or wrap round her shoulders, or fit round her waist,
Or that can be sewed on, or pinned on, or laced,
Or tied on with a string, or stitched on with a bow,
In front or behind, above or below;

WILLIAM ALLEN BUTLER 1825–1902

For bonnets, mantillas, capes, collars, and shawls;
Dresses for breakfasts, and dinners, and balls;
Dresses to sit in, and stand in, and walk in;
Dresses to dance in, and flirt in, and talk in;
Dresses in which to do nothing at all;
Dresses for Winter, Spring, Summer, and Fall—
All of them different in color and shape,
Silk, muslin, and lace, velvet, satin, and crape,
Brocade and broadcloth, and other material,
Quite as expensive and much more ethereal;
In short, for all things that could ever be thought of,
Or milliner, *modiste*, or tradesman be bought of,
    From ten-thousand-franc robes to twenty-sous frills;
In all quarters of Paris, and to every store,
While M'Flimsey in vain stormed, scolded, and swore,
    They footed the streets, and he footed the bills!

The last trip, their goods shipped by the steamer *Arägo*
Formed, M'Flimsey declares, the bulk of her cargo,
Not to mention a quantity kept from the rest,
Sufficient to fill the largest sized chest,
Which did not appear on the ship's manifest,
But for which the ladies themselves manifested
Such particular interest, that they invested
Their own proper persons in layers and rows
Of muslins, embroideries, worked under-clothes,
Gloves, handkerchiefs, scarfs, and such trifles as those;
Then, wrapped in great shawls, like Circassian beauties,
Gave *good-bye* to the ship, and *go by* to the duties.
Her relations at home all marvelled, no doubt,

WILLIAM ALLEN BUTLER 1825–1902

Miss Flora had grown so enormously stout
   For an actual belle and a possible bride;
But the miracle ceased when she turned inside out,
   And the truth came to light, and the dry-goods beside,
Which, in spite of Collector and Custom-House sentry,
Had entered the port without any entry.

And yet, though scarce three months have passed since
       the day
This merchandise went, on twelve carts, up Broadway,
This same Miss M'Flimsey, of Madison Square,
The last time we met was in utter despair,
Because she had nothing whatever to wear!

NOTHING TO WEAR! Now, as this is a true ditty,
   I do not assert—this, you know, is between us—
That she's in a state of absolute nudity,
   Like Powers' Greek Slave or the Medici Venus;
But I do mean to say, I have heard her declare,
   When at the same moment she had on a dress
   Which cost five hundred dollars, and not a cent less,
   And jewelry worth ten times more, I should guess,
That she had not a thing in the wide world to wear!

I should mention just here, that out of Miss Flora's
Two hundred and fifty or sixty adorers,
I had just been selected as he who should throw all
The rest in the shade, by the gracious bestowal
On myself, after twenty or thirty rejections,
Of those fossil remains which she called her "affections,"

WILLIAM ALLEN BUTLER 1825–1902

And that rather decayed, but well-known work of art,
Which Miss Flora persisted in styling her "heart."
So we were engaged. Our troth had been plighted,
   Not by moonbeam or starbeam, by fountain or grove,
But in a front parlor, most brilliantly lighted,
   Beneath the gas-fixtures, we whispered our love.
Without any romance, or raptures, or sighs,
Without any tears in Miss Flora's blue eyes,
Or blushes, or transports, or such silly actions,
It was one of the quietest business transactions,
With a very small sprinkling of sentiment, if any,
And a very large diamond imported by Tiffany.
On her virginal lips while I printed a kiss,
She exclaimed, as a sort of parenthesis,
And by way of putting me quite at my ease,
"You know I'm to polka as much as I please,
And flirt when I like—now, stop, don't you speak—
And you must not come here more than twice in the week,
Or talk to me either at party or ball,
But always be ready to come when I call;
So don't prose to me about duty and stuff,
If we don't break this off, there will be time enough
For that sort of thing; but the bargain must be
That, as long as I choose, I am perfectly free—
For this is a kind of engagement, you see,
Which is binding on you, but not binding on me."

Well, having thus wooed Miss M'Flimsey and gained her,
With the silks, crinolines, and hoops that contained her,
I had, as I thought, a contingent remainder

WILLIAM ALLEN BUTLER 1825–1902

At least in the property, and the best right
To appear as its escort by day and by night;
And it being the week of the Stuckup's grand ball—
   Their cards had been out for a fortnight or so,
   And set all the Avenue on the tiptoe—
I considered it only my duty to call,
   And see if Miss Flora intended to go.
I found her—as ladies are apt to be found,
When the time intervening between the first sound
Of the bell and the visitor's entry is shorter
Than usual—I found; I won't say I caught her—
Intent on the pier-glass, undoubtedly meaning
To see if perhaps it did n't need cleaning.
She turned as I entered—"Why, Harry, you sinner,
I thought that you went to the Flashers' to dinner!"
"So I did," I replied, "but the dinner is swallowed,
   And digested, I trust, for 't is now nine and more,
So, being relieved from that duty, I followed
   Inclination, which led me, you see, to your door;
And now will your ladyship so condescend
As just to inform me if you intend
Your beauty, and graces, and presence to lend
(All of which, when I own, I hope no one will borrow)
To the Stuckup's, whose party, you know, is to-morrow?"
The fair Flora looked up, with a pitiful air,
And answered quite promptly, "Why, Harry, *mon cher,*
I should like above all things to go with you there,
But really and truly—I 've nothing to wear."
"Nothing to wear! go just as you are;

WILLIAM ALLEN BUTLER 1825–1902

Wear the dress you have on, and you 'll be by far,
I engage, the most bright and particular star
  On the Stuckup horizon—" I stopped, for her eye,
Notwithstanding this delicate onset of flattery,
Opened on me at once a terrible battery
  Of scorn and amazement. She made no reply,
But gave a slight turn to the end of her nose—
  That pure Grecian feature—as much as to say,
"How absurd that any sane man should suppose
That a lady would go to a ball in the clothes,
  No matter how fine, that she wears every day!"
So I ventured again: "Wear your crimson brocade"—
(Second turn up of nose)—"That's too dark by a shade."
"Your blue silk"—"That's too heavy." "Your pink"—
        "That's too light."
"Wear tulle over satin"—"I can't endure white."
"Your rose-colored, then, the best of the batch"—
"I have n't a thread of point lace to match."
"Your brown *moire antique*"—"Yes, and look like a
        Quaker."
"The pearl-colored"—"I would, but that plaguy dress-
        maker
Has had it a week." "Then that exquisite lilac,
In which you would melt the heart of a Shylock"—
(Here the nose took again the same elevation)—
"I would n't wear that for the whole of creation."
"Why not? It 's my fancy, there 's nothing could strike it
    As more *comme il faut*"—"Yes, but, dear me, that lean
Sophronia Stuckup has got one just like it,

WILLIAM ALLEN BUTLER 1825–1902

  And I won't appear dressed like a chit of sixteen."
"Then that splendid purple, that sweet Mazarine;
That superb *point d'aiguille,* that imperial green,
That zephyr-like tarletan, that rich *grenadine*"—
"Not one of all which is fit to be seen,"
Said the lady, becoming excited and flushed.
"Then wear," I exclaimed, in a tone which quite crushed
  Opposition, "that gorgeous *toilette* which you sported
In Paris last spring, at the grand presentation,
When you quite turned the head of the head of the nation,
  And by all the grand court were so very much courted."
  The end of the nose was portentously tipped up,
And both the bright eyes shot forth indignation,
As she burst upon me with the fierce exclamation,
"I have worn it three times, at the least calculation,
  And that and most of my dresses are ripped up!"
Here I *ripped out* something, perhaps rather rash,
  Quite innocent, though; but, to use an expression
More striking than classic, it "settled my hash,"
  And proved very soon the last act of our session.
"Fiddlesticks, is it, sir? I wonder the ceiling
Does n't fall down and crush you—you men have no
    feeling;
You selfish, unnatural, illiberal creatures,
Who set yourselves up as patterns and preachers,
Your silly pretence—why, what a mere guess it is!
Pray, what do you know of a woman's necessities?
I have told you and shown you I 've nothing to wear,
And it 's perfectly plain you not only don't care,

WILLIAM ALLEN BUTLER 1825–1902

But you do not believe me"—(here the nose went still
    higher)—
"I suppose, if you dared, you would call me a liar.
Our engagement is ended, sir—yes, on the spot;
You're a brute, and a monster, and—I don't know what."
I mildly suggested the words Hottentot,
Pickpocket, and cannibal, Tartar, and thief,
As gentle expletives which might give relief;
But this only proved as a spark to the powder,
And the storm I had raised came faster and louder;
It blew and it rained, thundered, lightened, and hailed
Interjections, verbs, pronouns, till language quite failed
To express the abusive, and then its arrears
Were brought up all at once by a torrent of tears,
And my last faint, despairing attempt at an obs-
Ervation was lost in a tempest of sobs.

Well, I felt for the lady, and felt for my hat, too,
Improvised on the crown of the latter a tattoo,
In lieu of expressing the feelings which lay
Quite too deep for words, as Wordsworth would say;
Then, without going through the form of a bow,
Found myself in the entry—I hardly knew how,
On door-step and sidewalk, past lamp-post and square,
At home and up-stairs, in my own easy-chair;
  Poked my feet into slippers, my fire into blaze,
And said to myself, as I lit my cigar,
"Supposing a man had the wealth of the Czar
  Of the Russias to boot, for the rest of his days,

WILLIAM ALLEN BUTLER 1825–1902

On the whole, do you think he would have much to spare,
If he married a woman with nothing to wear?"

Since that night, taking pains that it should not be bruited
Abroad in society, I 've instituted
A course of inquiry, extensive and thorough,
On this vital subject, and find, to my horror,
That the fair Flora's case is by no means surprising,
 But that there exists the greatest distress
In our female community, solely arising
 From this unsupplied destitution of dress,
Whose unfortunate victims are filling the air
With the pitiful wail of "Nothing to wear."
Researches in some of the "Upper Ten" districts
Reveal the most painful and startling statistics,
Of which let me mention only a few:
In one single house, on the Fifth Avenue,
Three young ladies were found, all below twenty-two,
Who have been three whole weeks without anything new
In the way of flounced silks, and thus left in the lurch
Are unable to go to ball, concert, or church.
In another large mansion, near the same place,
Was found a deplorable, heart-rending case
Of entire destitution of Brussels point-lace.
In a neighboring block there was found, in three calls,
Total want, long continued, of camel's-hair shawls;
And a suffering family, whose case exhibits
The most pressing need of real ermine tippets;
One deserving young lady almost unable

WILLIAM ALLEN BUTLER 1825–1902

To survive for the want of a new Russian sable;
Still another, whose tortures have been most terrific
Ever since the sad loss of the steamer *Pacific,*
In which were engulfed, not friend or relation
(For whose fate she perhaps might have found consola-
    tion,
Or borne it, at least, with serene resignation),
But the choicest assortment of French sleeves and collars
Ever sent out from Paris, worth thousands of dollars,
And all as to style most *recherché* and rare,
The want of which leaves her with nothing to wear,
And renders her life so drear and dyspeptic
That she's quite a recluse, and almost a sceptic,
For she touchingly says that this sort of grief
Cannot find in Religion the slightest relief,
And Philosophy has not a maxim to spare
For victims of such overwhelming despair.
But the saddest, by far, of all these sad features
Is the cruelty practised upon the poor creatures
By husbands and fathers, real Bluebeards and Timons,
Who resist the most touching appeals made for diamonds
By their wives and their daughters, and leave them for
    days
Unsupplied with new jewelry, fans, or bouquets,
Even laugh at their miseries whenever they have a
    chance,
And deride their demands as useless extravagance.
One case of a bride was brought to my view,
Too sad for belief, but, alas! 't was too true,

WILLIAM ALLEN BUTLER 1825–1902

Whose husband refused, as savage as Charon,
To permit her to take more than ten trunks to Sharon.
The consequence was, that when she got there,
At the end of three weeks she had nothing to wear,
And when she proposed to finish the season
At Newport, the monster refused, out and out,
For his infamous conduct alleging no reason,
Except that the waters were good for his gout;
Such treatment as this was too shocking, of course,
And proceedings are now going on for divorce.

But why harrow the feelings by lifting the curtain
From these scenes of woe? Enough, it is certain,
Has here been disposed to stir up the pity
Of every benevolent heart in the city,
And spur up Humanity into a canter
To rush and relieve these sad cases instanter.
Won't somebody, moved by this touching description,
Come forward to-morrow and head a subscription?
Won't some kind philanthropist, seeing that aid is
So needed at once by these indigent ladies,
Take charge of the matter? Or won't Peter Cooper
The corner-stone lay of some new splendid super-
Structure, like that which to-day links his name
In the Union unending of Honor and Fame,
And found a new charity just for the care
Of these unhappy women with nothing to wear,
Which, in view of the cash which would daily be claimed,
The *Laying-out* Hospital well might be named?
Won't Stewart, or some of our dry-goods importers,

WILLIAM ALLEN BUTLER 1825–1902

Take a contract for clothing our wives and our daughters?
Or, to furnish the cash we supply these distresses,
And life's pathway strew with shawls, collars, and
    dresses,
For poor womankind, won't some venturesome lover
A new California somewhere discover?

O ladies, dear ladies, the next sunny day
Please trundle your hoops just out of Broadway,
From its whirl and its bustle, its fashion and pride,
And the temples of Trade which tower on each side,
To the alleys and lanes, where Misfortune and Guilt
Their children have gathered, their city have built;
Where Hunger and Vice, like twin beasts of prey,
  Have hunted their victims to gloom and despair;
Raise the rich, dainty dress, and the fine broidered skirt,
Pick your delicate way through the dampness and dirt,
  Grope through the dark dens, climb the rickety stair
To the garret, where wretches, the young and the old,
Half starved and half naked, lie crouched from the cold;
See those skeleton limbs, those frost-bitten feet,
All bleeding and bruised by the stones of the street;
Hear the sharp cry of childhood, the deep groans that
    swell
  From the poor dying creature who writhes on the floor;
Hear the curses that sound like the echoes of Hell,
  As you sicken and shudder and fly from the door;
Then home to your wardrobes, and say, if you dare—
Spoiled children of fashion—you 've nothing to wear!

WILLIAM ALLEN BUTLER 1825–1902

And O, if perchance there should be a sphere
Where all is made right which so puzzles us here,
Where the glare and the glitter and tinsel of Time
Fade and die in the light of that region sublime,
Where the soul, disenchanted of flesh and of sense,
Unscreened by its trappings and shows and pretence,
Must be clothed for the life and the service above,
With purity, truth, faith, meekness, and love,
O daughters of Earth! foolish virgins, beware!
Lest in that upper realm you have nothing to wear!

JOHN WILLIAMSON PALMER 1825–1896

The Fight at the San Jacinto

"Now for a brisk and cheerful fight!"
  Said Harman, big and droll,
As he coaxed his flint and steel for a light,
  And puffed at his cold clay bowl;
"For we are a skulking lot," says he,
  "Of land-thieves hereabout,
And these bold señors, two to one,
  Have come to smoke us out."

Santa Anna and Castillon,
  Almonte brave and gay,
Portilla red from Goliad,
  And Cos with his smart array.
Dulces and cigaritos,
  And the light guitar, ting-tum!
Sant' Anna courts siesta,
  And Sam Houston taps his drum.

The buck stands still in the timber—
  "Is it patter of nuts that fall?"
The foal of the wild mare whinnies—
  Did he hear the Comanche call?
In the brake by the crawling bayou
  The slinking she-wolves howl;
And the mustang's snort in the river sedge
  Has startled the paddling fowl.

JOHN WILLIAMSON PALMER 1825–1896

A soft, low tap, and a muffled tap,
   And a roll not loud nor long—
We would not break Sant' Anna's nap,
   Nor spoil Almonte's song.
Saddles and knives and rifles!
   Lord! but the men were glad
When Deaf Smith muttered "Alamo!"
   And Karnes hissed "Goliad!"

The drummer tucked his sticks in his belt,
   And the fifer gripped his gun.
Oh, for one free, wild, Texan yell,
   As we took the slope in a run!
But never a shout nor a shot we spent,
   Nor an oath nor a prayer, that day,
Till we faced the bravos, eye to eye,
   And then we blazed away.

Then we knew the rapture of Ben Milam,
   And the glory that Travis made,
With Bowie's lunge, and Crockett's shot,
   And Fannin's dancing blade;
And the heart of the fighter, bounding free
   In his joy so hot and mad—
When Millard charged for Alamo,
   Lamar for Goliad.

JOHN WILLIAMSON PALMER 1825–1896

Deaf Smith rode straight, with reeking spur,
   Into the shock and rout:
"I 've hacked and burned the bayou bridge;
   There 's no sneak's back-way out!"
Muzzle or butt for Goliad,
   Pistol and blade and fist!
Oh, for the knife that never glanced,
   And the gun that never missed!

Dulces and cigaritos,
   Song and the mandolin!
That gory swamp is a gruesome grove
   To dance fandangoes in.
We bridged the bog with the sprawling herd
   That fell in that frantic rout;
We slew and slew till the sun set red,
   And the Texan star flashed out.

JOHN WILLIAMSON PALMER 1825–1896

Stonewall Jackson's Way

Come, stack arms, men; pile on the rails;
   Stir up the camp-fire bright!
No growling if the canteen fails:
   We'll make a roaring night.
Here Shenandoah brawls along,
There burly Blue Ridge echoes strong,
To swell the Brigade's rousing song,
   Of Stonewall Jackson's Way.

We see him now—the queer slouched hat,
   Cocked o'er his eye askew;
The shrewd, dry smile; the speech so pat,
   So calm, so blunt, so true.
The "Blue-light Elder" knows 'em well:
Says he, "That's Banks; he's fond of shell.
Lord save his soul! we'll give him ——;" Well,
   That's Stonewall Jackson's Way.

Silence! Ground arms! Kneel all! Caps off!
   Old Marster's going to pray.
Strangle the fool that dares to scoff:
   Attention!—it's his way.
Appealing from his native sod,
In forma pauperis to God,
"Lay bare Thine arm! Stretch forth Thy rod!
   Amen!"—That's Stonewall's Way.

JOHN WILLIAMSON PALMER 1825–1896

He's in the saddle now. Fall in!
   Steady! the whole brigade.
Hill's at the ford, cut off; we'll win
   His way out, ball and blade.
What matter if our shoes are worn?
What matter if our feet are torn?
Quick step! we're with him before morn:
   That's Stonewall Jackson's Way.

The sun's bright lances rout the mists
   Of morning; and—By George!
Here's Longstreet, struggling in the lists,
   Hemmed in an ugly gorge.
Pope and his Dutchmen!—whipped before.
"Bay'nets and grape!" hear Stonewall roar.
Charge, Stuart! Pay off Ashby's score,
   In Stonewall Jackson's Way.

Ah, Maiden! wait and watch and yearn
   For news of Stonewall's band.
Ah, Widow! read, with eyes that burn,
   That ring upon thy hand.
Ah, Wife! sew on, pray on, hope on!
Thy life shall not be all forlorn.
The foe had better ne'er been born,
   That gets in Stonewall's Way.

RICHARD HENRY STODDARD 1825–1903

The Flight of Youth

There are gains for all our losses,
    There are balms for all our pain:
But when youth, the dream, departs,
It takes something from our hearts,
    And it never comes again.

We are stronger, and are better,
    Under manhood's sterner reign:
Still we feel that something sweet
Followed youth, with flying feet,
    And will never come again.

Something beautiful is vanished,
    And we sigh for it in vain:
We behold it everywhere,
On the earth, and in the air,
    But it never comes again.

RICHARD HENRY STODDARD 1825–1903

Without and Within

I.

The night is dark, and the winter winds
Go stabbing about with their icy spears;
The sharp hail rattles against the panes,
          And melts on my cheek like tears.

'T is a terrible night to be out of doors,
   But some of us must be, early and late;
We need n't ask who, for don't we know
          It has all been settled by Fate?

Not woman, but man. Give woman her flowers,
   Her dresses, her jewels, or what she demands:
The work of the world must be done by man,
          Or why has he brawny hands?

As I feel my way in the dark and cold,
   I think of the chambers warm and bright,
The nests where these delicate birds of ours
          Are folding their wings to-night.

Through the luminous windows, above and below,
   I catch a glimpse of the life they lead:
Some sew, some sing, others dress for the ball,
          While others, fair students, read.

RICHARD HENRY STODDARD 1825–1903

There's the little lady who bears my name,
   She sits at my table now, pouring her tea;
Does she think of me as I hurry home,
         Hungry and wet? Not she.

She helps herself to the sugar and cream
   In a thoughtless, dreamy, nonchalant way;
Her hands are white as the virgin rose
         That she wore on her wedding day.

My clumsy fingers are stained with ink,
   The badge of the Ledger, the mark of Trade;
But the money I give her is clean enough,
         In spite of the way it is made.

I wear out my life in the counting-room
   Over day-book and cash-book, Bought and Sold;
My brain is dizzy with anxious thought,
         My skin is as sallow as gold.

How does she keep the roses of youth
   Still fresh in her cheek? My roses are flown.
It lies in a nutshell—why do I ask?
         A woman's life is her own.

She gives me a kiss when we part for the day,
   Then goes to her music, blithe as a bird;
She reads it at sight, and the language, too,
         Though I know never a word.

RICHARD HENRY STODDARD 1825–1903

She sews a little, makes collars and sleeves,
   Or embroiders me slippers (always too small,)
Nets silken purses (for me to fill,)
        Often does nothing at all

But dream in her chamber, holding a flower,
   Or reading my letters—she'd better read me.
Even now, while I am freezing with cold,
        She is cosily sipping her tea.

If I ever reach home I shall laugh aloud
   At the sight of a roaring fire once more:
She must wait, I think, till I thaw myself,
        For the nightly kiss at the door.

I'll have with my dinner a bottle of port,
   To warm up my blood and soothe my mind;
Then a little music, for even I
        Like music—when I have dined.

I'll smoke a pipe in the easy-chair,
   And feel her behind patting my head;
Or drawing the little one on my knee,
        Chat till the hour for bed.

II

Will he never come? I have watched for him
   Till the misty panes are roughened with sleet;
I can see no more: shall I never hear
        The welcome sound of his feet?

RICHARD HENRY STODDARD 1825–1903

I think of him in the lonesome night,
   Tramping along with a weary tread,
And wish he were here by the cheery fire,
      Or I were there in his stead.

I sit by the grate, and hark for his step,
   And stare in the fire with a troubled mind;
The glow of the coals is bright in my face,
      But my shadow is dark behind.

I think of woman, and think of man,
   The tie that binds and the wrongs that part,
And long to utter in burning words
      What I feel to-night in my heart.

No weak complaint of the man I love,
   No praise of myself, or my sisterhood;
But—something that women understand—
      By men never understood.

Their natures jar in a thousand things;
   Little matter, alas, who is right or wrong,
She goes to the wall. "She is weak," they say—
      It is that which makes them strong.

Wherein am I weaker than Arthur, pray?
   He has, as he should, a sturdier frame,
And he labors early and late for me,
      But I—I could do the same.

RICHARD HENRY STODDARD 1825–1903

My hands are willing, my brain is clear,
   The world is wide, and the workers few;
But the work of the world belongs to man,
         There is nothing for woman to do!

Yes, she has the holy duties of home,
   A husband to love, and children to bear,
The softer virtues, the social arts,—
         In short, a life without care!

So our masters say. But what do they know
   Of our lives and feelings when they are away?
Our household duties, our petty tasks,
         The nothings that waste the day?

Nay, what do they care? 'T is enough for them
   That their homes are pleasant; they seek their ease:
One takes a wife to flatter his pride,
         Another to keep his keys.

They say they love us; perhaps they do,
   In a masculine way, as they love their wine:
But the soul of woman needs something more,
         Or it suffers at times like mine.

Not that Arthur is ever unkind
   In word or deed, for he loves me well;
But I fear he thinks me as weak as the rest—
         (And I may be, who can tell?)

RICHARD HENRY STODDARD 1825-1903

I should die if he changed, or loved me less,
   For I live at best but a restless life;
Yet he may, for they say the kindest men
        Grow tired of a sickly wife.

O, love me, Arthur, my lord, my life,
   If not for my love, and my womanly fears,
At least for your child. But I hear his step—
        He must not find me in tears.

A Woman's Poem

You say you love me, and you lay
   Your hand and fortune at my feet:
I thank you, sir, with all my heart,
        For love is sweet.

It is but little to you men,
   To whom the doors of Life stand wide;
But much, how much to woman! She
        Has naught beside.

You make the worlds wherein you move,
   You rule your tastes, or coarse, or fine;
Dine, hunt, or fish, or waste your gold
        At dice and wine.

RICHARD HENRY STODDARD 1825–1903

Our world (alas, you make that, too!)
   Is narrower, shut in four blank walls:
Know you, or care, what light is there?
              What shadow falls?

We read the last new novel out,
   And live in dream-land till it ends:
We write romantic school-girl notes,
              That bore our friends.

We learn to trill Italian songs,
   And thrum for hours the tortured keys:
We think it pleases you, and we
              But live to please.

We feed our birds, we tend our flowers,
   (Poor in-door things of sickly bloom,)
Or play the housewife in our gloves,
              And dust the room.

But some of us have hearts and minds,
   So much the worse for us and you;
For grant we seek a better life,
              What can we do?

We cannot build and sail your ships,
   Or drive your engines; we are weak,
And ignorant of the tricks of Trade.
              To think, and speak,

RICHARD HENRY STODDARD 1825–1903

Or write some earnest, stammering words
   Alone is ours, and that you hate;
So forced within ourselves again
              We sigh and wait.

Ah, who can tell the bitter hours,
   The dreary days, that women spend?
Their thoughts unshared, their lives unknown,
             Without a friend!

Without a friend? And what is he,
   Who, like a shadow, day and night,
Follows the woman he prefers—
             Lives in her sight?

Her lover, he: a gallant man,
   Devoted to her every whim;
He vows to die for her, so she
             Must live for him!

We should be very grateful, sir,
   That, when you 've nothing else to do,
You waste your idle hours on us—
             So kind of you!

Profuse in studied compliments,
   Your manners like your clothes are fine,
Though both at times are somewhat strong
             Of smoke and wine.

RICHARD HENRY STODDARD 1825–1903

What can we hope to know of you?
   Or you of us? We act our parts:
We love in jest: it is the play
          Of hands, not hearts!

You grant my bitter words are true
   Of others, not of you and me;
Your love is steady as a star:
          But we shall see.

You say you love me: have you thought
   How much those little words contain?
Alas, a world of happiness,
          And worlds of pain!

You know, or should, your nature now,
   Its needs and passions. Can I be
What you desire me? Do you find
          Your all in me?

You do. But have you thought that I
   May have my ways and fancies, too?
You love me well; but have you thought
          If I love you?

But think again. You know me not:
   I, too, may be a butterfly,
A costly parlor doll on show
          For you to buy.

RICHARD HENRY STODDARD 1825–1903

You trust me wholly? One word more.
   You see me young: they call me fair:
I think I have a pleasant face,
           And pretty hair.

But by and by my face will fade,
   It must with time, it may with care:
What say you to a wrinkled wife,
           With thin, gray hair?

You care not, you: in youth, or age,
   Your heart is mine, while life endures.
Is it so? Then, Arthur, here's my hand,
           My heart is yours.

LUCY LARCOM 1826–1893

Hannah Binding Shoes

   Poor lone Hannah,
Sitting at the window, binding shoes:
   Faded, wrinkled,
Sitting, stitching, in a mournful muse.
  Bright-eyed beauty once was she,
  When the bloom was on the tree:
   Spring and winter,
Hannah's at the window, binding shoes.

   Not a neighbor,
Passing nod or answer will refuse,
   To her whisper,
"Is there from the fishers any news?"
  Oh, her heart's adrift, with one
  On an endless voyage gone!
   Night and morning,
Hannah's at the window, binding shoes.

   Fair young Hannah,
Ben, the sunburnt fisher, gayly woos:
   Hale and clever,
For a willing heart and hand he sues.
  May-day skies are all aglow,
  And the waves are laughing so!
   For her wedding
Hannah leaves her window and her shoes.

LUCY LARCOM 1826–1893

May is passing:
'Mid the apple boughs a pigeon cooes.
    Hannah shudders,
For the mild southwester mischief brews.
  Round the rocks of Marblehead,
    Outward bound, a schooner sped:
      Silent, lonesome
Hannah's at the window, binding shoes.

'T is November,
Now no tear her wasted cheek bedews.
    From Newfoundland
Not a sail returning will she lose,
  Whispering hoarsely, "Fishermen,
    Have you, have you heard of Ben?"
      Old with watching,
Hannah's at the window, binding shoes.

Twenty winters
Bleach and tear the ragged shore she views.
    Twenty seasons:—
Never one has brought her any news.
  Still her dim eyes silently
    Chase the white sails o'er the sea:
      Hopeless, faithful,
Hannah's at the window, binding shoes.

ROBERT BARRY COFFIN 1826–1888

Ships at Sea

I have ships that went to sea
   More than fifty years ago;
None have yet come home to me,
   But are sailing to and fro.
I have seen them in my sleep,
Plunging through the shoreless deep,
With tattered sails and battered hulls,
While around them screamed the gulls,
     Flying low, flying low.

I have wondered why they stayed
   From me, sailing round the world;
And I've said, "I'm half afraid
   That their sails will ne'er be furled."
Great the treasures that they hold,
Silks, and plumes, and bars of gold;
While the spices which they bear
Fill with fragrance all the air,
     As they sail, as they sail.

Ah! each sailor in the port
   Knows that I have ships at sea,
Of the waves and winds the sport,
   And the sailors pity me.
Oft they come and with me walk,
Cheering me with hopeful talk,
Till I put my fears aside,
And, contented, watch the tide
     Rise and fall, rise and fall.

ROBERT BARRY COFFIN 1826–1888

I have waited on the piers,
   Gazing for them down the bay,
Days and nights for many years,
   Till I turned heart-sick away.
But the pilots, when they land,
Stop and take me by the hand,
Saying, "You will live to see
Your proud vessels come from sea,
     One and all, one and all."

So I never quite despair,
   Nor let hope or courage fail;
And some day, when skies are fair,
   Up the bay my ships will sail.
I shall buy then all I need,—
Prints to look at, books to read,
Horses, wines, and works of art,—
Everything except a heart.
     That is lost, that is lost.

Once when I was pure and young,
   Richer, too, than I am now,
Ere a cloud was o'er me flung,
   Or a wrinkle creased my brow,
There was one whose heart was mine;
But she's something now divine,
And though come my ships from sea,
They can bring no heart to me
     Evermore, evermore.

WILLIAM HAINES LYTLE 1826–1863

Antony and Cleopatra

I am dying, Egypt, dying!
  Ebbs the crimson life-tide fast,
And the dark Plutonian shadows
  Gather on the evening blast;
Let thine arm, O Queen, enfold me,
  Hush thy sobs and bow thine ear,
Listen to the great heart secrets
  Thou, and thou alone, must hear.

Though my scarred and veteran legions
  Bear their eagles high no more,
And my wrecked and scattered galleys
  Strew dark Actium's fatal shore;
Though no glittering guards surround me,
  Prompt to do their master's will,
I must perish like a Roman,
  Die the great Triumvir still.

Let not Cæsar's servile minions
  Mock the lion thus laid low;
'T was no foeman's arm that felled him,
  'T was his own that struck the blow:
His who, pillowed on thy bosom,
  Turned aside from glory's ray—
His who, drunk with thy caresses,
  Madly threw the world away.

WILLIAM HAINES LYTLE 1826–1863

Should the base plebeian rabble
   Dare assail my name at Rome,
Where the noble spouse Octavia
   Weeps within her widowed home,
Seek her; say the gods bear witness,—
   Altars, augurs, circling wings,—
That her blood, with mine commingled,
   Yet shall mount the throne of kings.

And for thee, star-eyed Egyptian—
   Glorious sorceress of the Nile!
Light the path to Stygian horrors,
   With the splendor of thy smile;
Give the Cæsar crowns and arches,
   Let his brow the laurel twine:
I can scorn the senate's triumphs,
   Triumphing in love like thine.

I am dying, Egypt, dying!
   Hark! the insulting foeman's cry;
They are coming—quick, my falchion!
   Let me front them ere I die.
Ah, no more amid the battle
   Shall my heart exulting swell;
Isis and Osiris guard thee—
   Cleopatra—Rome—farewell!

ETHELINDA (ELIOT) BEERS 1827–1879

All Quiet Along the Potomac

"All quiet along the Potomac," they say,
   "Except now and then a stray picket
Is shot, as he walks on his beat to and fro,
   By a rifleman hid in the thicket.
'T is nothing—a private or two now and then
   Will not count in the news of the battle;
Not an officer lost—only one of the men,
   Moaning out, all alone, the death-rattle."

All quiet along the Potomac to-night,
   Where the soldiers lie peacefully dreaming;
Their tents in the rays of the clear autumn moon,
   Or the light of the watch-fire, are gleaming.
A tremulous sigh of the gentle night-wind
   Through the forest leaves softly is creeping;
While stars up above, with their glittering eyes,
   Keep guard, for the army is sleeping.

There's only the sound of the lone sentry's tread,
   As he tramps from the rock to the fountain,
And thinks of the two in the low trundle-bed
   Far away in the cot on the mountain.
His musket falls slack; his face, dark and grim,
   Grows gentle with memories tender,
As he mutters a prayer for the children asleep,
   For their mother; may Heaven defend her!

ETHELINDA (ELIOT) BEERS 1827–1879

The moon seems to shine just as brightly as then,
  That night, when the love yet unspoken
Leaped up to his lips—when low-murmured vows
  Were pledged to be ever unbroken.
Then drawing his sleeve roughly over his eyes,
  He dashes off tears that are welling,
And gathers his gun closer up to its place,
  As if to keep down the heart-swelling.

He passes the fountain, the blasted pine-tree,
  The footstep is lagging and weary;
Yet onward he goes, through the broad belt of light,
  Toward the shade of the forest so dreary.
Hark! was it the night-wind that rustled the leaves?
  Was it moonlight so wondrously flashing?
It looked like a rifle . . . . "Ha! Mary, good-bye!"
  The red life-blood is ebbing and plashing.

All quiet along the Potomac to-night;
  No sound save the rush of the river;
While soft falls the dew on the face of the dead—
  The picket's off duty forever!

ROSE (TERRY) COOKE 1827–1892

The Two Villages

Over the river, on the hill,
Lieth a village white and still;
All around it the forest-trees
Shiver and whisper in the breeze;
Over it sailing shadows go
Of soaring hawk and screaming crow,
And mountain grasses, low and sweet,
Grow in the middle of every street.

Over the river, under the hill,
Another village lieth still;
There I see in the cloudy night
Twinkling stars of household light,
Fires that gleam from the smithy's door,
Mists that curl on the river-shore;
And in the roads no grasses grow,
For the wheels that hasten to and fro.

In that village on the hill
Never is sound of smithy or mill;
The houses are thatched with grass and flowers;
Never a clock to toll the hours;
The marble doors are always shut,
You cannot enter in hall or hut;
All the villagers lie asleep;
Never a grain to sow or reap;
Never in dreams to moan or sigh;
Silent and idle and low they lie.

ROSE (TERRY) COOKE 1827–1892

In that village under the hill,
When the night is starry and still,
Many a weary soul in prayer
Looks to the other village there,
And weeping and sighing, longs to go
Up to that home from this below;
Longs to sleep in the forest wild,
Whither have vanished wife and child,
And heareth, praying, this answer fall:
"Patience! that village shall hold ye all!"

GUY HUMPHREYS McMASTER 1829–1887

Carmen Bellicosum

In their ragged regimentals,
Stood the old Continentals,
    Yielding not,
While the grenadiers were lunging,
And like hail fell the plunging
    Cannon-shot;
    When the files
    Of the isles,
From the smoky night-encampment, bore the banner of the rampant
    Unicorn;
And grummer, grummer, grummer, rolled the roll of the drummer
    Through the morn!

Then with eyes to the front all,
And with guns horizontal,
    Stood our sires;
While the balls whistled deadly,
And in streams flashing redly
    Blazed the fires:
    As the roar
    On the shore
Swept the strong battle-breakers o'er the green-sodded acres
    Of the plain;
And louder, louder, louder, cracked the black gunpowder,
    Cracking amain!

GUY HUMPHREYS McMASTER 1829–1887

    Now like smiths at their forges
    Worked the red St. George's
        Cannoneers,
    And the villainous saltpetre
    Rang a fierce, discordant metre
        Round our ears:
        As the swift
        Storm-drift,
With hot sweeping anger, came the horse-guards' clangor
        On our flanks.
Then higher, higher, higher, burned the old-fashioned fire
        Through the ranks!

    Then the bare-headed Colonel
    Galloped through the white infernal
        Powder-cloud;
    And his broadsword was swinging,
    And his brazen throat was ringing
        Trumpet-loud;
        Then the blue
        Bullets flew,
And the trooper-jackets redden at the touch of the leaden
        Rifle-breath;
And rounder, rounder, rounder, roared the iron six-
    pounder,
        Hurling death!

CHARLES GRAHAM HALPINE 1829–1868

The Thousand and Thirty-Seven

Three years ago, to-day,
   We raised our hands to Heaven,
And, on the rolls of muster,
   Our names were thirty-seven;
There were just a thousand bayonets,
   And the swords were thirty-seven,
As we took our oath of service
   With our right hands raised to Heaven.

Oh, 't was a gallant day,
   In memory still adored.
That day of our sun-bright nuptials
   With the musket and the sword!
Shrill rang the fifes, the bugles blared,
   And beneath a cloudless heaven
Far flashed a thousand bayonets,
   And the swords were thirty-seven.

Of the thousand stalwart bayonets
   Two hundred march to-day;
Hundreds lie in Virginia swamps,
   And hundreds in Maryland clay;
While other hundreds—less happy—drag
   Their mangled limbs around,
And envy the deep, calm, blessed sleep
   Of the battle-field's holy ground.

CHARLES GRAHAM HALPINE 1829–1868

For the swords—one night a week ago,
   The remnant, just eleven—
Gathered around a banqueting-board
   With seats for thirty-seven.
There were two came in on crutches,
   And two had each but a hand,
To pour the wine and raise the cup
   As we toasted "Our Flag and Land!"

And the room seemed filled with whispers
   As we looked at the vacant seats,
And with choking throats we pushed aside
   The rich but untasted meats;
Then in silence we brimmed our glasses
   As we stood up—just eleven—
And bowed as we drank to the Loved and the Dead
   Who had made us thirty-seven!

HENRY TIMROD 1829–1867

Charleston

Calm as that second summer which precedes
    The first fall of the snow,
In the broad sunlight of heroic deeds,
    The City bides the foe.

As yet, behind their ramparts stern and proud,
    Her bolted thunders sleep,
Dark Sumter, like a battlemented cloud,
    Looms o'er the solemn deep.

No Calpe frowns from lofty cliff or scar
    To guard the holy strand;
But Moultrie holds in leash her dogs of war
    Above the level sand.

And down the dunes a thousand guns lie couched,
    Unseen, beside the flood—
Like tigers in some Orient jungle crouched
    That wait and watch for blood.

Meanwhile, through streets still echoing with trade,
    Walk grave and thoughtful men,
Whose hands may one day wield the patriot's blade
    As lightly as the pen.

And maidens, with such eyes as would grow dim
    Over a bleeding hound,
Seem each one to have caught the strength of him
    Whose sword she sadly bound.

HENRY TIMROD 1829–1867

Thus girt without and garrisoned at home,
    Day patient following day,
Old Charleston looks from roof and spire and dome,
    Across her tranquil bay.

Ships, through a hundred foes, from Saxon lands
    And spicy Indian ports,
Bring Saxon steel and iron to her hands,
    And Summer to her courts.

But still, along yon dim Atlantic line,
    The only hostile smoke
Creeps like a harmless mist above the brine,
    From some frail, floating oak.

Shall the Spring dawn, and she still clad in smiles,
    And with an unscathed brow,
Rest in the strong arms of her palm-crowned isles,
    As fair and free as now?

We know not; in the temple of the Fates
    God has inscribed her doom;
And, all untroubled in her faith, she waits
    The triumph or the tomb.

April, 1863.

HENRY TIMROD 1829–1867

Ode

[Sung on the occasion of decorating the graves of the Confederate dead at Magnolia Cemetery, Charleston, S. C., 1867.]

Sleep sweetly in your humble graves,
   Sleep, martyrs of a fallen cause;
Though yet no marble column craves
   The pilgrim here to pause.

In seeds of laurel in the earth
   The blossom of your fame is blown,
And somewhere, waiting for its birth,
   The shaft is in the stone!

Meanwhile, behalf the tardy years
   Which keep in trust your storied tombs,
Behold! your sisters bring their tears,
   And these memorial blooms.

Small tributes! but your shades will smile
   More proudly on these wreaths to-day,
Than when some cannon-moulded pile
   Shall overlook this bay.

Stoop, angels, hither from the skies!
   There is no holier spot of ground
Than where defeated valor lies,
   By mourning beauty crowned!

ELBRIDGE JEFFERSON CUTLER 1831–1870

The Volunteer

"At dawn," he said, "I bid them all farewell,
   To go where bugles call and rifles gleam."
And with the restless thought asleep he fell,
    And glided into dream.

A great hot plain from sea to mountain spread,—
   Through it a level river slowly drawn:
He moved with a vast crowd, and at its head
    Streamed banners like the dawn.

There came a blinding flash, a deafening roar,
   And dissonant cries of triumph and dismay;
Blood trickled down the river's reedy shore,
    And with the dead he lay.

The morn broke in upon his solemn dream,
   And still, with steady pulse and deepening eye,
"Where bugles call," he said, "and rifles gleam,
    I follow, though I die!"

ELIZABETH (AKERS) ALLEN 1832–1911

Rock Me to Sleep

Backward, turn backward, O Time, in your flight,
Make me a child again just for to-night!
Mother, come back from the echoless shore,
Take me again to your heart as of yore;
Kiss from my forehead the furrows of care,
Smooth the few silver threads out of my hair;
Over my slumbers your loving watch keep;—
Rock me to sleep, mother,—rock me to sleep!

Backward, flow backward, O tide of the years!
I am so weary of toil and of tears,—
Toil without recompense, tears all in vain,—
Take them, and give me my childhood again!
I have grown weary of dust and decay,—
Weary of flinging my soul-wealth away;
Weary of sowing for others to reap;—
Rock me to sleep, mother,—rock me to sleep!

Tired of the hollow, the base, the untrue,
Mother, O mother, my heart calls for you!
Many a summer the grass has grown green,
Blossomed and faded, our faces between:
Yet, with strong yearning and passionate pain,
Long I to-night for your presence again.
Come from the silence so long and so deep;—
Rock me to sleep, mother,—rock me to sleep!

ELIZABETH (AKERS) ALLEN 1832–1911

Over my heart, in the days that are flown,
No love like mother-love ever has shone;
No other worship abides and endures,—
Faithful, unselfish, and patient like yours:
None like a mother can charm away pain
From the sick soul and the world-weary brain.
Slumber's soft calms o'er my heavy lids creep;—
Rock me to sleep, mother,—rock me to sleep!

Come, let your brown hair, just lighted with gold,
Fall on your shoulders again as of old;
Let it drop over my forehead to-night,
Shading my faint eyes away from the light;
For with its sunny-edged shadows once more
Haply will throng the sweet visions of yore;
Lovingly, softly, its bright billows sweep;—
Rock me to sleep, mother,—rock me to sleep!

Mother, dear mother, the years have been long
Since I last listened your lullaby song:
Sing, then, and unto my soul it shall seem
Womanhood's years have been only a dream.
Clasped to your heart in a loving embrace,
With your light lashes just sweeping my face,
Never hereafter to wake or to weep;—
Rock me to sleep, mother,—rock me to sleep!

ELIZABETH (AKERS) ALLEN 1832–1911

Last

Friend, whose smile has come to be
Very precious unto me,
   Though I know I drank not first
   Of your love's bright fountain-burst,
Yet I grieve not for the past,
So you only love me last!

Other souls may find their joy
In the blind love of a boy:
   Give me that which years have tried,
   Disciplined and purified,—
Such as, braving sun and blast,
You will bring to me at last!

There are brows more fair than mine,
Eyes of more bewitching shine,
   Other hearts more fit, in truth,
   For the passion of your youth;
But, their transient empire past,
You will surely love me last!

Wing away your summer-time,
Find a love in every clime,
   Roam in liberty and light,—
   I shall never stay your flight;
For I know, when all is past
You will come to me at last!

ELIZABETH (AKERS) ALLEN 1832–1911

Change and flutter as you will,
I shall smile securely still;
   Patiently I trust and wait
    Though you tarry long and late;
Prize your spring till it be past,
Only, only love me last!

Left Behind

It was the autumn of the year!
The strawberry-leaves were red and sere,
October's airs were fresh and chill,
When, pausing on the windy hill,
The hill that overlooks the sea,
You talked confidingly to me,—
Me, whom your keen artistic sight
Has not yet learned to read aright,
Since I have veiled my heart from you,
And loved you better than you knew.

You told me of your toilsome past,
The tardy honors won at last,
The trials borne, the conquests gained,
The longed-for boon of Fame attained:
I knew that every victory
But lifted you away from me,—

ELIZABETH (AKERS) ALLEN 1832–1911

That every step of high emprise
But left me lowlier in your eyes:
I watched the distance as it grew,
And loved you better than you knew.

You did not see the bitter trace
Of anguish sweep across my face;
You did not hear my proud heart beat
Heavy and slow beneath your feet:
You thought of triumphs still unwon,
Of glorious deeds as yet undone;
And I, the while you talked to me,
I watched the gulls float lonesomely
Till lost amid the hungry blue,
And loved you better than you knew.

You walk the sunny side of Fate;
The wise world smiles, and calls you great;
The golden fruitage of success
Drops at your feet in plenteousness;
And you have blessings manifold,—
Renown and power, and friends and gold.
They build a wall between us twain
Which may not be thrown down again.
Alas! for I, the long years through,
Have loved you better than you knew.

ELIZABETH (AKERS) ALLEN 1832–1911

Your life's proud aim, your art's high truth,
Have kept the promise of your youth;
And while you won the crown which now
Breaks into bloom upon your brow,
My soul cried strongly out to you
Across the ocean's yearning blue,
While, unremembered and afar,
I watched you, as I watch a star
Through darkness struggling into view,
And loved you better than you knew.

I used to dream, in all these years
Of patient faith and silent tears,
That Love's strong hand would put aside
The barriers of place and pride,—
Would reach the pathless darkness through
And draw me softly up to you.
But that is past; if you should stray
Beside my grave some future day,
Perchance the violets o'er my dust
Will half betray their buried trust,
And say, their blue eyes full of dew,
"She loved you better than you knew."

GEORGE PRATT 1832–1875

A Pen of Steel

Give me a pen of steel!
   Away with the gray goose-quill!
I will grave the thoughts I feel
   With a fiery heart and will:
I will grave with the stubborn pen
   On the tablets of the heart,
Words never to fade again
   And thoughts that shall ne'er depart.

Give me a pen of steel!
   Hardened and bright and keen,—
To run like the chariot wheel,
   When the battle-flame is seen:—
And give me the warrior's heart,
   To struggle thro' night and day,
And to write with this thing of art
   Words clear as the lightning's play.

Give me a pen of steel!
   The softer age is done,
And the thoughts that lovers feel
   Have long been sought and won:—
No more of the gray goose-quill—
   No more of the lover's lay—
I have done with the minstrel's skill,
   And I change my path to-day.

GEORGE PRATT 1832–1875

Give me a pen of steel!
   I will tell to after-times
How nerve and iron will
   Are poured to the world in rhymes:—
How the soul is changed to power,
   And the heart is changed to flame,
In the space of a passing hour
   By poverty and shame!

Give me a pen of steel!—
   But even this shall rust,
The touch of time shall feel,
   And crumble away to dust:—
So perishes my heart,
   Corroding day by day—
And laid like the pen apart,
   Worn out and cast away!

EDMUND CLARENCE STEDMAN 1833–1906

Pan in Wall Street

A. D. 1867

Just where the Treasury's marble front
   Looks over Wall Street's mingled nations;
Where Jews and Gentiles most are wont
   To throng for trade and last quotations;
Where, hour by hour, the rates of gold
   Outrival, in the ears of people,
The quarter-chimes, serenely tolled
   From Trinity's undaunted steeple,—

Even there I heard a strange, wild strain
   Sound high above the modern clamor,
Above the cries of greed and gain,
   The curbstone war, the auction's hammer;
And swift, on Music's misty ways,
   It led, from all this strife for millions,
To ancient, sweet-do-nothing days
   Among the kirtle-robed Sicilians.

And as it stilled the multitude,
   And yet more joyous rose, and shriller,
I saw the minstrel, where he stood
   At ease against a Doric pillar:
One hand a droning organ played,
   The other held a Pan's-pipe (fashioned
Like those of old) to lips that made
   The reeds give out that strain impassioned.

EDMUND CLARENCE STEDMAN 1833–1906

'T was Pan himself had wandered here
    A-strolling through this sordid city,
And piping to the civic ear
    The prelude of some pastoral ditty!
The demigod had crossed the seas,—
    From haunts of shepherd, nymph, and satyr,
And Syracusan times,—to these
    Far shores and twenty centuries later.

A ragged cap was on his head;
    But—hidden thus—there was no doubting
That, all with crispy locks o'erspread,
    His gnarlèd horns were somewhere sprouting;
His club-feet, cased in rusty shoes,
    Were crossed, as on some frieze you see them,
And trousers, patched of divers hues,
    Concealed his crooked shanks beneath them.

He filled the quivering reeds with sound,
    And o'er his mouth their changes shifted,
And with his goat's-eyes looked around
    Where'er the passing current drifted;
And soon, as on Trinacrian hills
    The nymphs and herdsmen ran to hear him,
Even now the tradesmen from their tills,
    With clerks and porters, crowded near him.

EDMUND CLARENCE STEDMAN 1833-1906

The bulls and bears together drew
    From Jauncey Court and New Street Alley,
As erst, if pastorals be true,
    Came beasts from every wooded valley;
The random passers stayed to list,—
    A boxer Ægon, rough and merry,
A Broadway Daphnis, on his tryst
    With Nais at the Brooklyn Ferry.

A one-eyed Cyclops halted long
    In tattered cloak of army pattern,
And Galatea joined the throng,—
    A blowsy, apple-vending slattern;
While old Silenus staggered out
    From some new-fangled lunch-house handy,
And bade the piper, with a shout,
    To strike up Yankee Doodle Dandy!

A newsboy and a peanut-girl
    Like little Fauns began to caper:
His hair was all in tangled curl,
    Her tawny legs were bare and taper;
And still the gathering larger grew,
    And gave its pence and crowded nigher,
While aye the shepherd-minstrel blew
    His pipe, and struck the gamut higher.

EDMUND CLARENCE STEDMAN 1833–1906

O heart of Nature, beating still
   With throbs her vernal passion taught her,—
Even here, as on the vine-clad hill,
   Or by the Arethusan water!
New forms may fold the speech, new lands
   Arise within these ocean portals,
But Music waves eternal wands,—
   Enchantress of the souls of mortals!

So thought I,—but among us trod
   A man in blue, with legal baton,
And scoffed the vagrant demigod,
   And pushed him from the step I sat on.
Doubting I mused upon the cry,
   "Great Pan is dead!"—and all the people
Went on their ways:—and clear and high
   The quarter sounded from the steeple.

The Ballad of Lager Bier

In fallow college days, Tom Harland,
   We both have known the ways of Yale,
And talked of many a nigh and far land,
   O'er many a famous tap of ale.
There still they sing their Gaudeamus,
   And see the road to glory clear;
But taps, that in our day were famous,
   Have given place to Lager Bier.

EDMUND CLARENCE STEDMAN 1833–1906

Now, settled in this island-city,
    We let new fashions have their weight;
Though none too lucky—more 's the pity!—
    Can still beguile our humble state
By finding time to come together,
    In every season of the year,
In sunny, wet, or windy weather,
    And clink our mugs of Lager Bier.

On winter evenings, cold and blowing,
    'T is good to order " 'alf and 'alf";
To watch the fire-lit pewter glowing,
    And laugh a hearty English laugh;
Or even a sip of mountain whiskey
    Can raise a hundred phantoms dear
Of days when boyish blood was frisky,
    And no one heard of Lager Bier.

We 've smoked in summer with Oscanyan,
    Cross-legged in that defunct bazaar,
Until above our heads the banyan
    Or palm-tree seemed to spread afar;
And, then and there, have drunk his sherbet,
    Tinct with the roses of Cashmere:
That Orient calm! who would disturb it
    With Norseland calls for Lager Bier?

EDMUND CLARENCE STEDMAN 1833–1906

There's Paris chocolate,—nothing sweeter,
   At midnight, when the dying strain,
Just warbled by La Favorita,
   Still hugs the music-haunted brain;
Yet of all bibulous compoundings,
   Extracts or brewings, mixed or clear,
The best, in substance and surroundings,
   For frequent use, is Lager Bier.

Karl Schaeffer is a stalwart brewer,
   Who has above his vaults a hall,
Where—fresh-tapped, foaming, cool, and pure—
   He serves the nectar out to all.
Tom Harland, have you any money?
   Why, then, we'll leave this hemisphere,
This western land of milk and honey,
   For one that flows with Lager Bier.

Go, flaxen-haired and blue-eyed maiden,
   My German Hebe! hasten through
Yon smoke-cloud, and return thou laden
   With bread and cheese and bier for two.
Limburger suits this bearded fellow;
   His brow is high, his taste severe:
But I'm for Schweitzer, mild and yellow,
   To eat with bread and Lager Bier.

EDMUND CLARENCE STEDMAN 1833–1906

Ah, yes! the Schweitzer hath a savor
   Of marjoram and mountain thyme,
An odoriferous, Alpine flavor;
   You almost hear the cow-bells chime
While eating it, or, dying faintly,
   The *Ranz-des-vaches* entrance the ear,
Until you feel quite Swiss and saintly,
   Above your glass of Lager Bier.

Here come our drink, froth-crowned and sunlit,
   In goblets with high-curving arms,
Drawn from a newly opened runlet,
   As bier must be, to have its charms,
This primal portion each shall swallow
   At one draught, for a pioneer;
And thus a ritual usage follow
   Of all who honor Lager Bier.

Glass after glass in due succession,
   Till, borne through midriff, heart and brain,
He mounts his throne and takes possession,—
   The genial Spirit of the grain!
Then comes the old Berserker madness
   To make each man a priest and seer,
And, with a Scandinavian gladness,
   Drink deeper draughts of Lager Bier!

EDMUND CLARENCE STEDMAN 1833–1906

Go, maiden, fill again our glasses!
   While, with anointed eyes, we scan
The blouse Teutonic lads and lasses,
   The Saxon—Pruss—Bohemian,
The sanded floor, the cross-beamed gables,
   The ancient Flemish paintings queer,
The rusty cup-stains on the tables,
   The terraced kegs of Lager Bier.

And is it Göttingen or Gotha,
   Or Munich's ancient Wagner Brei,
Where each Bavarian drinks his quota,
   And swings a silver tankard high?
Or some ancestral Gast-Haus lofty
   In Nuremburg—of famous cheer
When Hans Sachs lived, and where, so oft, he
   Sang loud the praise of Lager Bier?

For even now some curious glamour
   Has brought about a misty change!
Things look, as in a moonlight dream, or
   Magician's mirror, quaint and strange.
Some weird, phantasmagoric notion
   Impels us backward many a year,
And far across the northern ocean,
   To Fatherlands of Lager Bier.

EDMUND CLARENCE STEDMAN 1833–1906

As odd a throng I see before us
   As ever haunted Brocken's height,
Carousing, with unearthly chorus,
   On any wild Walpurgis-night;
I see the wondrous art-creations!
   In proper guise they all appear,
And, in their due and several stations,
   Unite in drinking Lager Bier.

I see in yonder nook a trio:
   There's Doctor Faust, and, by his side,
Not half so love-distraught as Io,
   Is gentle Margaret, heaven-eyed;
That man in black beyond the waiter—
   I know him by his fiendish leer—
Is Mephistopheles, the traitor!
   And how he swigs his Lager Bier!

Strange if great Goethe should have blundered,
   Who says that Margaret slipt and fell
In Anno Domini Sixteen Hundred,
   Or thereabout; and Faustus,—well,
We won't deplore his resurrection,
   Since Margaret is with him here,
But, under her serene protection,
   May boldly drink our Lager Bier.

EDMUND CLARENCE STEDMAN 1833–1906

That bare-legged gypsy, small and lithy,
    Tanned like an olive by the sun,
Is little Mignon; sing us, prithee,
    Kennst du das Land, my pretty one!
Ah, no! she shakes her southern tresses,
    As half in doubt and more in fear;
Perhaps the elvish creature guesses
    We 've had too much of Lager Bier.

There moves, full-bodiced, ripe, and human,
    With merry smiles to all who come,
Karl Schaeffer's wife—the very woman
    Whom Rubens drew his Venus from!
But what a host of tricksome graces
    Play around our fairy Undine here,
Who pouts at all the bearded faces,
    And, laughing, brings the Lager Bier.

"Sit down, nor chase the vision farther,
    You 're tied to Yankee cities still!"
I hear you, but so much the rather
    Should Fancy travel where she will.
You let the dim ideals scatter;
    One puff, and lo! they disappear;
The comet, next, or some such matter,
    We 'll talk above our Lager Bier.

EDMUND CLARENCE STEDMAN 1833–1906

Now, then, your eyes begin to brighten,
   And marvellous theories to flow;
A philosophic theme you light on,
   And, spurred and booted, off you go!
If e'er—to drive Apollo's phaeton—
   I need an earthly charioteer,
This tall-browed genius I will wait on,
   And prime him first with Lager Bier.

But higher yet, in middle Heaven,
   Your steed seems taking flight, my friend;
You read the secret of the Seven,
   And on through trackless regions wend!
Don't vanish in the Milky Way, for
   This afternoon you're wanted here;
Come back! Come back! and help me pay for
   The bread and cheese and Lager Bier.

Edged Tools

Well, Helen, quite two years have flown
   Since that enchanted, dreamy night,
When you and I were left alone,
   And wondered whether they were right,
Who said that each the other loved;
   And thus debating, yes and no,
And half in earnest, as it proved,
   We bargained to pretend 't was so.

EDMUND CLARENCE STEDMAN 1833–1906

Two sceptic children of the world,
   Each with a heart engraven o'er
With broken love-knots, quaintly curled,
   Of hot flirtations held before;
Yet, somehow, either seemed to find,
   This time, a something more akin
To that young, natural love,—the kind
   Which comes but once, and breaks us in.

What sweetly stolen hours we knew,
   And frolics perilous as gay!
Though lit in sport, Love's taper grew
   More bright and burning day by day.
We knew each heart was only lent
   The other's ancient scars to heal:
The very thought a pathos blent
   With all the mirth we tried to feel.

How bravely, when the time to part
   Came with the wanton season's close,
Though nature with our mutual art
   Had mingled more than either chose,
We smothered Love, upon the verge
   Of folly, in one last embrace,
And buried him without a dirge,
   And turned, and left his resting-place.

EDMUND CLARENCE STEDMAN 1833–1906

Yet often (tell me what it means!)
   His spirit steals upon me here,
Far, far away from all the scenes
   His little lifetime held so dear;
He comes: I hear a mystic strain
   In which some tender memory lies;
I dally with your hair again;
   I catch the gleam of violet eyes.

Ah, Helen! how have matters been
   Since those rude obsequies, with you?
Say, is my partner in the sin
   A sharer of the penance too?
Again the vision's at my side:
   I drop my head upon my breast,
And wonder if he really died,
   And why his spirit will not rest.

The Undiscovered Country

   Could we but know
The land that ends our dark, uncertain travel,
   Where lie those happier hills and meadows low,—
Ah, if beyond the spirit's inmost cavil,
   Aught of that country could we surely know,
      Who would not go?

EDMUND CLARENCE STEDMAN 1833–1906

  Might we but hear
The hovering angels' high imagined chorus,
 Or catch, betimes, with wakeful eyes and clear,
One radiant vista of the realm before us,—
 With one rapt moment given to see and hear,
  Ah, who would fear?

  Were we quite sure
To find the peerless friend who left us lonely,
 Or there, by some celestial stream as pure,
To gaze in eyes that here were lovelit only,—
 This weary mortal coil, were we quite sure,
  Who would endure?

The World Well Lost

That year? Yes, doubtless I remember still,—
 Though why take count of every wind that blows!
'T was plain, men said, that Fortune used me ill
 That year,—the self-same year I met with Rose.

Crops failed; wealth took a flight; house, treasure, land,
 Slipped from my hold—thus plenty comes and goes.
One friend I had, but he too loosed his hand
 (Or was it I?) the year I met with Rose.

EDMUND CLARENCE STEDMAN 1833–1906

There was a war, I think; some rumor, too,
   Of famine, pestilence, fire, deluge, snows;
Things went awry. My rivals, straight in view,
   Throve, spite of all; but I,—I met with Rose.

That year my white-faced Alma pined and died:
   Some trouble vexed her quiet heart,—who knows?
Not I, who scarcely missed her from my side,
   Or aught else gone, the year I met with Rose.

Was there no more? Yes, that year life began:
   All life before a dream, false joys, light woes,—
All after-life compressed within the span
   Of that one year,—the year I met with Rose!

Si Jeunesse Savait!

When the veil from the eyes is lifted
   The seer's head is gray;
When the sailor to shore has drifted
   The sirens are far away.
Why must the clearer vision,
   The wisdom of Life's late hour,
Come, as in Fate's derision,
   When the hand has lost its power?
Is there a rarer being,
   Is there a fairer sphere

EDMUND CLARENCE STEDMAN 1833–1906

Where the strong are not unseeing,
    And the harvests are not sere;
Where, ere the seasons dwindle,
    They yield their due return;
Where the lamps of knowledge kindle
    While the flames of youth still burn?
O, for the young man's chances!
    O, for the old man's will!
Those flee while this advances,
    And the strong years cheat us still.

Provençal Lovers

Aucassin and Nicolette

Within the garden of Beaucaire
He met her by a secret stair,—
The night was centuries ago.
Said Aucassin, "My love, my pet,
These old confessors vex me so!
They threaten all the pains of hell
Unless I give you up, ma belle";—
Said Aucassin to Nicolette.

"Now, who should there in Heaven be
To fill your place, ma très-douce mie?
To reach that spot I little care!
There all the droning priests are met;

EDMUND CLARENCE STEDMAN 1833–1906

All the old cripples, too, are there
That unto shrines and altars cling
To filch the Peter-pence we bring";—
Said Aucassin to Nicolette.

"There are the barefoot monks and friars
With gowns well tattered by the briars,
The saints who lift their eyes and whine:
I like them not—a starveling set!
Who 'd care with folk like these to dine?
The other road 't were just as well
That you and I would take, ma belle!"—
Said Aucassin to Nicolette.

"To purgatory I would go
With pleasant comrades whom we know,
Fair scholars, minstrels, lusty knights
Whose deeds the land will not forget,
The captains of a hundred fights,
The men of valor and degree:
We 'll join that gallant company,"—
Said Aucassin to Nicolette.

"There, too, are jousts and joyance rare,
And beauteous ladies debonair,
The pretty dames, the merry brides,
Who with their wedded lords coquette
And have a friend or two besides,—
And all in gold and trappings gay,
With furs, and crests in vair and gray";—
Said Aucassin to Nicolette.

EDMUND CLARENCE STEDMAN 1833–1906

"Sweet players on the cithern strings,
And they who roam the world like kings,
Are gathered there, so blithe and free!
Pardie! I 'd join them now, my pet,
If you went also, ma douce mie!
The joys of heaven I 'd forego
To have you with me there below,"—
Said Aucassin to Nicolette.

Kearny at Seven Pines

So that soldierly legend is still on its journey,—
    That story of Kearny who knew not to yield!
'T was the day when with Jameson, fierce Berry, and Birney,
    Against twenty thousand he rallied the field.
Where the red volleys poured, where the clamor rose highest,
    Where the dead lay in clumps through the dwarf oak and pine,
Where the aim from the thicket was surest and nighest,—
    No charge like Phil Kearny's along the whole line.

When the battle went ill, and the bravest were solemn,
    Near the dark Seven Pines, where we still held our ground,
He rode down the length of the withering column,
    And his heart at our war-cry leapt up with a bound;

EDMUND CLARENCE STEDMAN 1833–1906

He snuffed, like his charger, the wind of the powder,—
  His sword waved us on and we answered the sign:
Loud our cheer as we rushed, but his laugh rang the louder,
  "There's the devil's own fun, boys, along the whole line!"

How he strode his brown steed! How we saw his blade brighten
  In the one hand still left,—and the reins in his teeth!
He laughed like a boy when the holidays heighten,
  But a soldier's glance shot from his visor beneath.
Up came the reserves to the mellay infernal,
  Asking where to go in,—through the clearing or pine?
"O, anywhere! Forward! 'T is all the same, Colonel:
  You'll find lovely fighting along the whole line!"

O, evil the black shroud of night at Chantilly,
  That hid him from sight of his brave men and tried!
Foul, foul sped the bullet that clipped the white lily,
  The flower of our knighthood, the whole army's pride!
Yet we dream that he still,—in that shadowy region
  Where the dead form their ranks at the wan drummer's sign,—
Rides on, as of old, down the length of his legion,
  And the word still is Forward! along the whole line.

EDMUND CLARENCE STEDMAN 1833–1906

Hypatia

'T is fifteen hundred years, you say,
   Since that fair teacher died
In learnèd Alexandria
   By the stone altar's side:—
The wild monks slew her, as she lay
   At the feet of the Crucified.

Yet in a prairie-town, one night,
   I found her lecture-hall,
Where bench and dais stood aright,
   And statues graced the wall,
And pendent brazen lamps the light
   Of classic days let fall.

A throng that watched the speaker's face
   And on her accents hung,
Was gathered there: the strength, the grace
   Of lands where life is young
Ceased not, I saw, with that blithe race
   From old Pelasgia sprung.

No civic crown the sibyl wore,
   Nor academic tire,
But shining skirts, that trailed the floor
   And made her stature higher;
A written scroll the lecturn bore,
   And flowers bloomed anigh her.

EDMUND CLARENCE STEDMAN 1833–1906

The wealth her honeyed speech had won
   Adorned her in our sight;
The silkworm for her sake had spun
   His cincture, day and night;
With broider-work and Honiton
   Her open sleeves were bright.

But still Hypatia's self I knew,
   And saw, with dreamy wonder,
The form of her whom Cyril slew
   (See Kingsley's novel, yonder)
Some fifteen centuries since, 't is true,
   And half a world asunder.

Her hair was coifed Athenian-wise,
   With one loose tress down-flowing;
Apollo's rapture lit her eyes,
   His utterance bestowing,—
A silver flute's clear harmonies
   On which a god was blowing.

Yet not of Plato's sounding spheres,
   And universal Pan,
She spoke; but searched historic years,
   The sisterhood to scan
Of women,—girt with ills and fears,—
   Slaves to the tyrant, Man.

EDMUND CLARENCE STEDMAN 1833–1906

Their crosiered banner she unfurled,
   And onward pushed her quest
Through golden ages of a world
   By their deliverance blest:—
At all who stay their hands she hurled
   Defiance from her breast.

I saw her burning words infuse
   A warmth through many a heart,
As still, in bright successive views,
   She drew her sex's part;
Discoursing, like the Lesbian Muse,
   On work, and song, and art.

Why vaunt, I thought, the past, or say
   The later is the less?
Our Sappho sang but yesterday,
   Of whom two climes confess
Heaven's flame within her wore away
   Her earthly loveliness.

So let thy wild heart ripple on,
   Brave girl, through vale and city!
Spare, of its listless moments, one
   To this, thy poet's ditty;
Nor long forbear, when all is done,
   Thine own sweet self to pity.

EDMUND CLARENCE STEDMAN 1833–1906

The priestess of the Sestian tower,
   Whose knight the sea swam over,
Among her votaries' gifts no flower
   Of heart's-ease could discover:
She died, but in no evil hour,
   Who, dying, clasped her lover.

The rose-tree has its perfect life
   When the full rose is blown;
Some height of womanhood the wife
   Beyond thy dream has known;
Set not thy head and heart at strife
   To keep thee from thine own.

Hypatia! thine essence rare
   The rarer joy should merit:
Possess thee of the common share
   Which lesser souls inherit:
All gods to thee their garlands bear,—
   Take one from Love and wear it!

JOHN JAMES INGALLS 1833–1900

Opportunity

"Master of human destinies am I!
Fame, love, and fortune on my footsteps wait.
Cities and fields I walk; I penetrate
Deserts and seas remote, and passing by
Hovel and mart and palace—soon or late
I knock unbidden once at every gate!

"If sleeping, wake—if feasting, rise before
I turn away. It is the hour of fate,
And they who follow me reach every state
Mortals desire, and conquer every foe
Save death; but those who doubt or hesitate,
Condemned to failure, penury, and woe,
Seek me in vain and uselessly implore.
I answer not, and I return no more!"

THOMAS BAILEY ALDRICH 1836–1907

Baby Bell

I

Have you not heard the poets tell
How came the dainty Baby Bell
Into this world of ours?
The gates of heaven were left ajar:
With folded hands and dreamy eyes,
Wandering out of Paradise,
She saw this planet, like a star,
Hung in the glistening depths of even—
Its bridges running to and fro,
O'er which the white-winged Angels go,
Bearing the holy Dead to heaven.
She touched a bridge of flowers—those feet,
So light they did not bend the bells
Of the celestial asphodels,
They fell like dew upon the flowers:
Then all the air grew strangely sweet.
And thus came dainty Baby Bell
Into this world of ours.

II

She came and brought delicious May;
The swallows built beneath the eaves;
Like sunlight, in and out the leaves
The robins went, the livelong day;
The lily swung its noiseless bell;
And on the porch the slender vine

THOMAS BAILEY ALDRICH 1836–1907

Held out its cups of fairy wine.
Oh, earth was full of singing-birds
And opening springtide flowers,
When the dainty Baby Bell
Came into this world of ours.

III

O Baby, dainty Baby Bell,
How fair she grew from day to day!
What woman-nature filled her eyes,
What poetry within them lay—
Those deep and tender twilight eyes,
So full of meaning, pure and bright
As if she yet stood in the light
Of those oped gates of Paradise.
And so we loved her more and more:
Ah, never in our hearts before
Was love so lovely born.
We felt we had a link between
This real world and that unseen—
The land beyond the morn;
And for the love of those dear eyes,
For love of her whom God led forth,
(The mother's being ceased on earth
When Baby came from Paradise,)—
For love of Him who smote our lives,
And woke the chords of joy and pain,
We said, *Dear Christ!*—our hearts bowed down
Like violets after rain.

THOMAS BAILEY ALDRICH 1836–1907

IV

And now the orchards, which were white
And pink with blossoms when she came,
Were rich in autumn's mellow prime;
The clustered apples burnt like flame,
The folded chestnut burst its shell,
The grapes hung purpling, range on range:
And time wrought just as rich a change
In little Baby Bell.
Her lissome form more perfect grew,
And in her features we could trace,
In softened curves, her mother's face.
Her angel-nature ripened too:
We thought her lovely when she came,
But she was holy, saintly now . . . .
Around her pale angelic brow
We saw a slender ring of flame.

V

God's hand had taken away the seal
That held the portals of her speech;
And oft she said a few strange words
Whose meaning lay beyond our reach.
She never was a child to us,
We never held her being's key;
We could not teach her holy things
Who was Christ's self in purity.

VI

It came upon us by degrees,
We saw its shadow ere it fell—
The knowledge that our God had sent
His messenger for Baby Bell.
We shuddered with unlanguaged pain,
And all our hopes were changed to fears,
And all our thoughts ran into tears
Like sunshine into rain.
We cried aloud in our belief,
"Oh, smite us gently, gently, God!
Teach us to bend and kiss the rod,
And perfect grow through grief."
Ah! how we loved her, God can tell;
Her heart was folded deep in ours.
Our hearts are broken, Baby Bell!

VII

At last he came, the messenger,
The messenger from unseen lands:
And what did dainty Baby Bell?
She only crossed her little hands,
She only looked more meek and fair!
We parted back her silken hair,
We wove the roses round her brow—
White buds, the summer's drifted snow—
Wrapt her from head to foot in flowers....
And thus went dainty Baby Bell
Out of this world of ours.

THOMAS BAILEY ALDRICH 1836–1907

Song from the Persian.

Ah! sad are they who know not love,
But, far from passion's tears and smiles,
Drift down a moonless sea, beyond
The silvery coasts of fairy isles.

And sadder they whose longing lips
Kiss empty air, and never touch
The dear warm mouth of those they love—
Waiting, wasting, suffering much.

But clear as amber, fine as musk,
Is life to those who, pilgrim-wise,
Move hand in hand from dawn to dusk,
Each morning nearer Paradise.

Ah, not for them shall angels pray!
They stand in everlasting light,
They walk in Allah's smile by day,
And slumber in his heart by night.

THOMAS BAILEY ALDRICH 1836–1907

Palabras Cariñosas

Good-night! I have to say good-night
To such a host of peerless things!
Good-night unto the slender hand
All queenly with its weight of rings;
Good-night to fond, uplifted eyes,
Good-night to chestnut braids of hair,
Good-night unto the perfect mouth,
And all the sweetness nestled there—
   The snowy hand detains me, then
   I'll have to say Good-night again!

But there will come a time, my love,
When, if I read our stars aright,
I shall not linger by this porch
With my farewells. Till then, good-night!
You wish the time were now? And I.
You do not blush to wish it so?
You would have blushed yourself to death
To own so much a year ago—
   What, both these snowy hands! ah, then
   I'll have to say Good-night again!

THOMAS BAILEY ALDRICH 1836–1907

In an Atelier

I pray you, do not turn your head;
And let your hands lie folded, so.
It was a dress like this, wine-red,
That troubled Dante, long ago.
You don't know Dante? Never mind.
He loved a lady wondrous fair—
His model? Something of the kind.
I wonder if she had your hair!

I wonder if she looked so meek,
And was not meek at all (my dear,
I want that side light on your cheek).
He loved her, it is very clear,
And painted her, as I paint you,
But rather better, on the whole
(Depress your chin; yes, that will do):
He was a painter of the soul!

(And painted portraits, too, I think,
In the Inferno—devilish good!
I 'd make some certain critics blink
Had I his method and his mood.)
Her name was (Fanny, let your glance
Rest there, by that majolica tray)—
Was Beatrice; they met by chance—
They met by chance, the usual way.

THOMAS BAILEY ALDRICH 1836–1907

(As you and I met, months ago,
Do you remember? How your feet
Went crinkle-crinkle on the snow
Along the bleak gas-lighted street!
An instant in the drug-store's glare
You stood as in a golden frame,
And then I swore it, then and there,
To hand your sweetness down to fame.)

They met, and loved, and never wed
(All this was long before our time),
And though they died, they are not dead—
Such endless youth gives mortal rhyme!
Still walks the earth, with haughty mien,
Pale Dante, in his soul's distress;
And still the lovely Florentine
Goes lovely in her wine-red dress.

You do not understand at all?
He was a poet; on his page
He drew her; and, though kingdoms fall,
This lady lives from age to age.
A poet—that means painter too,
For words are colors, rightly laid;
And they outlast our brightest hue,
For varnish cracks and crimsons fade.

The poets—they are lucky ones!
When *we* are thrust upon the shelves,
Our works turn into skeletons
Almost as quickly as ourselves;

THOMAS BAILEY ALDRICH 1836–1907

For our poor canvas peels at length,
At length is prized—when all is bare:
"What grace!" the critics cry, "what strength!"
When neither strength nor grace is there.

Ah, Fanny, I am sick at heart,
It is so little one can do;
We talk our jargon—live for Art!
I 'd much prefer to live for you.
How dull and lifeless colors are!
You smile, and all my picture lies:
I wish that I could crush a star
To make a pigment for your eyes.

Yes, child, I know, I am out of tune;
The light is bad; the sky is gray:
I paint no more this afternoon,
So lay your royal gear away.
Besides, you 're moody—chin on hand—
I know not what—not in the vein—
Not like Anne Bullen, sweet and bland:
You sit there smiling in disdain.

Not like the Tudor's radiant Queen,
Unconscious of the coming woe,
But rather as she might have been,
Preparing for the headsman's blow.
So, I have put you in a miff—
Sitting bolt-upright, wrist on wrist.
How *should* you look? Why, dear, as if—
Somehow—as if you 'd just been kissed!

THOMAS BAILEY ALDRICH 1836–1907

On Lynn Terrace

All day to watch the blue wave curl and break,
    All night to hear it plunging on the shore—
In this sea-dream such draughts of life I take,
        I cannot ask for more.

Behind me lie the idle life and vain,
    The task unfinished, and the weary hours;
That long wave softly bears me back to Spain
        And the Alhambra's towers!

Once more I halt in Andalusian Pass,
    To list the mule-bells jingling on the height;
Below, against the dull esparto grass,
        The almonds glimmer white.

Huge gateways, wrinkled, with rich grays and browns,
    Invite my fancy, and I wander through
The gable-shadowed, zigzag streets of towns
        The world's first sailors knew.

Or, if I will, from out this thin sea-haze
    Low-lying cliffs of lovely Calais rise;
Or yonder, with the pomp of olden days,
        Venice salutes my eyes.

Or some gaunt castle lures me up its stair;
    I see, far off, the red tiled hamlets shine,
And catch, through slits of windows here and there,
        Blue glimpses of the Rhine.

THOMAS BAILEY ALDRICH 1836–1907

Again I pass Norwegian fjord and fell,
  And through bleak wastes to where the sunset's fires
Light up the white-walled Russian citadel,
        The Kremlin's domes and spires.

And now I linger in green English lanes,
  By garden-plots of rose and heliotrope;
And now I face the sudden pelting rains
        On some lone Alpine slope.

Now at Tangier, among the packed bazaars,
  I saunter, and the merchants at the doors
Smile, and entice me: here are jewels like stars,
        And curved knives of the Moors;

Cloths of Damascus, strings of amber dates;
  What would Howadji—silver, gold, or stone?
Prone on the sun-scorched plain outside the gates
        The camels make their moan.

All this is mine, as I lie dreaming here,
  High on the windy terrace, day by day;
And mine the children's laughter, sweet and clear,
        Ringing across the bay.

For me the clouds; the ships sail by for me;
  For me the petulant sea-gull takes its flight;
And mine the tender moonrise on the sea,
        And hollow caves of night.

THOMAS BAILEY ALDRICH 1836–1907

On an Intaglio Head of Minerva

Beneath the warrior's helm, behold
   The flowing tresses of the woman!
Minerva, Pallas, what you will—
   A winsome creature, Greek or Roman.

Minerva? No! 't is some sly minx
   In cousin's helmet masquerading;
If not—then Wisdom was a dame
   For sonnets and for serenading!

I thought the goddess cold, austere,
   Not made for love's despairs and blisses:
Did Pallas wear her hair like that?
   Was Wisdom's mouth so shaped for kisses?

The Nightingale should be her bird,
   And not the Owl, big-eyed and solemn:
How very fresh she looks, and yet
   She's older far than Trajan's Column!

The magic hand that carved this face,
   And set this vine-work round it running,
Perhaps ere mighty Phidias wrought
   Had lost its subtle skill and cunning.

Who was he? Was he glad or sad,
   Who knew to carve in such a fashion?
Perchance he graved the dainty head
   For some brown girl that scorned his passion.

THOMAS BAILEY ALDRICH 1836–1907

Perchance, in some still garden-place,
    Where neither fount nor tree to-day is,
He flung the jewel at the feet
    Of Phryne, or perhaps 't was Lais.

But he is dust; we may not know
    His happy or unhappy story:
Nameless and dead these centuries,
    His work outlives him—there 's his glory!

Both man and jewel lay in earth
    Beneath a lava-buried city;
The countless summers came and went
    With neither haste, nor hate, nor pity.

Years blotted out the man, but left
    The jewel fresh as any blossom,
Till some Visconti dug it up—
    To rise and fall on Mabel's bosom!

Oh nameless brother! see how Time
    Your gracious handiwork has guarded:
See how your loving, patient art
    Has come, at last, to be rewarded.

Who would not suffer slights of men,
    And pangs of hopeless passion also,
To have his carven agate-stone
    On such a bosom rise and fall so!

Nocturne

Up to her chamber window
A slight wire trellis goes,
And up this Romeo's ladder
Clambers a bold white rose.

I lounge in the ilex shadows,
I see the lady lean,
Unclasping her silken girdle,
The curtain's folds between.

She smiles on her white-rose lover,
She reaches out her hand
And helps him in at the window—
I see it where I stand!

To her scarlet lip she holds him,
And kisses him many a time—
Ah, me! it was he that won her
Because he dared to climb!

NANCY (PRIEST) WAKEFIELD 1836–1870

Over the River

Over the river they beckon to me,—
   Loved ones who 've cross'd to the farther side;
The gleam of their snowy robes I see
   But their voices are drown'd in the rushing tide.
There 's one with ringlets of sunny gold,
   And eyes, the reflection of heaven's own blue;
He crossed in the twilight, gray and cold,
   And the pale mist hid him from mortal view.
We saw not the angels who met him there;
   The gates of the city we could not see;
Over the river, over the river,
   My brother stands waiting to welcome me.

Over the river, the boatman pale
   Carried another,—the household pet:
Her brown curls waved in the gentle gale—
   Darling Minnie! I see her yet.
She cross'd on her bosom her dimpled hands,
   And fearlessly enter'd the phantom bark;
We watch'd it glide from the silver sands,
   And all our sunshine grew strangely dark.
We know she is safe on the farther side,
   Where all the ransom'd and angels be;
Over the river, the mystic river,
   My childhood's idol is waiting for me.

NANCY (PRIEST) WAKEFIELD 1836–1870

For none return from those quiet shores,
    Who cross with the boatman cold and pale;
We hear the dip of the golden oars,
    And catch a gleam of the snowy sail,—
And lo! they have pass'd from our yearning heart;
    They cross the stream, and are gone for aye;
We may not sunder the veil apart,
    That hides from our vision the gates of day.
We only know that their barks no more
    May sail with us o'er life's stormy sea;
Yet somewhere, I know, on the unseen shore,
    They watch, and beckon, and wait for me.

And I sit and think, when the sunset's gold
    Is flushing river, and hill, and shore,
I shall one day stand by the water cold,
    And list for the sound of the boatman's oar;
I shall watch for a gleam of the flapping sail;
    I shall hear the boat as it gains the strand;
I shall pass from sight, with the boatman pale,
    To the better shore of the spirit land;
I shall know the loved who have gone before,—
    And joyfully sweet will the meeting be,
When over the river, the peaceful river,
    The Angel of Death shall carry me.

JOHN HAY 1838–1905

Jim Bludso of the Prairie Belle

Wall, no! I can't tell whar he lives,
   Because he don't live, you see;
Leastways, he's got out of the habit
   Of livin' like you and me.
Whar have you been for the last three year
   That you have n't heard folks tell
How Jimmy Bludso passed in his checks
   The night of the Prairie Belle?

He were n't no saint,—them engineers
   Is all pretty much alike,—
One wife in Natchez-under-the-Hill
   And another one here, in Pike;
A keerless man in his talk was Jim,
   And an awkward hand in a row,
But he never flunked, and he never lied,—
   I reckon he never knowed how.

And this was all the religion he had,—
   To treat his engine well;
Never be passed on the river;
   To mind the pilot's bell;
And if ever the Prairie Belle took fire,—
   A thousand times he swore
He 'd hold her nozzle agin the bank
   Till the last soul got ashore.

JOHN HAY 1838–1905

All boats has their day on the Mississip,
    And her day come at last,—
The Movastar was a better boat,
    But the Belle she *would n't* be passed.
And so she come tearin' along that night—
    The oldest craft on the line—
With a nigger squat on her safety-valve,
    And her furnace crammed, rosin and pine.

The fire bust out as she clared the bar,
    And burnt a hole in the night,
And quick as a flash she turned, and made
    For that willer-bank on the right.
There was runnin' and cussin', but Jim yelled out,
    Over all the infernal roar,
"I'll hold her nozzle agin the bank
    Till the last galoot's ashore."

Through the hot, black breath of the burnin' boat
    Jim Bludso's voice was heard,
And they all had trust in his cussedness,
    And knowed he would keep his word.
And, sure's you're born, they all got off
    Afore the smokestacks fell,—
And Bludso's ghost went up alone
    In the smoke of the Prairie Belle.

JOHN HAY 1838–1905

He were n't no saint,—but at jedgment
   I 'd run my chance with Jim,
'Longside of some pious gentlemen
   That would n't shook hands with him.
He seen his duty, a dead-sure thing,—
   And went for it thar and then;
And Christ ain't a going to be too hard
   On a man that died for men.

The Mystery of Gilgal

The darkest, strangest mystery
I ever read, or heern, or see,
Is 'long of a drink at Taggart's Hall,—
   Tom Taggart's of Gilgal.

I 've heern the tale a thousand ways,
But never could git through the maze
That hangs around that queer day's doin's;
   But I 'll tell the yarn to youans.

Tom Taggart stood behind his bar,
The time was fall, the skies was fa'r,
The neighbors round the counter drawed,
   And ca'mly drinked and jawed.

JOHN HAY   1838–1905

At last come Colonel Blood of Pike,
And old Jedge Phinn, permiscus-like,
And each, as he meandered in,
   Remarked, "A whisky-skin."

Tom mixed the beverage full and fa'r,
And slammed it, smoking, on the bar.
Some says three fingers, some says two,—
   I'll leave the choice to you.

Phinn to the drink put forth his hand;
Blood drew his knife, with accent bland,
"I ax yer parding, Mister Phinn—
   Jest drap that whisky skin."

No man high-toneder could be found
Than old Jedge Phinn the country round.
Says he, "Young man, the tribe of Phinns
   Knows their own whisky-skins!"

He went for his 'leven-inch bowie-knife:—
"I tries to foller a Christian life;
But I'll drap a slice of liver or two,
   My bloomin' shrub, with you."

They carved in a way that all admired,
Tell Blood drawed iron at last, and fired.
It took Seth Bludso 'twixt the eyes,
   Which caused him great surprise.

JOHN HAY 1838–1905

Then coats went off, and all went in;
Shots and bad language swelled the din;
The short, sharp bark of Derringers,
   Like bull-pups, cheered the furse.

They piled the stiffs outside the door;
They made, I reckon, a cord or more.
Girls went that winter, as a rule,
   Alone to spellin'-school.

I've sarched in vain, from Dan to Beer-
Sheba, to make this mystery clear;
But I end with *hit* as I did begin,—
   Who got the whisky-skin?

Hymn of the Knights Templars

Mother of God! as evening falls
   Upon the silent sea,
And shadows veil the mountain walls,
   We lift our souls to thee!
From lurking perils of the night,
   The desert's hidden harms,
From plagues that waste, from blasts that smite,
   Defend thy men-at-arms!

JOHN HAY 1838–1905

Mother of God! thy starry smile
    Still bless us from above!
Keep pure our souls from passion's guile,
    Our hearts from earthly love!
Still save each soul from guilt apart
    As stainless as each sword,
And guard undimmed in every heart
    The image of our Lord!

In desert march or battle's flame,
    In fortress and in field,
Our war-cry is thy holy name,
    Thy love our joy and shield!
And if we falter, let thy power
    Thy stern avenger be,
And God forget us in the hour
    We cease to think of thee!

Mother of God! the evening fades
    On wave and hill and lea,
And in the twilight's deepening shades
    We lift our souls to thee!
In passion's stress—the battle's strife,
    The desert's lurking harms,
Maid-Mother of the Lord of Life,
    Protect thy men-at-arms!

JAMES RYDER RANDALL 1839–1908

My Maryland

The despot's heel is on thy shore,
    Maryland!
His torch is at thy temple door,
    Maryland!
Avenge the patriotic gore
That flecked the streets of Baltimore,
And be the battle-queen of yore,
    Maryland, my Maryland!

Hark to an exiled son's appeal,
    Maryland!
My Mother State, to thee I kneel,
    Maryland!
For life and death, for woe and weal,
Thy peerless chivalry reveal,
And gird thy beauteous limbs with steel,
    Maryland, my Maryland!

Thou wilt not cower in the dust,
    Maryland!
Thy beaming sword shall never rust,
    Maryland!
Remember Carroll's sacred trust,
Remember Howard's warlike thrust,
And all thy slumberers with the just,
    Maryland, my Maryland!

JAMES RYDER RANDALL 1839–1908

Come! 't is the red dawn of the day,
    Maryland!
Come with thy panoplied array,
    Maryland!
With Ringgold's spirit for the fray,
With Watson's blood at Monterey,
With fearless Lowe and dashing May,
    Maryland, my Maryland!

Dear Mother, burst the tyrant's chain,
    Maryland!
Virginia should not call in vain,
    Maryland!
She meets her sisters on the plain,—
"*Sic semper!*" 't is the proud refrain
That baffles minions back amain,
    Maryland,
Arise in majesty again,
    Maryland, my Maryland!

Come! for thy shield is bright and strong,
    Maryland!
Come! for thy dalliance does thee wrong,
    Maryland!
Come to thine own heroic throng
Stalking with Liberty along,
And chant thy dauntless slogan-song,
    Maryland, my Maryland!

JAMES RYDER RANDALL 1839–1908

I see the blush upon thy cheek,
    Maryland!
For thou wast ever bravely meek,
    Maryland!
But lo! there surges forth a shriek,
From hill to hill, from creek to creek,
Potomac calls to Chesapeake,
    Maryland, my Maryland!

Thou wilt not yield the Vandal toll,
    Maryland!
Thou wilt not crook to his control,
    Maryland!
Better the fire upon thee roll,
Better the shot, the blade, the bowl,
Than crucifixion of the soul,
    Maryland, my Maryland!

I hear the distant thunder hum,
    Maryland!
The Old Line's bugle, fife and drum,
    Maryland!
She is not dead, nor deaf, nor dumb;
Huzza! she spurns the Northern scum!
She breathes! She burns! She'll come! She'll come!
    Maryland, my Maryland!

FRANCIS BRET HARTE 1839–1902

The Society upon the Stanislaus

I reside at Table Mountain, and my name is Truthful James;
I am not up to small deceit or any sinful games;
And I'll tell in simple language what I know about the row
That broke up our Society upon the Stanislow.

But first I would remark, that it is not a proper plan
For any scientific gent to whale his fellowman,
And, if a member don't agree with his peculiar whim,
To lay for that same member for to "put a head" on him.

Now nothing could be finer or more beautiful to see
Than the first six months' proceedings of that same Society,
Till Brown of Calaveras brought a lot of fossil bones
That he found within a tunnel near the tenement of Jones.

Then Brown he read a paper, and he reconstructed there,
From those same bones, an animal that was extremely rare;
And Jones then asked the chair for a suspension of the rules,
Till he could prove that those same bones was one of his lost mules.

FRANCIS BRET HARTE 1839–1902

Then Brown he smiled a bitter smile, and said he was at fault,
It seemed he had been trespassing on Jones's family vault;
He was a most sarcastic man, this quiet Mr. Brown,
And on several occasions he had cleaned out the town.

Now I hold it is not decent for a scientific gent
To say another is an ass,—at least, to all intent;
Nor should the individual who happens to be meant
Reply by heaving rocks at him, to any great extent.

Then Abner Dean of Angel's raised a point of order, when
A chunk of old red sandstone took him in the abdomen,
And he smiled a kind of sickly smile, and curled up on the floor,
And the subsequent proceedings interested him no more.

For, in less time than I write it, every member did engage
In a warfare with the remnants of a palæozoic age;
And the way they heaved those fossils in their anger was a sin,
Till the skull of an old mammoth caved the head of Thompson in.

And this is all I have to say of these improper games,
For I live at Table Mountain, and my name is Truthful James;
And I've told in simple language what I know about the row
That broke up our Society upon the Stanislow.

FRANCIS BRET HARTE 1839–1902

Plain Language from Truthful James
Table Mountain, 1870

Which I wish to remark,
   And my language is plain,
That for ways that are dark
   And for tricks that are vain,
The heathen Chinee is peculiar,
   Which the same I would rise to explain.

Ah Sin was his name;
   And I shall not deny,
In regard to the same,
   What that name might imply;
But his smile it was pensive and childlike,
   As I frequent remarked to Bill Nye.

It was August the third,
   And quite soft was the skies;
Which it might be inferred
   That Ah Sin was likewise;
Yet he played it that day upon William
   And me in a way I despise.

Which we had a small game,
   And Ah Sin took a hand:
It was Euchre. The same
   He did not understand;
But he smiled as he sat by the table,
   With the smile that was childlike and bland.

FRANCIS BRET HARTE 1839–1902

Yet the cards they were stocked
  In a way that I grieve,
And my feelings were shocked
  At the state of Nye's sleeve,
Which was stuffed full of aces and bowers,
  And the same with intent to deceive.

But the hands that were played
  By that heathen Chinee,
And the points that he made,
  Were quite frightful to see,—
Till at last he put down a right bower,
  Which the same Nye had dealt unto me.

Then I looked up at Nye,
  And he gazed upon me;
And he rose with a sigh,
  And said, "Can this be?
We are ruined by Chinese cheap labor,—"
  And he went for that heathen Chinee.

In the scene that ensued
  I did not take a hand,
But the floor it was strewed
  Like the leaves on the strand
With the cards that Ah Sin had been hiding,
  In the game "he did not understand."

In his sleeves, which were long,
    He had twenty-four jacks,—
Which was coming it strong,
    Yet I state but the facts;
And we found on his nails, which were taper,
    What is frequent in tapers,—that's wax.

Which is why I remark,
    And my language is plain,
That for ways that are dark
    And for tricks that are vain,
The heathen Chinee is peculiar,—
    Which the same I am free to maintain.

Dow's Flat
1856

Dow's Flat. That's its name;
    And I reckon that you
Are a stranger? The same?
    Well, I thought it was true,—
For thar is n't a man on the river as can't spot the place
    at first view.

It was called after Dow,—
    Which the same was an ass,—
And as to the how
    Thet the thing kem to pass,—
Jest tie up your hoss to that buckeye, and sit ye down
    here in the grass:

FRANCIS BRET HARTE 1839–1902

You see this 'yer Dow
    Hed the worst kind of luck;
He slipped up somehow
    On each thing thet he struck.
Why, ef he'd a straddled thet fence-rail, the derned
    thing 'd get up and buck.

He mined on the bar
    Till he could n't pay rates;
He was smashed by a car
    When he tunnelled with Bates;
And right on the top of his trouble kem his wife and five
    kids from the States.

It was rough,—mighty rough;
    But the boys they stood by,
And they brought him the stuff
    For a house, on the sly;
And the old woman,—well, she did washing, and took on
    when no one was nigh.

But this 'yer luck of Dow's
    Was so powerful mean
That the spring near his house
    Dried right up on the green;
And he sunk forty feet down for water, but nary a drop
    to be seen.

Then the bar petered out,
  And the boys would n't stay;
And the chills got about,
  And his wife fell away;
But Dow in his well kept a peggin' in his usual ridik-
    ilous way.

One day,—it was June,—
  And a year ago, jest,—
This Dow kem at noon
  To his work like the rest,
With a shovel and pick on his shoulder, and a derringer
    hid in his breast.

He goes to the well,
  And he stands on the brink,
And stops for a spell
  Jest to listen and think:
For the sun in his eyes (jest like this, sir!) you see,
    kinder made the cuss blink.

His two ragged gals
  In the gulch were at play,
And a gownd that was Sal's
  Kinder flapped on a bay:
Not much for a man to be leavin', but his all,—as I 've
    heer'd the folks say.

FRANCIS BRET HARTE 1839–1902

And—That's a peart hoss
   Thet you've got,—ain't it now?
What might be her cost?
   Eh? Oh!—Well, then, Dow—
Let's see,—well, that forty-foot grave was n't his, sir,
   that day, anyhow.

For a blow of his pick
   Sorter caved in the side,
And he looked and turned sick,
   Then he trembled and cried.
For you see the dern cuss had struck—"Water?"—Beg
   your parding, young man—there you lied!

It was *gold*,—in the quartz,
   And it ran all alike;
And I reckon five oughts
   Was the worth of that strike;
And that house with the coopilow's his'n,—which the
   same is n't bad for a Pike.

Thet's why it's Dow's Flat;
   And the thing of it is,
That he kinder got that
   Through sheer contrairiness:
For 't was *water* the derned cuss was seekin', and his
   luck made him certain to miss.

FRANCIS BRET HARTE 1839–1902

Thet 's so! Thar 's your way,
   To the left of yon tree;
But—a—look h'yur, say?
   Won't you come up to tea?
No? Well, then the next time you 're passin'; and ask
   after Dow,—and thet 's *me*.

"Jim"

Say there! P'r'aps
Some on you chaps
   Might know Jim Wild?
Well,—no offense:
Thar ain't no sense
   In gittin' riled!

Jim was my chum
   Up on the Bar:
That 's why I come
   Down from up yar,
Lookin' for Jim.
Thank ye, sir! *You*
Ain't of that crew,—
   Blest if you are!

Money? Not much:
   That ain't my kind;
I ain't no such.
   Rum? I don't mind,
Seein' it 's you.

FRANCIS BRET HARTE 1839–1902

Well, this yer Jim,—
Did you know him?
Jes' 'bout your size;
Same kind of eyes;—
Well, that is strange:
  Why, it's two year
  Since he came here,
Sick, for a change.

Well, here's to us:
  Eh?
The h— you say!
  Dead?
That little cuss?

What makes you star'
You over thar?
Can't a man drop
's glass in yer shop
But you must r'ar?
  It wouldn't take
  D—d much to break
You and your bar.

  Dead!
Poor—little—Jim!
Why, thar was me,
Jones, and Bob Lee,
Harry and Ben,—
No-account men:
Then to take *him!*

Well, thar—Good-by—
No more, sir—I—
  Eh?
What's that you say?
Why, dern it!—sho—
No? Yes! By Joe!
  Sold!
Sold! Why, you limb,
You ornery,
  Derned old
Long-legged Jim.

Chiquita

Beautiful! Sir, you may say so. Thar is n't her match
    in the county;
Is thar, old gal,—Chiquita, my darling, my beauty?
Feel of that neck, sir,—thar's velvet! Whoa! Steady,—
    ah, will you, you vixen!
Whoa! I say. Jack, trot her out; let the gentleman look
    at her paces.

Morgan!—She ain't nothin' else, and I 've got the papers
    to prove it.
Sired by Chippewa Chief, and twelve hundred dollars
    won't buy her.

FRANCIS BRET HARTE 1839–1902

Briggs of Tuolumne owned her. Did you know Briggs
 of Tuolumne?
Busted hisself in White Pine, and blew out his brains
 down in 'Frisco?

Hedn't no savey, hed Briggs. Thar, Jack! that'll do,
 quit that foolin'!
Nothin' to what she kin do, when she's got her work cut
 out before her.
Hosses is hosses, you know, and likewise, too, jockeys is
 jockeys;
And 't ain't ev'ry man as can ride as knows what a hoss
 has got in him.

Know the old ford on the Fork, that nearly got Flani-
 gan's leaders?
Nasty in daylight, you bet, and a mighty rough ford in
 low water!
Well, it ain't six weeks ago that me and the Jedge and
 his nevey
Struck for that ford in the night, in the rain, and the
 water all around us;

Up to our flanks in the gulch, and Rattlesnake Creek
 just a bilin',
Not a plank left in the dam, and nary a bridge on the
 river.
I had the gray, and the Jedge had his roan, and his
 nevey, Chiquita;
And after us trundled the rocks jest loosed from top of
 the cañon.

FRANCIS BRET HARTE 1839–1902

Lickity, lickity, switch, we came to the ford, and Chiquita
Buckled right down to her work, and, afore I could yell to her rider,
Took water jest at the ford; and there was the Jedge and me standing,
And twelve hundred dollars of hoss-flesh afloat, and a-driftin' to thunder!

Would ye b'lieve it? That night, that hoss, that ar' filly, Chiquita,
Walked herself into her stall, and stood there, all quiet and dripping:
Clean as a beaver or rat, with nary a buckle of harness,
Just as she swam the Fork,—that hoss, that ar' filly, Chiquita.

That's what I call a hoss! and—What did you say?— Oh! the nevey?
Drownded, I reckon,—leastways, he never kem back to deny it.
Ye see, the derned fool had no seat, ye couldn't have made him a rider;
And then, ye know, boys will be boys, and hosses—well, hosses is hosses!

FRANCIS BRET HARTE 1839–1902

What the Engines Said

Opening of the Pacific Railroad

What was it the Engines said,
Pilots touching,—head to head
Facing on the single track,
Half a world behind each back?
This is what the Engines said,
Unreported and unread.

With a prefatory screech,
In a florid Western speech,
Said the engine from the West,
"I am from Sierra's crest;
And, if altitude's a test,
Why, I reckon, it's confessed,
That I've done my level best."

Said the Engine from the East,
"They who work best talk the least.
S'pose you whistle down your brakes;
What you've done is no great shakes,—
Pretty fair,—but let our meeting
Be a different kind of greeting.
Let these folks with champagne stuffing,
Not their Engines, do the *puffing*.

FRANCIS BRET HARTE 1839–1902

"Listen! Where Atlantic beats
Shores of snow and summer heats;
Where the Indian autumn skies
Paint the woods with wampum dies,—
I have chased the flying sun,
Seeing all he looked upon,
Blessing all that he has blest,
Nursing in my iron breast
All his vivifying heat,
All his clouds about my crest;
And before my flying feet
Every shadow must retreat."

Said the Western Engine, "Phew!"
And a long, low whistle blew.
"Come, now, really that's the oddest
Talk for one so very modest.
You brag of your East. *You* do?
Why, *I* bring the East to *you!*
All the Orient, all Cathay,
Find through me the shortest way;
And the sun you follow here
Rises in my hemisphere.
Really,—if one must be rude,—
Length, my friend, ain't longitude."

FRANCIS BRET HARTE 1839–1902

Said the Union: "Don't reflect, or
I 'll run over some Director."
Said the Central: "I 'm Pacific;
But, when riled, I 'm quite terrific.
Yet to-day we shall not quarrel,
Just to show these folks this moral,
How two Engines—in their vision—
Once have met without collision."

That is what the Engines said,
Unreported and unread;
Spoken slightly through the nose,
With a whistle at the close.

ANONYMOUS

Home Wounded

Wheel me down by the meadow,
   Where no step but thine will pass;
Anchor me where the shadow
   Skims o'er the billowy grass:
Where the arbutus straggles over
   The slope of the spreading hill,
And the souls of hidden violets
   Their scented airs distil.

Saint, with your sweet composure,
   Lean your cool cheek 'gainst my hair;
My soul's in the fierce exposure
   Of fields where the dying are;
And even your hand can never
   Quiet this fever and pain,
Or soften the restless longing
   To share in the contest again.

O, to be here so idle!
   To sit like a clod in this chair,
With hands that ache for the bridle,
   With heart away in the war!
Instead of the long roll beating
   To hear but the tinkle of vines,
For the rush and whirl of the conflict
   Only the wail of the pines.

ANONYMOUS

Still midst the sounds of summer,
    Which freight the soft June air
With tender slumberous murmur,
    My soul hears the trumpet's blare.
What have I laid on the altar?
    Only a few drops of blood!
Small is the gift to offer
    For honor, freedom, God.

While by your side I dally,
    Still waits the slave in his chain.
Up, my faint pulse must rally
    Once more 'mid the leaden rain.
With kisses on lips, eyes and forehead,
    Sign me the sign of the Cross.
If my heart throb its last for our banner,
    Greater the gain than the loss.
If we gain—there'll be time for our wooing,
    In paths where the wild roses nod;
If we lose—I'll wait for you, dearest,
    'Neath the palms by the mount of our God.

EDWARD ROWLAND SILL 1841–1887

The Fool's Prayer

The royal feast was done; the King
   Sought some new sport to banish care,
And to his jester cried: "Sir Fool,
   Kneel now, and make for us a prayer!"

The jester doffed his cap and bells,
   And stood the mocking court before;
They could not see the bitter smile
   Behind the painted grin he wore.

He bowed his head, and bent his knee
   Upon the monarch's silken stool;
His pleading voice arose: "O Lord,
   Be merciful to me, a fool!

"No pity, Lord, could change the heart
   From red with wrong to white as wool;
The rod must heal the sin: but, Lord,
   Be merciful to me, a fool!

" 'T is not by guilt the onward sweep
   Of truth and right, O Lord, we stay;
'T is by our follies that so long
   We hold the earth from heaven away.

"These clumsy feet, still in the mire,
   Go crushing blossoms without end;
These hard, well-meaning hands we thrust
   Among the heart-strings of a friend.

EDWARD ROWLAND SILL 1841–1887

"The ill-timed truth we might have kept—
    Who knows how sharp it pierced and stung?
The word we had not sense to say—
    Who knows how grandly it had rung?

"Our faults no tenderness should ask,
    The chastening stripes must cleanse them all;
But for our blunders—oh, in shame
    Before the eyes of heaven we fall.

"Earth bears no balsam for mistakes;
    Men crown the knave, and scourge the tool
That did his will; but Thou, O Lord,
    Be merciful to me, a fool!"

The room was hushed; in silence rose
    The King, and sought his gardens cool,
And walked apart, and murmured low,
    "Be merciful to me, a fool!"

The Open Window

My tower was grimly builded,
    With many a bolt and bar,
"And here," I thought, "I will keep my life
    From the bitter world afar."

EDWARD ROWLAND SILL 1841–1887

Dark and chill was the stony floor,
   Where never a sunbeam lay,
And the mould crept up on the dreary wall,
   With its ghost touch, day by day.

One morn, in my sullen musings,
   A flutter and cry I heard;
And close at the rusty casement
   There clung a frightened bird.

Then back I flung the shutter
   That was never before undone,
And I kept till its wings were rested
   The little weary one.

But in through the open window,
   Which I had forgot to close,
There had burst a gush of sunshine
   And a summer scent of rose.

For all the while I had burrowed
   There in my dingy tower,
Lo! the birds had sung and the leaves had danced
   From hour to sunny hour.

And such balm and warmth and beauty
   Came drifting in since then,
That the window still stands open
   And shall never be shut again.

EDWARD ROWLAND SILL 1841–1887

To a Maid Demure

Often when the night is come,
With its quiet group at home,
While they broider, knit, or sew,
Read, or chat in voices low,
Suddenly you lift your eyes
With an earnest look, and wise;
But I cannot read their lore,—
Tell me less, or tell me more.

Like a picture in a book,
Pure and peaceful is your look,
Quietly you walk your ways;
Steadfast duty fills the days.
Neither tears nor fierce delights,
Feverish days nor tossing nights,
Any troublous dreams confess,—
Tell me more, or tell me less.

Swift the weeks are on the wing;
Years are brief, and love a thing
Blooming, fading, like a flower;
Wake and seize the little hour.
Give me welcome, or farewell;
Quick! I wait! And who can tell
What to-morrow may befall,—
Love me more, or not at all.

EDWARD ROWLAND SILL 1841–1887

Momentous Words

What spiteful chance steals unawares
   Wherever lovers come,
And trips the nimblest brain and scares
   The bravest feelings dumb?

We had one minute at the gate,
   Before the others came;
To-morrow it would be too late,
   And whose would be the blame!

I gazed at her, she glanced at me;
   Alas! the time sped by:
"How warm it is to-day!" said she;
   "It looks like rain," said I.

EDWARD ROWLAND SILL 1841-1887

The Lover's Song

Lend me thy fillet, Love!
   I would no longer see:
Cover mine eyelids close awhile,
   And make me blind like thee.

Then might I pass her sunny face,
   And know not it was fair;
Then might I hear her voice, nor guess
   Her starry eyes were there.

Ah! banished so from stars and sun—
   Why need it be my fate?
If only she might dream me good
   And wise, and be my mate!

Lend her thy fillet, Love!
   Let her no longer see:
If there is hope for me at all,
   She must be blind like thee.

EDWARD ROWLAND SILL 1841–1887

The Coup de Grace

    If I were very sure
That all was over betwixt you and me—
    That, while this endless absence I endure
With but one mood, one dream, one misery
Of waiting, you were happier to be free,—

    Then I might find again
In cloud and stream and all the winds that blow,
    Yea, even in the faces of my fellowmen,
The old companionship; and I might know
Once more the pulse of action, ere I go.

    But now I cannot rest,
While this one pleading, querulous tone without
    Breaks in and mars the music in my breast.
I open the closed door—lo! all about,
What seem your lingering footprints; then I doubt.

    Waken me from this sleep!
Strike fearless, let the naked truth-edge gleam!
    For while the beautiful old past I keep,
I am a phantom, and all mortals seem
But phantoms, and my life fades as a dream.

NORA PERRY 1841–1896

After the Ball

They sat and comb'd their beautiful hair,
   Their long, bright tresses, one by one,
As they laugh'd and talk'd in the chamber there,
   After the revel was done.

Idly they talk'd of waltz and quadrille,
   Idly they laugh'd, like other girls,
Who over the fire, when all is still,
   Comb out their braids and curls.

Robe of satin and Brussels lace,
   Knots of flowers and ribbons, too,
Scatter'd about in every place,
   For the revel is through.

And Maud and Madge in robes of white,
   The prettiest night-gowns under the sun,
Stockingless, slipperless, sit in the night,
   For the revel is done,—

Sit and comb their beautiful hair,
   Those wonderful waves of brown and gold,
Till the fire is out in the chamber there,
   And the little bare feet are cold.

Then out of the gathering winter chill,
   All out of the bitter St. Agnes weather,
While the fire is out and the house is still,
   Maud and Madge together,—

NORA PERRY 1841–1896

Maud and Madge in robes of white,
   The prettiest night-gowns under the sun,
Curtain'd away from the chilly night,
   After the revel is done,—

Float along in a splendid dream,
   To a golden gittern's tinkling tune,
While a thousand lustres shimmering stream
   In a palace's grand saloon.

Flashing of jewels and flutter of laces,
   Tropical odors sweeter than musk,
Men and women with beautiful faces,
   And eyes of tropical dusk;

And one face shining out like a star,
   One face haunting the dreams of each,
And one voice, sweeter than others are,
   Breaking into silvery speech,—

Telling, through lips of bearded bloom,
   An old, old story over again,
As down the royal banner'd room,
   To the golden gittern's strain,

Two and two, they dreamily walk,
   While an unseen spirit walks beside,
And all unheard in the lovers' talk,
   He claimeth one for a bride.

NORA PERRY 1841–1896

O Maud and Madge, dream on together,
   With never a pang of jealous fear!
For, ere the bitter St. Agnes weather
   Shall whiten another year,

Robed for the bridal, and robed for the tomb,
   Braided brown hair and golden tress,
There 'll be only one of you left for the bloom
   Of the bearded lips to press,—

Only one for the bridal pearls,
   The robe of satin and Brussels lace,—
Only one to blush through her curls
   At the sight of a lover's face.

O beautiful Madge, in your bridal white,
   For you the revel has just begun,
But for her who sleeps in your arms to-night
   The revel of Life is done!

But robed and crown'd with your saintly bliss,
   Queen of heaven and bride of the sun,
O beautiful Maud, you 'll never miss
   The kisses another hath won.

SIDNEY LANIER 1842–1881

Song of the Chattahoochee

Out of the hills of Habersham,
   Down the valleys of Hall,
I hurry amain to reach the plain,
Run the rapid and leap the fall,
Split at the rock and together again,
Accept my bed, or narrow or wide,
And flee from folly on every side
With a lover's pain to attain the plain
   Far from the hills of Habersham,
   Far from the valleys of Hall.

All down the hills of Habersham,
   All through the valleys of Hall,
The rushes cried *Abide, abide,*
The wilful waterweeds held me thrall,
The laving laurel turned my tide,
The ferns and the fondling grass said *Stay,*
The dewberry dipped for to work delay,
And the little reeds sighed *Abide, abide,*
   Here in the hills of Habersham,
   Here in the valleys of Hall.

High o'er the hills of Habersham,
   Veiling the valleys of Hall,
The hickory told me manifold
Fair tales of shade, the poplar tall
Wrought me her shadowy self to hold,

SIDNEY LANIER 1842–1881

The chestnut, the oak, the walnut, the pine,
Overleaning with flickering meaning and sign,
Said, *Pass not, so cold, these manifold*
 Deep shades of the hills of Habersham,
 These glades in the valleys of Hall.

And oft in the hills of Habersham,
 And oft in the valleys of Hall,
The white quartz shone, and the smooth brook-stone
Did bar me of passage with friendly brawl,
And many a luminous jewel lone
—Crystals clear or a-cloud with mist,
Ruby, garnet, and amethyst—
Made lures with the lights of streaming stone
 In the clefts of the hills of Habersham,
 In the beds of the valleys of Hall.

But oh, not the hills of Habersham,
 And oh, not the valleys of Hall
Avail: I am fain for to water the plain.
Downward the voices of Duty call—
Downward, to toil and be mixed with the main,
The dry fields burn, and the mills are to turn,
And a myriad flowers mortally yearn,
And the lordly main from beyond the plain
 Calls o'er the hills of Habersham,
 Calls through the valleys of Hall.

SIDNEY LANIER 1842–1881

The Marshes of Glynn

Glooms of the live-oaks, beautiful-braided and woven
With intricate shades of the vines that myriad-cloven
Clamber the forks of the multiform boughs,—
      Emerald twilights,—
      Virginal shy lights,
Wrought of the leaves to allure to the whisper of vows,
When lovers pace timidly down through the green colonnades
Of the dim sweet woods, of the dear dark woods,
  Of the heavenly woods and glades,
That run to the radiant marginal sand-beach within
      The wide sea-marshes of Glynn;—

Beautiful glooms, soft dusks in the noonday fire,—
Wildwood privacies, closets of lone desire,
Chamber from chamber parted with wavering arras of leaves,—
Cells for the passionate pleasure of prayer to the soul that grieves,
Pure with a sense of the passing of saints through the wood,
Cool for the dutiful weighing of ill with good;—

O braided dusks of the oak and woven shades of the vine,
While the riotous noonday sun of the June-day long did shine
Ye held me fast in your heart and I held you fast in mine;

SIDNEY LANIER 1842–1881

But now when the noon is no more, and riot is rest,
And the sun is a-wait at the ponderous gate of the West,
And the slant yellow beam down the wood-aisle doth seem
Like a lane into heaven that leads from a dream,—
Ay, now, when my soul all day hath drunken the soul of
    the oak,
And my heart is at ease from men, and the wearisome
    sound of the stroke
    Of the scythe of time and trowel of trade is
    low,
    And belief overmasters doubt, and I know that I
    know,
    And my spirit is grown to a lordly great compass
    within,
That the length and the breadth and the sweep of the
    marshes of Glynn
Will work me no fear like the fear they have wrought me
    of yore
When length was fatigue, and when breadth was but
    bitterness sore,
And when terror and shrinking and dreary unnamable
    pain
Drew over me out of the merciless miles of the plain,—

Oh, now, unafraid, I am fain to face
  The vast sweet visage of space.
To the edge of the wood I am drawn, I am drawn,
Where the gray beach glimmering runs, as a belt of the
    dawn,

For a mete and a mark
　　　　To the forest dark:—
　　　　　　So:
Affable live-oak, leaning low,—
Thus—with your favor—soft, with a reverent hand,
(Not lightly touching your person, Lord of the land!)
Bending your beauty aside, with a step I stand
On the firm-packed sand,
　　　　　Free
By a world of marsh that borders a world of sea.
　　Sinuous southward and sinuous northward the shimmering band
　　　Of the sand-beach fastens the fringe of the marsh to the folds of the land.
Inward and outward to northward and southward the beach-lines linger and curl
As a silver-wrought garment that clings to and follows the firm sweet limbs of a girl.
Vanishing, swerving, evermore curving again into sight,
Softly the sand-beach wavers away to a dim gray looping of light.
And what if behind me to westward the wall of the woods stands high?
The world lies east: how ample, the marsh and the sea and the sky!
A league and a league of marsh-grass, waist-high, broad in the blade,
Green, and all of a height, and unflecked with a light or a shade,

SIDNEY LANIER 1842–1881

Stretch leisurely off, in a pleasant plain,
To the terminal blue of the main.

Oh, what is abroad in the marsh and the terminal sea?
    Somehow my soul seems suddenly free
From the weighing of fate and the sad discussion of sin,
By the length and the breadth and the sweep of the
    marshes of Glynn.

Ye marshes, how candid and simple and nothing-with-
    holding and free
Ye publish yourselves to the sky and offer yourselves to
    the sea!
Tolerant plains, that suffer the sea and the rains and the
    sun,
Ye spread and span like the catholic man who hath
    mightily won
God out of knowledge and good out of infinite pain
And sight out of blindness and purity out of a stain.

As the marsh-hen secretly builds on the watery sod,
Behold I will build me a nest on the greatness of God:
I will fly in the greatness of God as the marsh-hen flies
In the freedom that fills all the space 'twixt the marsh
    and the skies:
By so many roots as the marsh-grass sends in the sod
I will heartily lay me a-hold on the greatness of God:
Oh, like to the greatness of God is the greatness within
The range of the marshes, the liberal marshes of Glynn.

And the sea lends large, as the marsh: lo, out of his
    plenty the sea
Pours fast: full soon the time of the flood tide must be:
Look how the grace of the sea doth go
About and about through the intricate channels that flow
    Here and there,
        Everywhere,
Till his waters have flooded the uttermost creeks and the
    low-lying lanes,
And the marsh is meshed with a million veins,
That like as with rosy and silvery essences flow
    In the rose-and-silver evening glow.
        Farewell, my lord Sun!
The creeks overflow: a thousand rivulets run
'Twixt the roots of the sod; the blades of the marsh-grass
    stir;
Passeth a hurrying sound of wings that westward whirr;
Passeth, and all is still; and the currents cease to run;
And the sea and the marsh are one.

How still the plains of the waters be!
The tide is in his ecstasy;
The tide is at his highest height;
    And it is night.

And now from the Vast of the Lord will the waters of
    sleep
Roll in on the souls of men,
But who will reveal to our waking ken

SIDNEY LANIER 1842–1881

The forms that swim and the shapes that creep
        Under the waters of sleep?
And I would I could know what swimmeth below when
    the tide comes in
On the length and the breadth of the marvellous marshes
    of Glynn.

RICHARD WATSON GILDER 1844–1909

A Woman's Thought

I am a woman—therefore I may not
Call to him, cry to him,
Fly to him,
Bid him delay not!

Then when he comes to me, I must sit quiet;
Still as a stone—
All silent and cold.
If my heart riot—
Crush and defy it!
Should I grow bold,
Say one dear thing to him,
All my life fling to him,
Cling to him—
What to atone
Is enough for my sinning!
This were the cost to me,
This were my winning—
That he were lost to me.

Not as a lover
At last if he part from me,
Tearing my heart from me,
Hurt beyond cure—
Calm and demure
Then must I hold me,
In myself fold me,

RICHARD WATSON GILDER 1844–1909

Lest he discover;
Showing no sign to him
By look of mine to him
What he has been to me—
How my heart turns to him,
Follows him, yearns to him,
Prays him to love me.

Pity me, lean to me,
Thou God above me!

The River Inn

The night was black and drear
Of the last day of the year.
Two guests to the river inn
Came, from the wide world's bound—
One with clangor and din,
The other without a sound.

"Now hurry, servants and host!
Get the best that your cellars boast.
White be the sheets and fine,
And the fire on the hearthstone bright;
Pile the wood, and spare not the wine,
And call him at morning light."

"But where is the silent guest?
In what chamber shall she rest?
In this! Should she not go higher?
'T is damp, and the fire is gone."
"You need not kindle the fire,
You need not call her at dawn."

Next morn he sallied forth
On his journey to the North.
Oh, bright the sunlight shone
Through boughs that the breezes stir;
But for her was lifted a stone
Under the churchyard fir.

Reform

I

Oh, how shall I help to right the world that is going
    wrong!
And what can I do to hurry the promised time of peace!
The day of work is short and the night of sleep is long;
And whether to pray or preach, or whether to sing a song,
To plow in my neighbor's field, or to seek the golden
    fleece,
Or to sit with my hands in my lap, and wish that ill
    would cease!

RICHARD WATSON GILDER 1844–1909

II

I think, sometimes, it were best just to let the Lord alone;
I am sure some people forget He was here before they came;
Tho' they say it is all for His glory, 't is a good deal more for their own,
That they peddle their petty schemes, and blate and babble and groan.
I sometimes think it were best, and a man were little to blame,
Should he pass on his silent way nor mix with the noisy shame.

Noël

Star-dust and vaporous light,—
    The mist of worlds unborn,—
A shuddering in the awful night
    Of winds that bring the morn.

Now comes the dawn: the circling earth;
    Creatures that fly and crawl;
And Man, that last, imperial birth;
    And Christ, the flower of all.

RICHARD WATSON GILDER 1844–1909

Songs

I

Not from the whole wide world I chose thee—
  Sweetheart, light of the land and the sea!
The wide, wide world could not inclose thee,
  For thou art the whole wide world to me.

II

Years have flown since I knew thee first,
  And I know thee as water is known of thirst;
Yet I knew thee of old at the first sweet sight,
  And thou art strange to me, Love, to-night.

Ah, Be Not False

Ah, be not false, sweet Splendor!
  Be true, be good;
Be wise as thou art tender;
  Be all that Beauty should.

Not lightly be thy citadel subdued;
  Not ignobly, not untimely.
Take praise in solemn mood;
  Take love sublimely.

RICHARD WATSON GILDER 1844–1909

The Heroic Age

He speaks not well who doth his time deplore,
Naming it new and little and obscure,
Ignoble and unfit for lofty deeds.
All times were modern in the time of them,
And this no more than others. Do thy part
Here in the living day, as did the great
Who made old days immortal! So shall men,
Gazing long back to this far-looming hour,
Say: "Then the time when men were truly men;
Tho' wars grew less, their spirits met the test
Of new conditions; conquering civic wrong;
Saving the state anew by virtuous lives;
Guarding the country's honor as their own,
And their own as their country's and their sons';
Proclaiming service the one test of worth;
Defying leagued fraud with single truth;
Knights of the spirit; warriors in the cause
Of justice absolute 'twixt man and man;
Not fearing loss; and daring to be pure.
When error through the land raged like a pest,
They calmed the madness caught from mind to mind
By wisdom drawn from eld, and counsel sane;
And as the martyrs of the ancient world
Gave Death for man, so nobly gave they Life:
Those the great days, and that the heroic age."

   Athens, 1896.

Dear Old London

When I was broke in London in the fall of '89,
I chanced to spy in Oxford Street this tantalizing sign,—
"A Splendid Horace cheap for Cash!" Of course I had
    to look
Upon the vaunted bargain, and it was a noble book!
A finer one I 've never seen, nor can I hope to see,—
The first edition, richly bound, and clean as clean can be;
And, just to think, for three-pounds-ten I might have had
    that Pine,
When I was broke in London in the fall of '89!

Down at Noseda's, in the Strand, I found, one fateful
    day,
A portrait that I pined for as only maniac may,—
A print of Madame Vestris (she flourished years ago,
Was Bartolozzi's daughter, and a thoroughbred, you
    know).
A clean and handsome print it was, and cheap at thirty
    bob,—
That 's what I told the salesman, as I choked a rising sob;
But I hung around Noseda's as it were a holy shrine,
When I was broke in London in the fall of '89.

At Davey's, in Great Russell Street, were autographs
    galore,
And Mr. Davey used to let me con that precious store.
Sometimes I read what warriors wrote, sometimes a king's
    command,
But oftener still a poet's verse, writ in a meagre hand.

EUGENE FIELD 1850–1895

Lamb, Byron, Addison, and Burns, Pope, Johnson, Swift,
   and Scott,—
It needed but a paltry sum to comprehend the lot;
Yet, though Friend Davey marked 'em down, what could
   I but decline?
For I was broke in London in the fall of '89.

Of antique swords and spears I saw a vast and dazzling
   heap
That Curio Fenton offered me at prices passing cheap;
And, oh, the quaint old bureaus, and the warming-pans
   of brass,
And the lovely hideous freaks I found in pewter and in
   glass!
And, oh, the sideboards, candlesticks, the cracked old
   china plates,
The clocks and spoons from Amsterdam that antedate all
   dates!
Of such superb monstrosities I found an endless mine
When I was broke in London in the fall of '89.

O ye that hanker after boons that others idle by,—
The battered things that please the soul, though they may
   vex the eye,—
The silver plate and crockery all sanctified with grime,
The oaken stuff that has defied the tooth of envious Time,
The musty tomes, the speckled prints, the mildewed bills
   of play,
And other costly relics of malodorous decay,—

Ye only can appreciate what agony was mine
When I was broke in London in the fall of '89.

When, in the course of natural things, I go to my reward,
Let no imposing epitaph my martyrdoms record;
Neither in Hebrew, Latin, Greek, nor any classic tongue,
Let my ten thousand triumphs over human griefs be sung;
But in plain Anglo-Saxon—that he may know who seeks
What agonizing pangs I've had while on the hunt for freaks—
Let there be writ upon the slab that marks my grave this line:
"Deceased was broke in London in the fall of '89."

In Amsterdam

    Mynheer Hans Von Der Bloom has got
    A majazin in Kalverstraat,
    Where one may buy for sordid gold
    Wares quaint and curious, new and old.
    Here are antiquities galore,—
    The jewels which Dutch monarchs wore,
    Swords, teacups, helmets, platters, clocks,
    Bright Dresden jars, dull Holland crocks,
    And all those joys I might rehearse
    That please the eye, but wreck the purse.

EUGENE FIELD 1850–1895

I most admired an ancient bed,
With ornate carvings at its head,—
A massive frame of dingy oak,
Whose curious size and mould bespoke
Prodigious age. "How much?" I cried.
"Ein tousand gildens," Hans replied;
And then the honest Dutchman said
A king once owned that glorious bed,—
King Fritz der Foorst, of blessed fame,
Had owned and slept within the same!

Then long I stood and mutely gazed,
By reminiscent splendors dazed,
And I had bought it right away,
Had I the wherewithal to pay.
But, lacking of the needed pelf,
I thus discoursed within myself:
"O happy Holland! where's the bliss
That can approximate to this
Possession of the rare antique
Which maniacs hanker for and seek?
My native land is full of stuff
That's good, but is not old enough.
Alas! it has no oaken beds
Wherein have slumbered royal heads,
No relic on whose face we see
The proof of grand antiquity."

Thus reasoned I a goodly spell
Until, perchance, my vision fell
Upon a trademark at the head
Of Fritz der Foorst's old oaken bed,—
A rampant wolverine, and round
This strange device these words I found:
"Patent Antique. Birkey & Gay,
Grand Rapids, Michigan, U. S. A."

At present I'm not saying much
About the simple, guileless Dutch;
And as it were a loathsome spot
I keep away from Kalverstraat,
Determined when I want a bed
In which hath slept a royal head
I'll patronize no middleman,
But deal direct with Michigan.

The Bibliomaniac's Prayer

Keep me, I pray, in wisdom's way
   That I may truths eternal seek;
I need protecting care to-day,—
   My purse is light, my flesh is weak.
So banish from my erring heart
   All baleful appetites and hints
Of Satan's fascinating art,
   Of first editions, and of prints.

Direct me in some godly walk
   Which leads away from bookish strife,
That I with pious deed and talk
   May extra-illustrate my life.

But if, O Lord, it pleaseth Thee
   To keep me in temptation's way,
I humbly ask that I may be
   Most notably beset to-day;
Let my temptation be a book,
   Which I shall purchase, hold, and keep,
Whereon when other men shall look,
   They'll wail to know I got it cheap.
Oh, let it such a volume be
   As in rare copperplates abounds,
Large paper, clean, and fair to see,
   Uncut, unique, unknown to Lowndes.

Dibdin's Ghost

Dear wife, last midnight, whilst I read
   The tomes you so despise,
A spectre rose beside the bed,
   And spake in this true wise:
"From Canaan's beatific coast
   I've come to visit thee,
For I am Frognall Dibdin's ghost,"
   Says Dibdin's ghost to me.

I bade him welcome, and we twain
   Discussed with buoyant hearts
The various things that appertain
   To bibliomaniac arts.
"Since you are fresh from t' other side,
   Pray tell me of that host
That treasured books before they died,"
   Says I to Dibdin's ghost.

"They 've entered into perfect rest;
   For in the life they 've won
There are no auctions to molest,
   No creditors to dun.
Their heavenly rapture has no bounds
   Beside that jasper sea;
It is a joy unknown to Lowndes,"
   Says Dibdin's ghost to me.

Much I rejoiced to hear him speak
   Of biblio-bliss above,
For I am one of those who seek
   What bibliomaniacs love.
"But tell me, for I long to hear
   What doth concern me most,
Are wives admitted to that sphere?"
   Says I to Dibdin's ghost.

"The women folk are few up there;
   For 't were not fair, you know,
That they our heavenly joy should share
   Who vex us here below.

The few are those who have been kind
   To husbands such as we;
They knew our fads, and did n't mind,"
   Says Dibdin's ghost to me.

"But what of those who scold at us
   When we would read in bed?
Or, wanting victuals, make a fuss
   If we buy books instead?
And what of those who 've dusted not
   Our motley pride and boast,—
Shall they profane that sacred spot?"
   Says I to Dibdin's ghost.

"Oh, no! they tread that other path,
   Which leads where torments roll,
And worms, yes, bookworms, vent their wrath
   Upon the guilty soul.
Untouched of bibliomaniac grace,
   That saveth such as we,
They wallow in that dreadful place,"
   Says Dibdin's ghost to me.

"To my dear wife will I recite
   What things I 've heard you say;
She 'll let me read the books by night
   She 's let me buy by day.
For we together by and by
   Would join that heavenly host;
She 's earned a rest as well as I,"
   Says I to Dibdin's ghost.

EUGENE FIELD 1850–1895

The Tea-Gown

My lady has a tea-gown
   That is wondrous fair to see,—
It is flounced and ruffed and plaited and puffed,
   As a tea-gown ought to be;
And I thought she must be jesting
   Last night at supper when
She remarked, by chance, that it came from France,
   And had cost but two pounds ten.

Had she told me fifty shillings,
   I might (and would n't you?)
Have referred to that dress in a way folks express
   By an eloquent dash or two;
But the guileful little creature
   Knew well her tactics when
She casually said that that dream in red
   Had cost but two pounds ten.

Yet our home is all the brighter
   For that dainty, sentient thing,
That floats away where it properly may,
   And clings where it ought to cling;
And I count myself the luckiest
   Of all us married men
That I have a wife whose joy in life
   Is a gown at two pounds ten.

EUGENE FIELD 1850–1895

It is n't the gown compels me
  Condone this venial sin;
It 's the pretty face above the lace,
  And the gentle heart within.
And with her arms about me
  I say, and say again,
" 'T was wondrous cheap,"—and I think a heap
  Of that gown at two pounds ten!

The Little Peach

A little peach in the orchard grew,—
A little peach of emerald hue;
Warmed by the sun and wet by the dew,
        It grew.

One day, passing that orchard through,
That little peach dawned on the view
Of Johnny Jones and his sister Sue—
        Them two.

Up at that peach a club they threw—
Down from the stem on which it grew
Fell that peach of emerald hue.
        Mon Dieu!

John took a bite and Sue a chew,
And then the trouble began to brew,—
Trouble the doctor could n't subdue.
        Too true!

Under the turf where the daisies grew
They planted John and his sister Sue,
And their little souls to the angels flew,—
        Boo hoo!

What of that peach of the emerald hue,
Warmed by the sun, and wet by the dew?
Ah, well, its mission on earth is through.
        Adieu!

Lydia Dick

When I was a boy at college,
Filling up with classic knowledge,
    Frequently I wondered why
Old Professor Demas Bentley
Used to praise so eloquently
    "Opera Horatii."

Toiling on a season longer
Till my reasoning powers got stronger,
    As my observation grew,
I became convinced that mellow,
Massic-loving poet fellow,
    Horace, knew a thing or two.

EUGENE FIELD 1850–1895

Yes, we sophomores figured duly
That, if we appraised him truly,
   Horace must have been a brick;
And no wonder that with ranting
Rhymes he went a-gallivanting
   Round with sprightly Lydia Dick!

For that pink of female gender
Tall and shapely was, and slender,
   Plump of neck and bust and arms;
While the raiment that invested
Her so jealously suggested
   Certain more potential charms.

Those dark eyes of hers that fired him,
Those sweet accents that inspired him,
   And her crown of glorious hair,—
These things baffle my description:
I should have a fit conniption
   If I tried; so I forbear.

Maybe Lydia had her betters;
Anyway, this man of letters
   Took that charmer as his pick.
Glad—yes, glad I am to know it!
I, a *fin de siècle* poet,
   Sympathize with Lydia Dick!

EUGENE FIELD 1850–1895

Often in my arbor shady
I fall thinking of that lady,
   And the pranks she used to play;
And I 'm cheered,—for all we sages
Joy when from those distant ages
   Lydia dances down our way.

Otherwise some folks might wonder,
With good reason, why in thunder
   Learned professors, dry and prim,
Find such solace in the giddy
Pranks that Horace played with Liddy
   Or that Liddy played on him.

Still this world of ours rejoices
In those ancient singing voices,
   And our hearts beat high and quick,
To the cadence of old Tiber
Murmuring praise of roistering Liber
   And of charming Lydia Dick.

Still Digentia, downward flowing,
Prattleth to the roses blowing
   By the dark, deserted grot.
Still Soracte, looming lonely,
Watcheth for the coming only
   Of a ghost that cometh not.

EUGENE FIELD 1850–1895

The Preference Declared

Horace Ode I. 38

Boy, I detest the Persian pomp;
    I hate those linden-bark devices;
And as for roses, holy Moses!
    They can't be got at living prices!
Myrtle is good enough for us,—
    For *you,* as bearer of my flagon;
For *me,* supine beneath this vine,
    Doing my best to get a jag on!

Grandma's Prayer

I pray that, risen from the dead,
    I may in glory stand—
A crown, perhaps, upon my head,
    But a needle in my hand.

I've never learned to sing or play,
    So let no harp be mine;
From birth unto my dying day,
    Plain sewing's been my line.

Therefore, accustomed to the end
    To plying useful stitches,
I'll be content if asked to mend
    The little angels' breeches.

EUGENE FIELD 1850–1895

The Duel

The gingham dog and the calico cat
Side by side on the table sat;
'T was half-past twelve, and (what do you think!)
Nor one nor t' other had slept a wink!
    The old Dutch clock and the Chinese plate
    Appeared to know as sure as fate
There was going to be a terrible spat.
    (I was n't there; I simply state
    What was told to me by the Chinese plate!)

The gingham dog went "bow-wow-wow!"
And the calico cat replied "mee-ow!"
The air was littered, an hour or so,
With bits of gingham and calico,
    While the old Dutch clock in the chimney-place
    Up with its hands before its face,
For it always dreaded a family row!
    (Never mind: I 'm only telling you
    What the old Dutch clock declares is true!)

The Chinese plate looked very blue,
And wailed, "Oh, dear! what shall we do!"
But the gingham dog and the calico cat
Wallowed this way and tumbled that,
    Employing every tooth and claw
    In the awfullest way you ever saw—
And, oh! how the gingham and calico flew!
    (Don't fancy I exaggerate—
    I got my news from the Chinese plate!)

EUGENE FIELD 1850–1895

Next morning where the two had sat
They found no trace of dog or cat;
And some folks think unto this day
That burglars stole that pair away!
   But the truth about the cat and pup
   Is this: they ate each other up!
Now what do you really think of that!
   (The old Dutch clock it told me so,
   And that is how I came to know.)

MARC COOK 1854–1882

Her Opinion of the Play

Do I like it? I think it just splendid!
   You see how I speak out my mind,
And I think 't would be better if men did
   The same when they feel so inclined.
But no, you 're all dumb as an oyster,
   You critics who sit here and stare,
Looking grave as a monk in his cloister—
   You have n't laughed once, I declare!

I 'm sure there 's been lots that is jolly,
   And more that 's exciting, you 'll own;
Why, I pity the poor hero's folly
   As if he were some one I 'd known!
And was n't it grand and heroic
   When he shielded that friendless girl Sue?
'T would have quickened the pulse of a stoic,
   But of course, sir, it could n't rouse you!

And then for the villain De Lancey—
   Now, does n't he act with a dash?
Such art and such delicate fancy,
   And—did you observe his moustache?
He made my very blood tingle
   When he threw himself down on his knees—
Do you know if he 's married or single?
   Yes, the villain—there, laugh if you please!

MARC COOK 1854–1882

I admit I know nothing of "action,"
   Of "unities," "plot," and the rest,
But the play gives complete satisfaction,
   And that is a good enough test.
Yes, I know you will pick it to pieces
   In your horribly savage review,
But, for me, its interest increases
   Because 't will be censured by you!

I should think 't would be awfully jolly
   For the author to make such a hit;
How he pricks all the bubbles of folly
   With his sharp little needle of wit!
I am sure he is perfectly charming,
   Or he could never write such a play—
(I declare, sir, it 's really alarming
   To have you sit staring that way!)

And oh, if I only were brighter,
   And not such a poor little dunce,
I should so like to meet with the writer,
   For I know I should love him at once.
Yes, I should, though you think it audacious,
   And I 'd tell him so, too, which is more,
And—*you* are the author?—good gracious!
   Why did n't you say so before?

The Way to Arcady

Oh, what's the way to Arcady,
  To Arcady, to Arcady;
Oh, what's the way to Arcady,
  Where all the leaves are merry?

Oh, what's the way to Arcady?
The spring is rustling in the tree—
The tree the wind is blowing through—
  It sets the blossoms flickering white.
I knew not skies could burn so blue
  Nor any breezes blow so light.
They blow an old-time way for me,
Across the world to Arcady.

Oh, what's the way to Arcady?
Sir Poet, with the rusty coat,
Quit mocking of the song-bird's note.
How have you heart for any tune,
You with the wayworn russet shoon?
Your scrip, a-swinging by your side,
Gapes with a gaunt mouth hungry-wide.
I'll brim it well with pieces red,
If you will tell the way to tread.

Oh, I am bound for Arcady,
And if you but keep pace with me
You tread the way to Arcady.

HENRY CUYLER BUNNER 1855–1896

And where away lies Arcady,
And how long yet may the journey be?

Ah, that (quoth he) I do not know—
Across the clover and the snow—
Across the frost, across the flowers—
Through summer seconds and winter hours,
I've trod the way my whole life long,
  And know not now where it may be;
My guide is but the stir to song,
That tells me I cannot go wrong,
  Or clear or dark the pathway be
  Upon the road to Arcady.

But how shall I do who cannot sing?
  I was wont to sing, once on a time—
There is never an echo now to ring
  Remembrance back to the trick of rhyme.

'T is strange you cannot sing (quoth he),
The folk all sing in Arcady.

But how may he find Arcady
Who hath nor youth nor melody?

What, know you not, old man (quoth he)—
  Your hair is white, your face is wise—
  That Love must kiss that Mortal's eyes
Who hopes to see fair Arcady?

HENRY CUYLER BUNNER 1855–1896

No gold can buy you entrance there;
But beggared Love may go all bare—
No wisdom won with weariness;
But Love goes in with Folly's dress—
No fame that wit could ever win;
But only Love may lead Love in
   To Arcady, to Arcady.

Ah, woe is me, through all my days
   Wisdom and wealth I both have got,
And fame and name, and great men's praise;
   But Love, ah, Love! I have it not.
There was a time, when life was new—
   But far away, and half forgot—
I only know her eyes were blue;
   But Love—I fear I knew it not.
We did not wed, for lack of gold,
And she is dead, and I am old.
All things have come since then to me,
Save Love, ah, Love! and Arcady.

Ah, then I fear we part (quoth he),
My way's for Love and Arcady.

But you, you fare alone, like me;
   The gray is likewise in your hair.
   What love have you to lead you there,
To Arcady, to Arcady?

HENRY CUYLER BUNNER 1855–1896

Ah, no, not lonely do I fare;
   My true companion's Memory.
With Love he fills the Spring-time air;
   With Love he clothes the Winter tree.
Oh, past this poor horizon's bound
   My song goes straight to one who stands—
Her face all gladdening at the sound—
   To lead me to the Spring-green lands,
To wander with enlacing hands.
The songs within my breast that stir
Are all of her, are all of her.
My maid is dead long years (quoth he),
She waits for me in Arcady.

Oh, yon's the way to Arcady,
   To Arcady, to Arcady;
Oh, yon's the way to Arcady,
   Where all the leaves are merry.

HENRY CUYLER BUNNER 1855–1896

She Was a Beauty

She was a beauty in the days
  When Madison was President:
And quite coquettish in her ways—
  On conquests of the heart intent.

  Grandpapa, on his right knee bent,
Wooed her in stiff, old-fashioned phrase—
She was a beauty in the days
  When Madison was President.

And when your roses where hers went
Shall go, my Rose, who date from Hayes,
  I hope you'll wear her sweet content
Of whom tradition lightly says:
She was a beauty in the days
  When Madison was President.

Feminine

She might have known it in the earlier Spring,
  That all my heart with vague desire was stirred;
And, ere the Summer winds had taken wing,
  I told her; but she smiled and said no word.

The Autumn's eager hand his red gold grasped,
  And she was silent; till from skies grown drear
Fell soft one fine, first snow-flake, and she clasped
  My neck and cried, "Love, we have lost a year!"

HENRY CUYLER BUNNER 1855-1896

Candor

October—A Wood

"I know what you 're going to say," she said,
   And she stood up looking uncommonly tall;
   "You are going to speak of the hectic Fall,
And say you 're sorry the summer 's dead.
   And no other summer was like it, you know,
   And can I imagine what made it so?
Now are n't you, honestly?" "Yes," I said.

"I know what you 're going to say," she said;
   "You are going to ask if I forget
   That day in June when the woods were wet,
And you carried me"—here she dropped her head—
   "Over the creek; you are going to say,
   Do I remember that horrid day.
Now are n't you, honestly?" "Yes," I said.

"I know what you 're going to say," she said;
   "You are going to say that since that time
   You have rather tended to run to rhyme,
And"—her clear glance fell and her cheek grew
      red—
   "And have I noticed your tone was queer?—
   Why, everybody has seen it here!—
Now are n't you, honestly?" "Yes," I said.

"I know what you 're going to say," I said;
  "You 're going to say you 've been much annoyed,
  And I 'm short of tact—you will say devoid—
And I 'm clumsy and awkward, and call me Ted,
  And I bear abuse like a dear old lamb,
  And you 'll have me, anyway, just as I am.
Now are n't you, honestly?"
        "Ye-es," she said.

Wed

For these white arms about my neck—
  For the dainty room, with its ordered grace—
For my snowy linen without a fleck—
  For the tender charm of this uplift face—

For the softened light and the homelike air—
  The low luxurious cannel fire—
The padded ease of my chosen chair—
  The devoted love that discounts desire—

I sometimes think, when Twelve is struck
  By the clock on the mantel, tinkling clear,
I would take—and thank the gods for the luck—
  One single hour with the boys and the beer.

Where the sawdust scent of a cheap saloon
  Is mingled with malt; where each man smokes,
Where they sing the street songs out of tune,
  Talk Art, and bandy ephemeral jokes.

By Jove, I do! And all the time
  I know not a man that is there to-night
But would barter his brains to be where I 'm—
  And I 'm well aware that the beggars are right.

The Chaperon

I take my chaperon to the play—
  She thinks she 's taking me.
And the gilded youth who owns the box,
  A proud young man is he—
But how would his young heart be hurt
  If he could only know
  That not for his sweet sake I go
  Nor yet to see the trifling show;
But to see my chaperon flirt.

Her eyes beneath her snowy hair
  They sparkle young as mine;
There 's scarce a wrinkle in her hand
  So delicate and fine.
And when my chaperon is seen,
  They come from everywhere—
  The dear old boys with silvery hair,
  With old-time grace and old-time air,
To greet their old-time queen.

They bow as my young Midas here
    Will never learn to bow
(The dancing-masters do not teach
    That gracious reverence now);
With voices quavering just a bit,
    They play their old parts through,
    They talk of folk who used to woo,
    Of hearts that broke in 'fifty-two—
Now none the worse for it.

And as those aged crickets chirp
    I watch my chaperon's face,
And see the dear old features take
    A new and tender grace—
And in her happy eyes I see
    Her youth awakening bright,
    With all its hope, desire, delight—
    Ah, me! I wish that I were quite
As young—as young as she!

Chakey Einstein

Pharaoh, King of Egypt's land,
Held you in his cruel hand,
Till the Appointed of the Lord
Led you forth and drowned his horde.
Cushan, Eglon's Moabites,
Jabin, then the Midianites,

HENRY CUYLER BUNNER 1855–1896

Ammonite and Philistine
Held you, by decree divine.
Shishak spoiled you—but the list
Fades in dim tradition's mist—
And on history's page we see
One long tale of misery,
Century after century through—
Chains and lashes for the Jew.
Haman and Antiochus,
Herod, Roman Socius,
Spoiled you, crushed you, various ways,
Till the dawn of Christian days;
Since which time your wrongs and shame
Have remained about the same.
Whipped and chained, your teeth pulled out;
English cat and Russian knout
Made familiar with your back—
When you were n't upon the rack—
Marked for scorn of Christian men;
Pilfered, taxed, and taxed again;
Pilloried, prisoned, burnt and stoned,
Stripped of even the clothes you owned;
Child of Torture, Son of Shame,
Robbed of even a father's name—
In this year of Christian grace,
What's your state and what's your place?
Why, you're rich and strong and gay—
Chakey Einstein, owff Broadway!

HENRY CUYLER BUNNER 1855–1896

Myriad signs along the street
Israelitish names repeat.
Lichtenstein and Morgenroth
Sell the pants and sell the coat;
Minzesheimer, Isaacs, Meyer,
Levy, Lehman, Simon, Speyer—
These may just suggest a few
Specimens of Broadway Jew—
And these gentlemen have made
Quite their own the Dry-gootz Trade.
Surely you 're on top to-day,
Chakey Einstein, owff Broadway!

Fat and rich you are, and loud;
Fond of being in a crowd;
Fond of diamonds and rings;
Fond of haberdashers' things;
Fond of color, fond of noise;
Fond of treating "owl der boys"
(Yet, it 's only fair to state,
For yourself, most temperate);
Fond of women, fond of song;
Fond of bad cigars, and strong;
Fond, too much, of Brighton's Race
(Where you 're wholly out of place,
For no Jew in Time's long course
Knew one thing about a horse);
Fond of life, and fond of fun
(Once your "beezness" wholly done);

HENRY CUYLER BUNNER 1855-1896

Open-handed, generous, free,
Full of Christian charity
(Far more full than he who pokes
At your avarice his jokes);
Fond of friends, and ever kind
To the sick and lame and blind
(And, though loud you else may be,
Silent in your charity);
Fond of Mrs. Einstein and
Her too-numerous infant band,
Ever willing they should share
Your enjoyment everywhere—
What of you is left to say,
Chakey Einstein, owff Broadway?

Though you're spurned in some hotels,
You have kin among the swells—
Great musicians, poets true,
Painters, singers not a few,
Own their cousinship to you:
And all England, so they say,
Yearly blooms on Primrose Day
All in memory of a Jew
Of the self-same race as you;
Greatest leader ever known
Since the Queen came to her throne;
Bismarck's only equal foe,
With a thrust for every blow,
One who rose from place to place

HENRY CUYLER BUNNER 1855–1896

To lead the Anglo-Saxon race,
One whose statecraft wise and keen
Made an Empress of a Queen—
You 've your share in Primrose Day,
Chakey Einstein, owff Broadway!

Well, good friend, we look at you
And behold the Conquering Jew:
In despite of all the years
Filled with agonies and fears;
In despite of stake and chain;
In despite of Rome and Spain;
'Spite of prison, rack, and lash,
You are here and you 've the cash:
You are Trade's uncrownèd king—
You are mostly everything—
Only one small joke, O Jew!
Has the Christian world on you—
When your son, your first-born boy,
Solomon, your fond heart's joy,
Grows to manhood's years, he 'll wed
One a Christian born and bred;
Blue of blood, of lineage old,
Who will take him for his gold—
That 's not all—so far the joke
Is upon the Christian folk.
But, dear Chakey, when he goes
In his proper Sabbath clo'es,
To the House of Worship, he

And his little family,
He will pass the synagogue,
And upon his way will jog
To a Church, wherein his pew
Will bear a name unknown to you—
One quite unknown in old B'nai B'rith—
Eynston maybe—maybe Smith.
That's just as sure as day is day—
Chakey Einstein, owff Broadway!

Atlantic City

O City that is not a city, unworthy the prefix Atlantic,
Forlornest of watering-places, and thoroughly Philadelphian!
In thy despite I sing, with a bitter and deep detestation—
A detestation born of a direful and dinnerless evening,
Spent in thy precincts unhallowed—an evening I trust may recur not.
Never till then did I know what was meant by the word god-forsaken:
Thou its betokening hast taught me, being the chiefest example.
Thou art the scorned of the gods; thy sand from their sandals is shaken;
Thee have they left in their wrath to thy uninteresting extensiveness,

Barren and bleak and big; a wild aggregation of barracks,
Miscalled hotels, and of dovecotes denominate cottages;
A confusion of ugly girls, of sand, and of health-bearing breezes,
With one unending plank-walk for a true Philadelphia "attraction."
City ambitiously named, why, with inducements delusive,
Is the un-Philadelphian stranger lured to thy desert pretentious?
'T is not alone that thy avenues, broad and unpaved and unending,
Re-echo yet with the obsolete music of "Pinafore,"
Whistled in various keys by the rather too numerous negro;
'T is not alone that Propriety—Propriety too Philadelphian—
Over thee stretches an ægis of wholly superfluous virtue;
That thou art utterly good; hast no single vice to redeem thee;
'T is not alone that thou art provincial in all things, and petty;
And that the dullness of death is gay, compared to thy dullness—
'T is not alone for these things that my curse is to rest upon thee:
But for a sin that crowns thee with perfect and eminent badness;

Sets thee alone in thy shame, the unworthiest town on
    the sea-coast:
This: that thou dinest at Noon, and then in a manner
    barbarian,
Soupless and wineless and coffeeless, untimely and wholly
    indecent—
As is the custom, I learn, in Philadelphia proper.
I rose and I fled from thy Supper; I said: "I will get me
    a Dinner!"
Vainly I wandered thy streets: thy eating-places ungodly
Knew not the holiness of Dinner; in all that evening I
    dined not;
But in a strange low lair, infested of native mechanics,
Bolted a fried beefsteak for the physical need of my
    stomach.
And for them that have fried that steak, in Aides' lowest
    back-kitchen
May they eternally broil, by way of a warning to others.
During my wanderings, I met, and hailed with delight
    one Italian,
A man with a name from "Pasquale"—the chap sung by
    Tagliapietra—
He knew what it was to dine; he comprehended my
    yearnings;
But the spell was also on him; the somnolent spell Phila-
    delphian;
And his hostelry would not be open till Saturday next;
    and I cursed him.

Now this is not *too* much to ask, God knows, that a mortal
    should want a
Pint of Bordeaux to his dinner, and a small cigarette
    for a climax:
But, these things being denied him, where then is your
    Civilization?
O Coney Island! of old I have reviled and blasphemed
    thee,
For that thou dowsest thy glim at an hour that is un-
    metropolitan;
That thy frequenters' feet turn townwards ere striketh
    eleven,
When the returning cars are filled with young men and
    maidens,
Most of the maidens asleep on the young men's cindery
    shoulders—
Yea, but I spake as a fool, insensate, disgruntled, un-
    grateful:
Thee will I worship henceforth in appreciative humility:
Luxurious and splendid and urban, glorious and gaslit
    and gracious,
Gathering from every land thy gay and ephemeral ten-
    antry,
From the Greek who hails thee, "Thalatta!" to the rustic
    who murmurs, "My Golly!"
From the Bowery youth who requests his sweetheart to
    "look at them billers!"
To the Gaul whom thy laughing waves almost persuade
    to immersion:

HENRY CUYLER BUNNER 1855–1896

O Coney Island, thou art the weary citizen's heaven—
A heaven to dine, not die in, joyful and restful and
       clamful,
Better one hour of thee than an age of Atlantic City!

Da Capo

Short and sweet, and we've come to the end of it—
   Our poor little love lying cold.
Shall no sonnet, then, ever be penned of it?
   Nor the joys and pains of it told?
How fair was its face in the morning,
   How close its caresses at noon,
How its evening grew chill without warning,
       Unpleasantly soon!

I can't say just how we began it—
   In a blush, or a smile, or a sigh;
Fate took but an instant to plan it;
   It needs but a moment to die.
Yet—remember that first conversation,
   When the flowers you had dropped at your feet
I restored. The familiar quotation
       Was—"Sweets to the sweet."

Oh, their delicate perfume has haunted
   My senses a whole season through.
If there *was* one soft charm that you wanted
   The violets lent it to you.
I whispered you, life was but lonely:
   A cue which you graciously took;
And your eyes learned a look for me only—
       A very nice look.

And sometimes your hand would touch *my* hand,
   With a sweetly particular touch;
You said many things in a sigh, and
   Made a look express wondrously much.
We smiled for the mere sake of smiling,
   And laughed for no reason but fun;
Irrational joys; but beguiling—
       And all that is done!

We were idle, and played for a moment
   At a game that now neither will press:
I cared not to find out what "No" meant;
   Nor your lips to grow yielding with "Yes."
Love is done with and dead; if there lingers
   A faint and indefinite ghost,
It is laid with this kiss on your fingers—
       A jest at the most.

HENRY CUYLER BUNNER 1855–1896

'T is a commonplace, stale situation,
   Now the curtain comes down from above
On the end of our little flirtation—
   A travesty romance; for Love,
If he climbed in disguise to your lattice,
   Fell dead of the first kisses' pain:
But one thing is left us now; that is—
      Begin it again.

Just a Love-Letter

"'Miss Blank—at Blank.' Jemima, let it go!"
                                      —*Austin Dobson.*

               New York, July 20, 1883.
DEAR GIRL:
      The town goes on as though
     It thought you still were in it;
   The gilded cage seems scarce to know
     That it has lost its linnet;
   The people come, the people pass;
     The clock keeps on a-ticking:
   And through the basement plots of grass
     Persistent weeds are pricking.

I thought 't would never come—the Spring—
   Since you had left the City:
But on the snow-drifts lingering
   At last the skies took pity,
Then Summer's yellow warmed the sun,
   Daily decreasing distance—
I really don't know how 't was done
   Without your kind assistance.

Aunt Van, of course, still holds the fort:
   I 've paid the call of duty;
She gave me one small glass of port—
   'T was '34 and fruity.
The furniture was draped in gloom
   Of linen brown and wrinkled;
I smelt in spots about the room
   The pungent camphor sprinkled.

I sat upon the sofa, where
   You sat and dropped your thimble—
You know—you said you did n't care;
   But I was nobly nimble.
On hands and knees I dropped, and tried
   To—well, I tried to miss it:
You slipped your hand down by your side—
   You knew I meant to kiss it!

HENRY CUYLER BUNNER 1855–1896

Aunt Van, I fear we put to shame
    Propriety and precision:
But, praised be Love, that kiss just came
    Beyond your line of vision.
Dear maiden aunt! the kiss, more sweet
    Because 't is surreptitious,
You never stretched a hand to meet,
    So dimpled, dear, delicious.

I sought the Park last Saturday;
    I found the Drive deserted;
The water-trough beside the way
    Sad and superfluous spurted.
I stood where Humboldt guards the gate,
    Bronze, bumptious, stained and streaky—
There sat a sparrow on his pate,
    A sparrow chirp and cheeky.

Ten months ago! ten months ago!—
    It seems a happy second,
Against a life-time lone and slow,
    By Love's wild time-piece reckoned—
You smiled, by Aunt's protecting side,
    Where thick the drags were massing,
On one young man who did n't ride,
    But stood and watched you passing.

HENRY CUYLER BUNNER 1855–1896

I haunt Purssell's—to his amaze—
   Not that I care to eat there;
But for the dear clandestine days
   When we two had to meet there.
Oh, blessed is that baker's bake,
   Past cavil and past question;
I ate a bun for your sweet sake,
   And Memory helped Digestion.

The Norths are at their Newport ranch;
   Van Brunt has gone to Venice;
Loomis invites me to the Branch,
   And lures me with lawn-tennis.
O bustling barracks by the sea!
   O spiles, canals, and islands!
Your varied charms are naught to me—
   My heart is in the Highlands!

My paper trembles in the breeze
   That all too faintly flutters
Among the dusty city trees,
   And through my half-closed shutters:
A northern captive in the town,
   Its native vigor deadened,
I hope that, as it wandered down,
   Your dear pale cheek it reddened.

HENRY CUYLER BUNNER 1855–1896

I 'll write no more. A *vis-à-vis*
   In halcyon vacation
Will sure afford a much more free
   Mode of communication;
I 'm tantalized and cribbed and checked
   In making love by letter:
I know a style more brief, direct—
   And generally better!

RICHARD HOVEY 1864–1900

The Wander-Lovers

Down the world with Marna!
That's the life for me!
Wandering with the wandering wind,
Vagabond and unconfined!
Roving with the roving rain
Its unboundaried domain!
Kith and kin of wander-kind,
Children of the sea!

Petrels of the sea-drift!
Swallows of the lea!
Arabs of the whole wide girth
Of the wind-encircled earth!
In all climes we pitch our tents,
Cronies of the elements,
With the secret lords of birth
Intimate and free.

All the seaboard knows us
From Fundy to the Keys;
Every bend and every creek
Of abundant Chesapeake;
Ardise hills and Newport coves
And the far-off orange groves,
Where Floridian oceans break,
Tropic tiger seas.

RICHARD HOVEY 1864–1900

Down the world with Marna,
Tarrying there and here!
Just as much at home in Spain
As in Tangier or Touraine!
Shakespeare's Avon knows us well,
And the crags of Neufchâtel;
And the ancient Nile is fain
Of our coming near.

Down the world with Marna,
Daughter of the air!
Marna of the subtle grace,
And the vision in her face!
Moving in the measures trod
By the angels before God!
With her sky-blue eyes amaze
And her sea-blue hair!

Marna with the trees' life
In her veins a-stir!
Marna of the aspen heart
Where the sudden quivers start!
Quick-responsive, subtle, wild!
Artless as an artless child,
Spite of all her reach of art!
Oh, to roam with her!

RICHARD HOVEY 1864–1900

Marna with the wind's will,
Daughter of the sea!
Marna of the quick disdain,
Starting at the dream of stain!
At a smile with love aglow,
At a frown a statued woe,
Standing pinnacled in pain
Till a kiss sets free!

Down the world with Marna,
Daughter of the fire!
Marna of the deathless hope,
Still alert to win new scope
Where the wings of life may spread
For a flight unhazarded!
Dreaming of the speech to cope
With the heart's desire!

Marna of the far quest
After the divine!
Striving ever for some goal
Past the blunder-god's control!
Dreaming of potential years
When no day shall dawn in fears!
That's the Marna of my soul,
Wander-bride of mine!

RICHARD HOVEY 1864–1900

At the End of Day

There is no escape by the river,
There is no flight left by the fen;
We are compassed about by the shiver
Of the night of their marching men.
Give a cheer!
For our hearts shall not give way.
Here's to a dark to-morrow,
And here's to a brave to-day!

The tale of their hosts is countless,
And the tale of ours a score;
But the palm is naught to the dauntless,
And the cause is more and more.
Give a cheer!
We may die, but not give way.
Here's to a silent morrow,
And here's to a stout to-day!

God has said: "Ye shall fail and perish;
But the thrill ye have felt to-night
I shall keep in my heart and cherish
When the worlds have passed in night."
Give a cheer!
For the soul shall not give way.
Here's to the greater to-morrow
That is born of a great to-day!

RICHARD HOVEY 1864–1900

Now shame on the craven truckler
And the puling things that mope!
We've a rapture for our buckler
That outwears the wings of hope.
Give a cheer!
For our joy shall not give way.
Here's in the teeth of to-morrow
To the glory of to-day!

The Sea Gypsy

I am fevered with the sunset,
I am fretful with the bay,
For the wander-thirst is on me
And my soul is in Cathay.

There's a schooner in the offing,
With her topsails shot with fire,
And my heart has gone aboard her
For the Islands of Desire.

I must forth again to-morrow!
With the sunset I must be
Hull down on the trail of rapture
In the wonder of the sea.

RICHARD HOVEY 1864–1900

Launa Dee

Weary, oh, so weary
With it all!
Sunny days or dreary—
How they pall!
Why should we be heroes,
Launa Dee,
Striving to no winning?
Let the world be Zero's!
As in the beginning
Let it be.

What good comes of toiling,
When all's done?
Frail green sprays for spoiling
Of the sun;
Laurel leaf or myrtle,
Love or fame—
Ah, what odds what spray, sweet?
Time, that makes life fertile,
Makes its blooms decay, sweet,
As they came.

Lie here with me dreaming,
Cheek to cheek,
Lithe limbs twined and gleaming,
Brown and sleek;
Like two serpents coiling
In their lair.

RICHARD HOVEY 1864–1900

Where's the good of wreathing
Sprays for Time's despoiling?
Let me feel your breathing
In my hair.

You and I together—
Was it so?
In the August weather
Long ago!
Did we kiss and fellow,
Side by side,
Till the sunbeams quickened
From our stalks great yellow
Sunflowers, till we sickened
There and died?

Were we tigers creeping
Through the glade
Where our prey lay sleeping,
Unafraid,
In some Eastern jungle?
Better so.
I am sure the snarling
Beasts could never bungle
Life as men do, darling,
Who half know.

Ah, if all of life, love,
Were the living!
Just to cease from strife, love,
And from grieving;

Let the swift world pass us,
You and me,
Stilled from all aspiring,—
Sinai nor Parnassus
Longer worth desiring,
Launa Dee!

Just to live like lilies
In the lake!
Where no thought nor will is,
To mistake!
Just to lose the human
Eyes that weep!
Just to cease from seeming
Longer man and woman!
Just to reach the dreaming
And the sleep!

Unmanifest Destiny

To what new fates, my country, far
   And unforeseen of foe or friend,
Beneath what unexpected star,
   Compelled to what unchosen end,

Across the sea that knows no beach
   The Admiral of Nations guides
Thy blind obedient keels to reach
   The harbor where thy future rides!

RICHARD HOVEY 1864–1900

The guns that spoke at Lexington
   Knew not that God was planning then
The trumpet word of Jefferson
   To bugle forth the rights of men.

To them that wept and cursed Bull Run,
   What was it but despair and shame?
Who saw behind the cloud the sun?
   Who knew that God was in the flame?

Had not defeat upon defeat,
   Disaster on disaster come,
The slave's emancipated feet
   Had never marched behind the drum.

There is a Hand that bends our deeds
   To mightier issues than we planned,
Each son that triumphs, each that bleeds,
   My country, serves Its dark command.

I do not know beneath what sky
   Nor on what seas shall be thy fate;
I only know it shall be high,
   I only know it shall be great.

RICHARD HOVEY 1864–1900

Voices of Unseen Spirits

From "Taliesin: a Masque"

Here falls no light of sun nor stars;
   No stir nor striving here intrudes;
No moan nor merry-making mars
   The quiet of these solitudes.

Submerged in sleep, the passive soul
   Is one with all the things that seem;
Night blurs in one confusèd whole
   Alike the dreamer and the dream.

O dwellers in the busy town!
   For dreams you smile, for dreams you weep.
Come out, and lay your burdens down!
   Come out; there is no God but Sleep.

Sleep, and renounce the vital day;
   For evil is the child of life.
Let be the will to live, and pray
   To find forgetfulness of strife.

Beneath the thicket of these leaves
   No light discriminates each from each.
No Self that wrongs, no Self that grieves
   Hath longer deed nor creed nor speech.

Sleep on the mighty Mother's breast!
   Sleep, and no more be separate!
Then, one with Nature's ageless rest,
   There shall be no more sin to hate.

RICHARD HOVEY 1864–1900

Faith and Fate

To horse, my dear, and out into the night!
Stirrup and saddle and away, away!
Into the darkness, into the affright,
Into the unknown on our trackless way!
Past bridge and town missiled with flying feet,
Into the wilderness our riding thrills;
The gallop echoes through the startled street,
And shrieks like laughter in the demoned hills;
Things come to meet us with fantastic frown,
And hurry past with maniac despair;
Death from the stars looks ominously down—
Ho, ho, the dauntless riding that we dare!
    East, to the dawn, or west or south or north!
    Loose rein upon the neck of Fate—and forth!

WILLIAM VAUGHN MOODY 1869–1910

An Ode in Time of Hesitation

(After seeing at Boston the statue of Robert Gould Shaw, killed while storming Fort Wagner, July 18, 1863, at the head of the first enlisted negro regiment, the 54th Massachusetts.)

I

Before the solemn bronze Saint Gaudens made
To thrill the heedless passer's heart with awe,
And set here in the city's talk and trade
To the good memory of Robert Shaw,
This bright March morn I stand,
And hear the distant spring come up the land;
Knowing that what I hear is not unheard
Of this boy soldier and his negro band,
For all their gaze is fixed so stern ahead,
For all the fatal rhythm of their tread.
The land they died to save from death and shame
Trembles and waits, hearing the spring's great name,
And by her pangs these resolute ghosts are stirred.

II

Through street and mall the tides of people go
Heedless; the trees upon the Common show
No hint of green; but to my listening heart
The still earth doth impart
Assurance of her jubilant emprise,

And it is clear to my long-searching eyes
That love at last has might upon the skies.
The ice is runneled on the little pond;
A telltale patter drips from off the trees;
The air is touched with southland spiceries,
As if but yesterday it tossed the frond
Of pendent mosses where the live-oaks grow
Beyond Virginia and the Carolines,
Or had its will among the fruits and vines
Of aromatic isles asleep beyond
Florida and the Gulf of Mexico.

III

Soon shall the Cape Ann children shout in glee,
Spying the arbutus, spring's dear recluse;
Hill lads at dawn shall hearken the wild goose
Go honking northward over Tennessee;
West from Oswego to Sault Sainte-Marie,
And on to where the Pictured Rocks are hung,
And yonder where, gigantic, willful, young,
Chicago sitteth at the northwest gates,
With restless violent hands and casual tongue
Moulding her mighty fates,
The Lakes shall robe them in ethereal sheen;
And like a larger sea, the vital green
Of springing wheat shall vastly be outflung
Over Dakota and the prairie states.
By desert people immemorial

WILLIAM VAUGHN MOODY 1869–1910

On Arizonan mesas shall be done
Dim rites unto the thunder and the sun;
Nor shall the primal gods lack sacrifice
More splendid, when the white Sierras call
Unto the Rockies straightway to arise
And dance before the unveiled ark of the year,
Sounding their windy cedars as for shawms,
Unrolling rivers clear
For flutter of broad phylacteries;
While Shasta signals to Alaskan seas
That watch old sluggish glaciers downward creep,
To fling their icebergs thundering from the steep,
And Mariposa through the purple calms
Gazes at far Hawaii crowned with palms
Where East and West are met,—
A rich seal on the ocean's bosom set
To say that East and West are twain,
With different loss and gain:
The Lord hath sundered them; let them be sundered yet.

IV

Alas! what sounds are these that come
Sullenly over the Pacific seas,—
Sounds of ignoble battle, striking dumb
The season's half-awakened ecstasies?
Must I be humble, then,
Now when my heart hath need of pride?
Wild love falls on me from these sculptured men;

By loving much the land for which they died
I would be justified.
My spirit was away on pinions wide
To soothe in praise of her its passionate mood
And ease it of its ache of gratitude.
Too sorely heavy is the debt they lay
On me and the companions of my day.
I would remember now
My country's goodliness, make sweet her name.
Alas! what shade art thou
Of sorrow or of blame
Liftest the lyric leafage from her brow,
And pointest a slow finger at her shame?

V

Lies! lies! It cannot be! The wars we wage
Are noble, and our battles still are won
By justice for us, ere we lift the gage.
We have not sold our loftiest heritage.
The proud republic hath not stooped to cheat
And scramble in the market-place of war;
Her forehead weareth yet its solemn star.
Here is her witness: this, her perfect son,
This delicate and proud New England soul
Who leads despisèd men, with just-unshackled feet,
Up the large ways where death and glory meet,
To show all peoples that our shame is done,
That once more we are clean and spirit-whole.

VI

Crouched in the sea fog on the moaning sand
All night he lay, speaking some simple word
From hour to hour to the slow minds that heard,
Holding each poor life gently in his hand
And breathing on the base rejected clay
Till each dark face shone mystical and grand
Against the breaking day;
And lo, the shard the potter cast away
Was grown a fiery chalice crystal-fine
Fulfilled of the divine
Great wine of battle wrath by God's ring-finger stirred.
Then upward, where the shadowy bastion loomed
Huge on the mountain in the wet sea light,
Whence now, and now, infernal flowerage bloomed,
Bloomed, burst, and scattered down its deadly seed,—
They swept, and died like freemen on the height,
Like freemen, and like men of noble breed;
And when the battle fell away at night
By hasty and contemptuous hands were thrust
Obscurely in a common grave with him
The fair-haired keeper of their love and trust.
Now limb doth mingle with dissolvèd limb
In nature's busy old democracy
To flush the mountain laurel when she blows
Sweet by the southern sea,
And heart with crumbled heart climbs in the rose:—
The untaught hearts with the high heart that knew

This mountain fortress for no earthly hold
Of temporal quarrel, but the bastion old
Of spiritual wrong,
Built by an unjust nation sheer and strong,
Expugnable but by a nation's rue
And bowing down before that equal shrine
By all men held divine,
Whereof his band and he were the most holy sign.

VII

O bitter, bitter shade!
Wilt thou not put the scorn
And instant tragic question from thine eyes?
Do thy dark brows yet crave
That swift and angry stave—
Unmeet for this desirous morn—
That I have striven, striven to evade?
Gazing on him, must I not deem they err
Whose careless lips in street and shop aver
As common tidings, deeds to make his cheek
Flush from the bronze, and his dead throat to speak?
Surely some elder singer would arise,
Whose harp hath leave to threaten and to mourn
Above this people when they go astray.
Is Whitman, the strong spirit, overworn?
Has Whittier put his yearning wrath away?
I will not and I dare not yet believe!
Though furtively the sunlight seems to grieve,
And the spring-laden breeze

WILLIAM VAUGHN MOODY 1869–1910

Out of the gladdening west is sinister
With sounds of nameless battle overseas;
Though when we turn and question in suspense
If these things be indeed after these ways,
And what things are to follow after these,
Our fluent men of place and consequence
Fumble and fill their mouths with hollow phrase,
Or for the end-all of deep arguments
Intone their dull commercial liturgies—
I dare not yet believe! My ears are shut!
I will not hear the thin satiric praise
And muffled laughter of our enemies,
Bidding us never sheathe our valiant sword
Till we have changed our birthright for a gourd
Of wild pulse stolen from a barbarian's hut;
Showing how wise it is to cast away
The symbols of our spiritual sway,
That so our hands with better ease
May wield the driver's whip and grasp the jailer's keys.

VIII

Was it for this our fathers kept the law?
This crown shall crown their struggle and their ruth?
Are we the eagle nation Milton saw
Mewing its mighty youth,
Soon to possess the mountain winds of truth,
And be a swift familiar of the sun
Where aye before God's face his trumpets run?

Or have we but the talons and the maw,
And for the abject likeness of our heart
Shall some less lordly bird be set apart?—
Some gross-billed wader where the swamps are fat?
Some gorger in the sun?   Some prowler with the bat?

IX

Ah, no!
We have not fallen so.
We are our fathers' sons: let those who lead us know!
'T was only yesterday sick Cuba's cry
Came up the tropic wind, "Now help us, for we die!"
Then Alabama heard,
And rising, pale, to Maine and Idaho
Shouted a burning word,
Proud state with proud impassioned state conferred,
And at the lifting of a hand sprang forth,
East, west, and south, and north,
Beautiful armies.   Oh, by the sweet blood and young
Shed on the awful hillslope at San Juan,
By the unforgotten names of eager boys
Who might have tasted girls' love and been stung
With the old mystic joys
And starry griefs, now the spring nights come on,
But that the heart of youth is generous,—
We charge you, ye who lead us,
Breathe on their chivalry no hint of stain!
Turn not their new-world victories to gain!

WILLIAM VAUGHN MOODY 1869–1910

One least leaf plucked for chaffer from the bays
Of their dear praise,
One jot of their pure conquest put to hire,
The implacable republic will require;
With clamor, in the glare and gaze of noon,
Or subtly, coming as a thief at night,
But surely, very surely, slow or soon
That insult deep we deeply will requite.
Tempt not our weakness, our cupidity!
For save we let the island men go free,
Those baffled and dislaureled ghosts
Will curse us from the lamentable coasts
Where walk the frustrate dead.
The cup of trembling shall be drainèd quite,
Eaten the sour bread of astonishment,
With ashes of the hearth shall be made white
Our hair, and wailing shall be in the tent;
Then on your guiltier head
Shall our intolerable self-disdain
Wreak suddenly its anger and its pain;
For manifest in that disastrous light
We shall discern the right
And do it, tardily.—O ye who lead,
Take heed!
Blindness we may forgive, but baseness we will smite.

WILLIAM VAUGHN MOODY 1869–1910

Gloucester Moors

A mile behind is Gloucester town
Where the fishing fleets put in,
A mile ahead the land dips down
And the woods and farms begin.
Here, where the moors stretch free
In the high blue afternoon,
Are the marching sun and talking sea,
And the racing winds that wheel and flee
On the flying heels of June.

Jill-o'er-the-ground is purple blue,
Blue is the quaker maid,
The wild geranium holds its dew
Long in the boulder's shade.
Wax-red hangs the cup
From the huckleberry boughs,
In barberry bells the gray moths sup,
Or where the choke-cherry lifts high up
Sweet bowls for their carouse.

Over the shelf of the sandy cove
Beach-peas blossom late.
By copse and cliff the swallows rove
Each calling to his mate.
Seaward the sea-gulls go,
And the land-birds all are here;
That green-gold flash was a vireo,
And yonder flame where the marsh-flags grow
Was a scarlet tanager.

WILLIAM VAUGHN MOODY 1869–1910

This earth is not the steadfast place
We landsmen build upon;
From deep to deep she varies pace,
And while she comes is gone.
Beneath my feet I feel
Her smooth bulk heave and dip;
With velvet plunge and soft upreel
She swings and steadies to her keel
Like a gallant, gallant ship.

These summer clouds she sets for sail,
The sun is her masthead light,
She tows the moon like a pinnace frail
Where her phosphor wake churns bright.
Now hid, now looming clear,
On the face of the dangerous blue
The star fleets tack and wheel and veer,
But on, but on does the old earth steer
As if her port she knew.

God, dear God! Does she know her port,
Though she goes so far about?
Or blind astray, does she make her sport
To brazen and chance it out?
I watched when her captains passed:
She were better captainless.
Men in the cabin, before the mast,
But some were reckless and some aghast.
And some sat gorged at mess.

WILLIAM VAUGHN MOODY 1869–1910

By her battened hatch I leaned and caught
Sounds from the noisome hold,—
Cursing and sighing of souls distraught
And cries too sad to be told.
Then I strove to go down and see;
But they said, "Thou art not of us!"
I turned to those on the deck with me
And cried, "Give help!" But they said, "Let be:
Our ship sails faster thus."

Jill-o'er-the-ground is purple blue,
Blue is the quaker-maid,
The alder-clump where the brook comes through
Breeds cresses in its shade.
To be out of the moiling street
With its swelter and its sin!
Who has given to me this sweet,
And given my brother dust to eat?
And when will his wage come in?

Scattering wide or blown in ranks,
Yellow and white and brown,
Boats and boats from the fishing banks
Come home to Gloucester town.
There is cash to purse and spend,
There are wives to be embraced,
Hearts to borrow and hearts to lend,
And hearts to take and keep to the end,—
O little sails, make haste!

WILLIAM VAUGHN MOODY 1869–1910

But thou, vast outbound ship of souls,
What harbor town for thee?
What shapes, when thy arriving tolls,
Shall crowd the banks to see?
Shall all the happy shipmates then
Stand singing brotherly?
Or shall a haggard ruthless few
Warp her over and bring her to,
While the many broken souls of men
Fester down in the slaver's pen,
And nothing to say or do?

INDEX

INDEX OF TITLES

After the Ball	Perry	477
Ah, Be Not False	Gilder	492
Alas!	Cary	345
All Quiet Along the Potomac	Beers	383
Alnwick Castle	Halleck	14
American Flag, The	Drake	69
Annabel Lee	Poe	186
Antony and Cleopatra	Lytle	381
Arsenal at Springfield, The	Longfellow	113
Atlantic City	Bunner	525
At the End of Day	Hovey	539
Auf Wiedersehen	Lowell	302
Baby Bell	Aldrich	427
Babylonian Captivity, The	Barlow	3
Ballad of Lager Bier, The	Stedman	406
Ballad of the Oysterman, The	Holmes	216
Barbara Frietchie	Whittier	163
Barclay of Ury	Whittier	139
Battle-Field, The	Bryant	53
Bells, The	Poe	182
Bereavement	Saxe	250
Black Eyes	Story	264
Battle-Hymn of the Republic	Howe	317
Bibliomaniac's Prayer, The	Field	498
Bivouac of the Dead, The	O'Hara	332
Borrowing	Emerson	86
Brahma	Emerson	87
Burns	Halleck	18
Candor	Bunner	517
Carmen Bellicosum	McMaster	387
Celestial Army	Read	337
Chakey Einstein	Bunner	520
Chambered Nautilus, The	Holmes	226

INDEX OF TITLES

Chaperon, The	Bunner	519
Charleston	Timrod	391
Chiquita	Harte	462
Cleopatra	Story	253
Concord Hymn	Emerson	85
Connecticut	Halleck	30
Conqueror's Grave, The	Bryant	60
Conqueror Worm, The	Poe	180
Coup de Grace, The	Sill	476
Courtin', The	Lowell	270
Credidimus Jovem Regnare	Lowell	307
Crowded Street, The	Bryant	56
Cumberland, The	Longfellow	131
Da Capo	Bunner	529
Days	Emerson	84
Day is Done, The	Longfellow	119
Deacon's Masterpiece, The	Holmes	218
Dear Old London	Field	494
Death of the Flowers, The	Bryant	46
Dedication of "In War Time"	Whittier	159
Dibdin's Ghost	Field	499
Dilemma, The	Holmes	195
Dixie	Pike	230
Dow's Flat	Harte	456
Duel, The	Field	508
Early Rising	Saxe	240
Edged Tools	Stedman	413
Egyptian Serenade	Curtis	343
Endymion	Longfellow	108
Evening	Doane	72
Excelsior	Longfellow	111
Fable	Emerson	83
Faith	Palmer	168
Faith and Fate	Hovey	546
Fancy Shot, The	Shanly	237

INDEX OF TITLES

Feminine	Bunner	516
Fight at the San Jacinto, The	Palmer	361
Flight of Youth, The	Stoddard	366
Florence Vane	Cooke	251
Fool's Prayer, The	Sill	470
Footsteps of Angels	Longfellow	96
Forest Hymn, A	Bryant	40
Freedom for the Mind	Garrison	88
Future Life, The	Bryant	55
Gloucester Moors	Moody	556
Grandma's Prayer	Field	507
Hannah Binding Shoes	Larcom	377
Haunted Palace, The	Poe	178
Health, A	Pinkney	74
Her Epitaph	Parsons	326
Heri, Cras, Hodie	Emerson	86
Her Opinion of the Play	Cook	510
Heroic Age, The	Gilder	493
Home, Sweet Home	Payne	34
Home Wounded	Anonymous	468
Hour of Peaceful Rest, The	Tappan	35
Humble-Bee, The	Emerson	80
Hymn of the Knights Templars	Hay	447
Hypatia	Stedman	422
Ichabod	Whittier	146
In Amsterdam	Field	496
In an Atelier	Aldrich	433
Incognita of Raphael, The	Butler	346
In Sorrow	Hastings	8
In the Rain	Story	266
"Jim"	Harte	460
Jim Bludso of the Prairie Belle	Hay	443
June	Bryant	44
Just a Love-Letter	Bunner	531
Kearny at Seven Pines	Stedman	420

INDEX OF TITLES

L'Abbate	Story	260
Last	Allen	397
Last Leaf, The	Holmes	193
Latter Day, The	Hastings	7
Launa Dee	Hovey	541
Left Behind	Allen	398
Lexington	Holmes	203
Life on the Ocean Wave, A	Sargent	239
Lines on the Death of S. O. Torrey	Whittier	144
Little Peach, The	Field	503
Love in a Cottage	Willis	90
Love to the Church	Dwight	1
Lover's Song, The	Sill	475
Lydia Dick	Field	504
Maidenhood	Longfellow	109
Marco Bozzaris	Halleck	10
Marshes of Glynn, The	Lanier	482
Mary Booth	Parsons	325
Maud Muller	Whittier	148
Milton's Prayer of Patience	Howell	232
Mint Julep, The	Hoffman	93
Momentous Words	Sill	474
Monterey	Hoffman	92
Music-Grinders, The	Holmes	200
My Aunt	Holmes	197
My Lost Youth	Longfellow	127
My Maryland	Randall	449
My Playmate	Whittier	153
Mystery of Gilgal, The	Hay	445
Nearer Home	Cary	344
Nocturne	Aldrich	440
Noël	Gilder	491
Nothing to Wear	Butler	348
Nuremberg	Longfellow	115
Obituary	Parsons	327

INDEX OF TITLES

O Captain! My Captain!	Whitman	321
O Listen to the Sounding Sea	Curtis	342
Ode	Timrod	393
Ode in Time of Hesitation, An	Moody	547
Ode recited at the Harvard Commemoration	Lowell	286
"Oh Mother of a Mighty Race"	Bryant	58
Old Burying-Ground, The	Whittier	155
On a Bust of Dante	Parsons	323
On an Intaglio Head of Minerva	Aldrich	438
On Lending a Punch-Bowl	Holmes	206
On Lynn Terrace	Aldrich	436
On the Death of Joseph Rodman Drake	Halleck	25
Open Window, The	Sill	471
Opportunity	Ingalls	426
Orpheus and Eurydice	Saxe	245
Our Orders	Howe	318
Over the River	Wakefield	441
Palabras Cariñosas	Aldrich	432
Palinode	Lowell	303
Pan in Wall Street	Stedman	403
Paradisi Gloria	Parsons	328
Parting, A	Pinkney	76
Parting Word, The	Holmes	210
Past, The	Bryant	48
Pen of Steel, A	Pratt	401
Petition, The	Lowell	306
Philosopher to His Love, The	Holmes	215
Plain Language from Truthful James	Harte	454
Planting of the Apple-Tree, The	Bryant	63
Poet	Emerson	85
Polyphemus and Ulysses	Saxe	242
Praxiteles and Phryne	Story	258
Preference Declared, The	Field	507
Present Crisis, The	Lowell	275
Private Devotion	Brown	6

INDEX OF TITLES

Problem, The	Emerson	77
Proem to Edition of 1847	Whittier	133
Provençal Lovers	Stedman	418
Psalm of Life, The	Longfellow	95
"Qui Vive"	Holmes	223
Randolph of Roanoke	Whittier	134
Raven, The	Poe	170
Red Jacket	Halleck	26
Reform	Gilder	490
Resignation	Longfellow	123
Rhodora, The	Emerson	79
River Inn, The	Gilder	489
Rocked in the Cradle of the Deep	Willard	9
Rock Me to Sleep	Allen	395
Sacrifice	Emerson	86
Saint Peray	Parsons	329
Sea Gypsy, The	Hovey	540
Seaweed	Longfellow	121
Serenade, A	Pinkney	73
Shakespeare	Emerson	86
Sheridan's Ride	Read	339
She Was a Beauty	Bunner	516
Ships at Sea	Coffin	379
Si Jeunesse Savait!	Stedman	417
Skeleton in Armor, The	Longfellow	99
Snowdrop	Story	267
Snow-Shower, The	Bryant	66
Society upon the Stanislaus, The	Harte	452
Some Things Love Me	Read	336
Song	Pinkney	73
Song	Lowell	274
Song from the Persian	Aldrich	431
Song of Marion's Men	Bryant	51
Song of the Chattahoochee	Lanier	480

INDEX OF TITLES

Song of the Silent Land	Longfellow	98
Songs	Gilder	492
Spring Song	Curtis	343
Star and the Water-Lily, The	Holmes	213
Star-Spangled Banner, The	Key	4
Stonewall Jackson's Way	Palmer	364
Summons, The	Howe	319
Tea-Gown, The	Field	502
Telepathy	Lowell	306
Thanatopsis	Bryant	36
Thousand and Thirty-Seven, The	Halpine	389
To a Maid Demure	Sill	473
To a Waterfowl	Bryant	39
To Eva	Emerson	84
To Helen	Poe	192
To One in Paradise	Poe	177
To the Portrait of "A Lady"	Holmes	199
Two Villages, The	Cooke	385
Ulalume	Poe	188
Under the Washington Elm, Cambridge	Holmes	225
Undiscovered Country, The	Stedman	415
Unmanifest Destiny	Hovey	543
Unseen Spirits	Willis	89
Village Blacksmith, The	Longfellow	106
Voiceless, The	Holmes	224
Voice of the Loyal North, A	Holmes	228
Voices of Unseen Spirits	Hovey	545
Volunteer, The	Cutler	394
Wander-Lovers, The	Hovey	536
Warden of the Cinque Ports, The	Longfellow	125
Washers of the Shroud, The	Lowell	282
Watchers, The	Whittier	160
Way to Arcady, The	Bunner	512
Wed	Bunner	518
What the Engines Said	Harte	465

INDEX OF TITLES

What Mr. Robinson Thinks	Lowell	268
What the Birds Said	Whittier	166
Widow's Song, The	Pinkney	76
Winter Wish, A	Messinger	234
Without and Within	Lowell	304
Without and Within	Stoddard	367
Woman's Poem, A	Stoddard	372
Woman's Thought, A	Gilder	488
World Well Lost, The	Stedman	416

www.bookjungle.com *email: sales@bookjungle.com fax: 630-214-0564 mail: Book Jungle PO Box 2226 Champaign, IL 61825*

The Codes Of Hammurabi And Moses
W. W. Davies

QTY

The discovery of the Hammurabi Code is one of the greatest achievements of archaeology, and is of paramount interest, not only to the student of the Bible, but also to all those interested in ancient history...

Religion   **ISBN:** *1-59462-338-4*   Pages:132
MSRP $12.95

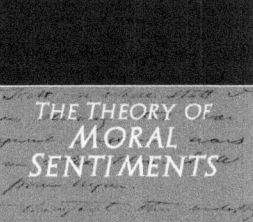

The Theory of Moral Sentiments
Adam Smith

QTY

This work from 1749. contains original theories of conscience amd moral judgment and it is the foundation for systemof morals.

Philosophy   **ISBN:** *1-59462-777-0*   Pages:536
MSRP $19.95

Jessica's First Prayer
Hesba Stretton

QTY

In a screened and secluded corner of one of the many railway-bridges which span the streets of London there could be seen a few years ago, from five o'clock every morning until half past eight, a tidily set-out coffee-stall, consisting of a trestle and board, upon which stood two large tin cans, with a small fire of charcoal burning under each so as to keep the coffee boiling during the early hours of the morning when the work-people were thronging into the city on their way to their daily toil...

Pages:84

Childrens   **ISBN:** *1-59462-373-2*   *MSRP $9.95*

My Life and Work
Henry Ford

QTY

Henry Ford revolutionized the world with his implementation of mass production for the Model T automobile. Gain valuable business insight into his life and work with his own auto-biography... "We have only started on our development of our country we have not as yet, with all our talk of wonderful progress, done more than scratch the surface. The progress has been wonderful enough but..."

Pages:300

Biographies/   **ISBN:** *1-59462-198-5*   *MSRP $21.95* www.bookjungle.com *email: sales@bookjungle.com fax: 630-214-0564 mail: Book Jungle PO Box 2226 Champaign, IL 61825*

The Art of Cross-Examination
Francis Wellman

QTY

I presume it is the experience of every author, after his first book is published upon an important subject, to be almost overwhelmed with a wealth of ideas and illustrations which could readily have been included in his book, and which to his own mind, at least, seem to make a second edition inevitable. Such certainly was the case with me; and when the first edition had reached its sixth impression in five months, I rejoiced to learn that it seemed to my publishers that the book had met with a sufficiently favorable reception to justify a second and considerably enlarged edition. ..

Reference   ISBN: *1-59462-647-2*   Pages:412   MSRP *$19.95*

On the Duty of Civil Disobedience
Henry David Thoreau

QTY

Thoreau wrote his famous essay, On the Duty of Civil Disobedience, as a protest against an unjust but popular war and the immoral but popular institution of slave-owning. He did more than write—he declined to pay his taxes, and was hauled off to gaol in consequence. Who can say how much this refusal of his hastened the end of the war and of slavery ?

Law   ISBN: *1-59462-747-9*   Pages:48   MSRP *$7.45*

Dream Psychology Psychoanalysis for Beginners
Sigmund Freud

QTY

Sigmund Freud, born Sigismund Schlomo Freud (May 6, 1856 - September 23, 1939), was a Jewish-Austrian neurologist and psychiatrist who co-founded the psychoanalytic school of psychology. Freud is best known for his theories of the unconscious mind, especially involving the mechanism of repression; his redefinition of sexual desire as mobile and directed towards a wide variety of objects; and his therapeutic techniques, especially his understanding of transference in the therapeutic relationship and the presumed value of dreams as sources of insight into unconscious desires.

Psychology   ISBN: *1-59462-905-6*   Pages:196   MSRP *$15.45*

The Miracle of Right Thought
Orison Swett Marden

QTY

Believe with all of your heart that you will do what you were made to do. When the mind has once formed the habit of holding cheerful, happy, prosperous pictures, it will not be easy to form the opposite habit. It does not matter how improbable or how far away this realization may see, or how dark the prospects may be, if we visualize them as best we can, as vividly as possible, hold tenaciously to them and vigorously struggle to attain them, they will gradually become actualized, realized in the life. But a desire, a longing without endeavor, a yearning abandoned or held indifferently will vanish without realization.

Self Help   ISBN: *1-59462-644-8*   Pages:360   MSRP *$25.45*

www.bookjungle.com email: sales@bookjungle.com fax: 630-214-0564 mail: Book Jungle PO Box 2226 Champaign, IL 61825

QTY

	Title	ISBN	Price
☐	**The Rosicrucian Cosmo-Conception Mystic Christianity** by *Max Heindel*	ISBN: 1-59462-188-8	$38.95
	The Rosicrucian Cosmo-conception is not dogmatic, neither does it appeal to any other authority than the reason of the student. It is: not controversial, but is: sent forth in the, hope that it may help to clear...	New Age/Religion Pages 646	
☐	**Abandonment To Divine Providence** by *Jean-Pierre de Caussade*	ISBN: 1-59462-228-0	$25.95
	"The Rev. Jean Pierre de Caussade was one of the most remarkable spiritual writers of the Society of Jesus in France in the 18th Century. His death took place at Toulouse in 1751. His works have gone through many editions and have been republished...	Inspirational/Religion Pages 400	
☐	**Mental Chemistry** by *Charles Haanel*	ISBN: 1-59462-192-6	$23.95
	Mental Chemistry allows the change of material conditions by combining and appropriately utilizing the power of the mind. Much like applied chemistry creates something new and unique out of careful combinations of chemicals the mastery of mental chemistry...	New Age Pages 354	
☐	**The Letters of Robert Browning and Elizabeth Barret Barrett 1845-1846 vol II** by *Robert Browning* and *Elizabeth Barrett*	ISBN: 1-59462-193-4	$35.95
		Biographies Pages 596	
☐	**Gleanings In Genesis (volume I)** by *Arthur W. Pink*	ISBN: 1-59462-130-6	$27.45
	Appropriately has Genesis been termed "the seed plot of the Bible" for in it we have, in germ form, almost all of the great doctrines which are afterwards fully developed in the books of Scripture which follow...	Religion/Inspirational Pages 420	
☐	**The Master Key** by *L. W. de Laurence*	ISBN: 1-59462-001-6	$30.95
	In no branch of human knowledge has there been a more lively increase of the spirit of research during the past few years than in the study of Psychology, Concentration and Mental Discipline. The requests for authentic lessons in Thought Control, Mental Discipline and...	New Age/Business Pages 422	
☐	**The Lesser Key Of Solomon Goetia** by *L. W. de Laurence*	ISBN: 1-59462-092-X	$9.95
	This translation of the first book of the "Lernegton" which is now for the first time made accessible to students of Talismanic Magic was done, after careful collation and edition, from numerous Ancient Manuscripts in Hebrew, Latin, and French...	New Age/Occult Pages 92	
☐	**Rubaiyat Of Omar Khayyam** by *Edward Fitzgerald*	ISBN:1-59462-332-5	$13.95
	Edward Fitzgerald, whom the world has already learned, in spite of his own efforts to remain within the shadow of anonymity, to look upon as one of the rarest poets of the century, was born at Bredfield, in Suffolk, on the 31st of March, 1809. He was the third son of John Purcell...	Music Pages 172	
☐	**Ancient Law** by *Henry Maine*	ISBN: 1-59462-128-4	$29.95
	The chief object of the following pages is to indicate some of the earliest ideas of mankind, as they are reflected in Ancient Law, and to point out the relation of those ideas to modern thought.	Religiom/History Pages 452	
☐	**Far-Away Stories** by *William J. Locke*	ISBN: 1-59462-129-2	$19.45
	"Good wine needs no bush, but a collection of mixed vintages does. And this book is just such a collection. Some of the stories I do not want to remain buried for ever in the museum files of dead magazine-numbers an author's not unpardonable vanity..."	Fiction Pages 272	
☐	**Life of David Crockett** by *David Crockett*	ISBN: 1-59462-250-7	$27.45
	"Colonel David Crockett was one of the most remarkable men of the times in which he lived. Born in humble life, but gifted with a strong will, an indomitable courage, and unremitting perseverance...	Biographies/New Age Pages 424	
☐	**Lip-Reading** by *Edward Nitchie*	ISBN: 1-59462-206-X	$25.95
	Edward B. Nitchie, founder of the New York School for the Hard of Hearing, now the Nitchie School of Lip-Reading, Inc, wrote "LIP-READING Principles and Practice". The development and perfecting of this meritorious work on lip-reading was an undertaking...	How-to Pages 400	
☐	**A Handbook of Suggestive Therapeutics, Applied Hypnotism, Psychic Science** by *Henry Munro*	ISBN: 1-59462-214-0	$24.95
		Health/New Age/Health/Self-help Pages 376	
☐	**A Doll's House: and Two Other Plays** by *Henrik Ibsen*	ISBN: 1-59462-112-8	$19.95
	Henrik Ibsen created this classic when in revolutionary 1848 Rome. Introducing some striking concepts in playwriting for the realist genre, this play has been studied the world over.	Fiction/Classics/Plays 308	
☐	**The Light of Asia** by *sir Edwin Arnold*	ISBN: 1-59462-204-3	$13.95
	In this poetic masterpiece, Edwin Arnold describes the life and teachings of Buddha. The man who was to become known as Buddha to the world was born as Prince Gautama of India but he rejected the worldly riches and abandoned the reigns of power when...	Religion/History/Biographies Pages 170	
☐	**The Complete Works of Guy de Maupassant** by *Guy de Maupassant*	ISBN: 1-59462-157-8	$16.95
	"For days and days, nights and nights, I had dreamed of that first kiss which was to consecrate our engagement, and I knew not on what spot I should put my lips..."	Fiction/Classics Pages 240	
☐	**The Art of Cross-Examination** by *Francis L. Wellman*	ISBN: 1-59462-309-0	$26.95
	Written by a renowned trial lawyer, Wellman imparts his experience and uses case studies to explain how to use psychology to extract desired information through questioning.	How-to/Science/Reference Pages 408	
☐	**Answered or Unanswered?** by *Louisa Vaughan*	ISBN: 1-59462-248-5	$10.95
	Miracles of Faith in China	Religion Pages 112	
☐	**The Edinburgh Lectures on Mental Science (1909)** by *Thomas*	ISBN: 1-59462-008-3	$11.95
	This book contains the substance of a course of lectures recently given by the writer in the Queen Street Hail, Edinburgh. Its purpose is to indicate the Natural Principles governing the relation between Mental Action and Material Conditions...	New Age/Psychology Pages 148	
☐	**Ayesha** by *H. Rider Haggard*	ISBN: 1-59462-301-5	$24.95
	Verily and indeed it is the unexpected that happens! Probably if there was one person upon the earth from whom the Editor of this, and of a certain previous history, did not expect to hear again...	Classics Pages 380	
☐	**Ayala's Angel** by *Anthony Trollope*	ISBN: 1-59462-352-X	$29.95
	The two girls were both pretty, but Lucy who was twenty-one who supposed to be simple and comparatively unattractive, whereas Ayala was credited, as her Bombwhat romantic name might show, with poetic charm and a taste for romance. Ayala when her father died was nineteen...	Fiction Pages 484	
☐	**The American Commonwealth** by *James Bryce*	ISBN: 1-59462-286-8	$34.45
	An interpretation of American democratic political theory. It examines political mechanics and society from the perspective of Scotsman James Bryce	Politics Pages 572	
☐	**Stories of the Pilgrims** by *Margaret P. Pumphrey*	ISBN: 1-59462-116-0	$17.95
	This book explores pilgrims religious oppression in England as well as their escape to Holland and eventual crossing to America on the Mayflower, and their early days in New England...	History Pages 268	

www.bookjungle.com email: sales@bookjungle.com fax: 630-214-0564 mail: Book Jungle PO Box 2226 Champaign, IL 61825

			QTY
The Fasting Cure by *Sinclair Upton*	ISBN: *1-59462-222-1*	**$13.95**	
In the Cosmopolitan Magazine for May, 1910, and in the Contemporary Review (London) for April, 1910, I published an article dealing with my experiences in fasting. I have written a great many magazine articles, but never one which attracted so much attention... New Age/Self Help/Health Pages 164			
Hebrew Astrology by *Sepharial*	ISBN: *1-59462-308-2*	**$13.45**	
In these days of advanced thinking it is a matter of common observation that we have left many of the old landmarks behind and that we are now pressing forward to greater heights and to a wider horizon than that which represented the mind-content of our progenitors... Astrology Pages 144			
Thought Vibration or The Law of Attraction in the Thought World	ISBN: *1-59462-127-6*	**$12.95**	
by **William Walker Atkinson**	*Psychology/Religion Pages 144*		
Optimism by *Helen Keller*	ISBN: *1-59462-108-X*	**$15.95**	
Helen Keller was blind, deaf, and mute since 19 months old, yet famously learned how to overcome these handicaps, communicate with the world, and spread her lectures promoting optimism. An inspiring read for everyone... Biographies/Inspirational Pages 84			
Sara Crewe by *Frances Burnett*	ISBN: *1-59462-360-0*	**$9.45**	
In the first place, Miss Minchin lived in London. Her home was a large, dull, tall one, in a large, dull square, where all the houses were alike, and all the sparrows were alike, and where all the door-knockers made the same heavy sound... Childrens/Classic Pages 88			
The Autobiography of Benjamin Franklin by *Benjamin Franklin*	ISBN: *1-59462-135-7*	**$24.95**	
The Autobiography of Benjamin Franklin has probably been more extensively read than any other American historical work, and no other book of its kind has had such ups and downs of fortune. Franklin lived for many years in England, where he was agent... Biographies/History Pages 332			

Name	
Email	
Telephone	
Address	
City, State ZIP	

☐ Credit Card   ☐ Check / Money Order

Credit Card Number	
Expiration Date	
Signature	

Please Mail to: Book Jungle
　　　　　　　　　PO Box 2226
　　　　　　　　　Champaign, IL 61825
or Fax to: 　　630-214-0564

ORDERING INFORMATION

web: *www.bookjungle.com*
email: *sales@bookjungle.com*
fax: *630-214-0564*
mail: *Book Jungle PO Box 2226 Champaign, IL 61825*
or PayPal *to sales@bookjungle.com*

Please contact us for bulk discounts

DIRECT-ORDER TERMS

20% Discount if You Order Two or More Books
Free Domestic Shipping!
Accepted: Master Card, Visa, Discover, American Express

www.ingramcontent.com/pod-product-compliance
Lightning Source LLC
Chambersburg PA
CBHW060502300426
44112CB00017B/2521